I had morning coffee out in the yard with the shop crew. When everyone had left and gone back to work, I stayed sitting on the saw horse, soaking in the sun of this _____ the old man I have become.

My mind _____ years, 63 to be ____, to the _____ when I first sailed into Que_____

Qussett in _____ quiet place, the small harb_____ hardly a soul in sight, on t_____ 1944 ____.

Atlantis Stories
Before the Mast on a
Sailing Research Vessel
1944-1948

The fog co_____ ashore, so that the small boat yard was hardly noticeable until we rowed right up to the small wharf.

The Eldred house was barely visable in the haze on the hill above the yard.

"God, what a lonely place" I said to Capt Verge when I returned to "Segochet". I hope we go to Falmouth Harbor soon."

As I had rowed the owner, Mr Peterson ashore, he told me Segotchet" would probably lay in the harbor for about two weeks before moving on to Falmouth. He also said it "should not be too bad for you, as Charlie Eldred has a couple of daughters your age"

Photo courtesy WHOI Archives © Woods Hole Oceanographic Institution.

ATLANTIS STORIES

Before the Mast on a Sailing Research Vessel

1944-1948

by William B. Cooper

Woods Hole Historical Museum

Editors:
Arthur G. Gaines, Jr.
Jay Burnett

Design and production:
Barbara M. Whitehead

Published by The Woods Hole Historical Collection
the publishing division of the
Woods Hole Historical Museum
P.O. Box 185
Woods Hole, Massachusetts 02543
Printed in Canada

ISBN 0-9611374-9-5

Dedicated to the many unacknowledged men and women

who crew the oceanographic vessels,

who make the equipment work,

and who spend

months at sea.

∽

Photo courtesy WHOI Archives © Woods Hole Oceanographic Institution.

Contents

Photo courtesy WHOI Archives © Woods Hole Oceanographic Institution.

Editors' Foreword

BILL COOPER wrote this book as a collection of memoirs over a period of many years, starting as early as 1980, but mainly after the mid-1990s. His memoirs of the *Atlantis* years were written in longhand, and later typed by his wife Judy (who made the first round of editorial adjustments). Over the years, most of these stories became familiar to Bill's friends and family as shoptalk or dinnertime verbal accounts, often presented in the Swedish-English vernacular. In fact it was Bill's son Douglas who encouraged his father to put the stories in writing. Bill's last entry was written on November 25, 2010, a month before his death at age 83.

Some of these anecdotes have been published before: in *Woods Hole Passage,* a community newsletter and creative writing periodical (now defunct); in *Spritsail, a Journal of the History of Falmouth and Vicinity* (now in its 27th year) published by the Woods Hole Historical Museum; and in *Woods Hole Reflections,* a book celebrating the history of Woods Hole edited by the late Mary Lou Smith. Bill also related some of his memories at a session of "Woods Hole Conversations", an oral history program of the Woods Hole Historical Museum. We believe the present work is the most comprehensive collection of Bill's writings.

After Bill's death, his wife Judy Cooper brought the typed manuscript to us suspecting that we would like to read it. It quickly became evident that the memoirs presented a unique and skillfully written perspective of life aboard a sailing oceanographic research vessel, a fascinating record of the professional Scandinavian seamen and their stories, and a special view of late- and post- World War II activities at Woods Hole through 1948. The manuscript also chronicles the coming of age of a young man, hungry for seagoing knowledge and adventure. His story is set in the worldwide convulsion of World War II.

Those of us who knew Bill see in his writings the origins of many qualities he exemplified in life—independence, love of boat design and construction, skill in sailing, uncompromising insistence on fair play, respect for protocol and history, a passion for teaching, and, occasionally, the squall of his temper. As those who knew Bill read these passages, we hear his voice once again.

Bill did not record his memoirs in chronological order, but rather as they came to mind, sometimes prompted by an event or date. As editors we saw our role largely to put Bill's record in chronological order, where appropriate, to make it more coherent to the reader, and to remove occasional redundancy. We have added sidebars to enlarge on certain aspects Bill mentions but does not elaborate on, such as in science and history. Shorter notes by the editors are enclosed in brackets [ ].

Although many photo copies were included in Bill's original manuscript, few of these copies were of publication quality. Therefore, we went through the extensive photo archives of the Woods Hole Oceanographic Institution and other collections and, where available, selected high quality digital photographs as substitutes or additions. In the interest of full disclosure, some of the photos were not taken on Bill's cruises, although all are accurately captioned.

Two points of clarification: in this book the term "squarehead" refers, in Bill's words, to that old-school Scandinavian sailor, "that most excellent breed of seaman". Bill was moved by their expertise and professionalism, their work ethic and shipboard code, their wit, and their quiet acceptance of hardship. In the context of this book there is no pejorative intended in the term. Bill would never have countenanced calumny of these fine men.

Secondly, the full name of the Woods Hole Oceanographic Institution is sometimes shortened to "the Oceanographic" or the "Institution". In more recent years the acronym "WHOI" has been applied. We use all four terms in this book.

Arthur G. Gaines, Jr.
Jay Burnett
Editors

Preface

WILLIAM BERNARD COOPER, JR. was born in Brooklyn, New York, in the late winter of 1927. His father, William senior, was a New York Cooper, so it is claimed, of James Fennimore Cooper and Cooper Union fame. His mother, a young Irish immigrant, was at the time of young William's birth most likely already infected with tuberculosis. While he was still a toddler, his mother Katherine became a victim of the disease leaving William motherless. At the age of two he fell on some broken glass and badly cut his right knee. The doctors, concerned about William's status of infection due to his exposure to his mother, became highly suspect of the wound to his knee. Fearing he could have contracted tuberculosis of the bone they removed the entire joint and fused the femur to the tibia. As a result, young Bill, as his father called him, was left with a rigid right leg that was also six inches short. After two years recuperating in a New York hospital, Bill emerged a cheerful, determined, though handicapped, boy.

To those who knew him later in life, it was clear that Bill never thought of himself as handicapped and never let it hinder him from what he wanted to do. His family and close friends, even though they knew he was different, didn't think of him as physically impaired. Bill often said that when he was a young boy he saw another boy in a wheel chair and was horrified. He resolved to never use a wheel chair or any aid. Bill would go on to become an extremely physically capable man. He would run fast, ride a bicycle, ice skate and ride horses. He sailed on ships, worked in shipyards, and built houses. Bill knew that if he gave in, and listened to the doctors, he would become a cripple.

Though living in New York City, as a young boy Bill dreamed of going to sea. His father would take him down to the docks to see the great ocean liners as they came and went in their heyday of the 1930s. In later life he would recall them by name: the British *Queen Mary,* the German *Europa,* the Italian *Rex,* and his favorite, the beautiful French liner *Normandie.* In the summer of 1941 Bill and his high school buddy made a plot to run away to sea. Their plan was to make their way to Nova Scotia and join a British merchantman. When they realized how far they would have to travel, sleeping outdoors in the cold, with almost no money, they gave up on their dream.

When Bill was sixteen his father's new wife decided that Bill had to go. His father sent him to work on a ranch in upper New York State. Even though he grew up essentially motherless, and with this change became effectively fatherless, he thrived. At the ranch Bill learned to ride horses and work with real cowboys. Still, inexplicably, he yearned for the sailor's life. Along with the sea he had long been drawn to New England which he thought of as steeped in history. Cape Cod was, in his young mind, the ideal place.

Though offered a chance to go to Texas he, and two restless girls from the ranch, decided to travel to the Cape in March of 1944. Their destination was Provincetown, as everyone said that was "the" Cape Cod town. After two days of traveling they arrived in Provincetown and were greeted by naval ships in the harbor, quaint cottages, wooden sidewalks, and very few people. The older girl, while exploring the rest of the Cape, was introduced to John R. Peterson, a professional wrestler who owned the Cape Codder Hotel in Falmouth. Known as "Big Boy", he also owned a 45' schooner and was looking to hire a "boy" to serve as crew. Bill leapt at the chance and in April traveled with Mr. Peterson to Maine where the schooner was lying.

At this point we can pick up the story in Bill's own words.

Douglas Cooper

I had morning coffee out in the yard with the shop crew. When everyone had left and gone back to work, I stayed sitting on the saw-horse, soaking in the sun of this ___ the old man I have become.

My mind ___ years, 63 to be exact, to the ___ en I first sailed into Qus___

Qussett in ___ quiet place, the small harb___ hardly a soul in sight, on t___ ___ 44 ___,

The fog con___ ___ ashore, so that the small boat yard was hardly noticeable until we rowed right up to the small wharf. The Eldred house was barely visable in the haze on the hill above the yard.

"God, what a lonely place" I said to Capt Verge when I returned to "Segochet". I hope we go to Falmouth Harbor soon."

As I had rowed the owner, Mr Peterson ashore, he told me Segotchet" would probably lay in the harbor for about two weeks before moving on to Falmouth. He also said it "should not be too bad for you, as Charlie Eldred has a couple of daughters your age"

Atlantis Stories

Before the Mast on a

Sailing Research Vessel

1944-1948

Photo courtesy WHOI Archives © Woods Hole Oceanographic Institution.

Prologue

I N M I D - A P R I L, 1944, I found myself at 17 years of age travelling downeast to Maine from Falmouth, Massachusetts, in a station wagon with John R. Peterson and Bob Tilton. Our destination was Thomaston, where Mr. Peterson had a small schooner which he had purchased earlier that spring being put in commission. I rode in the back seat of the station wagon with a six-cylinder Chrysler marine engine. We had left the Cape early in the morning and, after clearing Boston, we worked our way downeast along old Route 1, probably the only good road to Maine those days.

We stopped in Freeport, Maine, and Mr. Peterson and Bob Tilton took me into a store, L.L. Bean, a name and place that of course meant nothing to me. At 17 years of age, I had never been any farther than 100 miles or so from where I had been born in Brooklyn, New York. In my youth, we considered any kid who had been to more than two states a sophisticated traveler.

I was going all the way to Maine to join Mr. Peterson's schooner as the "boy" to help his professional captain, Enos Verge, prepare the schooner for her trip down to the Cape. How it was that I ended up in the station wagon at that time, with these two men, virtually strangers, is another story.

Mr. Peterson and Bob Tilton talked about boats and engines most of the trip. I understood very little of what was said at the time, though I had an all-consuming interest, even then, in ships, boats, and the sea. Looking back now, I realize that it was during that ride from Falmouth to Thomaston that my real life began. Bob Tilton, I found out later, was a famous striped bass fishing guide from the island of Cuttyhunk, but I had no idea where that was at that time.

We worked our way downeast, and stopped the first night in Waldoboro, on the long uphill grade on Route 1 before Moody's Diner, at a little farmhouse that was right out of the nineteenth century. The house belonged to an old lady, Lucy Ryder, the sister as I remember of the man that managed Mr. Peterson's hotel, the Cape Codder. His name was Denny Hunt, a real nice man, as I was to discover most Mainers were. The farmhouse had a large black iron coal stove in the kitchen and also a smaller stove in the "parlor" as they called it. The kitchen sink, made of stone, had a hand pump, something I had never seen before, and the outhouse was out back through a long passage in an adjoining shed. There was no plumbing in the house.

The thing that amazed me, a boy from New York City, was the hand-crank telephone. I could hardly believe it was real. We had supper by kerosene lamp light and, after a short conversation, all went to bed. Mrs. Ryder made a bed for me on the couch in the parlor, near the coal stove, where she said I would be "nice and warm." It can be cold in Maine in mid-April, but I slept soundly that night. The next morning, after a first-class breakfast of ham, eggs and griddlecakes cooked by Denny Hunt (I have always loved breakfast), we got underway for Thomaston.

For my younger readers, I want to point out that the United States, especially New England, before World War II, was not as prosperous as it is today. When I first saw Thomaston it had known better days, but did not look to my eyes any worse than most of the other places I had been. Mr. Peterson's little schooner was laying next to the Dunn & Elliot coal wharf on the St. George River in Thomaston, near where the highway bridge crosses the river. The coal wharf and storage shed no longer exist. The schooner, named *Segochet,* was about 46 feet long. She was built in Thomaston by Enos Morse about 1930. She was supposed to be an exact model of a Gloucester fishing schooner. She was gaff-rigged, with both a fore and main topmast. Painted black, with a white deck house and light green pine deck, she was a salty-looking vessel and I was thrilled. We met *Segochet's* professional captain, Enos Verge, who was a Thomaston native about 65 years old. He had been a yacht captain for the last ten years or so. Up to that time he had been a fisherman most of his life.

I had stowed my bag in *Segochet's* small fo'c'sle when a new dragger came down the river from Gray's yard above the highway bridge. She was about 75 feet in length and turned out to be the *Puritan* of Gloucester. *Puritan* lay outboard of us while some work was done in preparation for her passage to Gloucester. Her owner soon arrived and Mr. Peterson introduced Ben Pine to Bob Tilton, Captain Verge, and me. Captain Pine, as I remember, was a large man with light gray hair, very confident in himself and very cheerful. It was only later that I learned that Captain Ben Pine was, at that time, the owner and skipper of the famous Gloucester schooner *Gertrude L. Thebaud*.

Segochet had a square trunk hatch on her fore deck that led to the fo'c'sle, and as I was about to descend into the fo'c'sle, I lifted the hatch cover off the coaming and, not knowing any better, placed it upside down on the deck. Captain Pine noticed this and it brought him up "all standing". "Don't ever place a hatch cover on deck upside down", he told me. "It is bad luck and the vessel will be lost for sure." This was my first lesson in the superstitions of the sea, and I have never placed a hatch cover upside down on a boat since that time.

Bob Tilton, who was a superb cook, went below and fired up the Shipmate coal stove in the galley and before long had a nice fish chowder cooking. We had brought stores with us and Bob organized and stowed things away, cooking the chowder at the same time. To accompany the chowder, he tried out some salt pork. It was the first time I had ever had salt pork that way, and I love it to this day.

Mr. Peterson and Bob Tilton stayed overnight aboard *Segochet*, and the next morning, after a hearty breakfast, were ready to return to Falmouth. The Chrysler engine had been unloaded on to the wharf, and the owner and captain had discussions with the boss from Gray's yard in regard to changing the cockpit, work on the stern, and installing the engine.

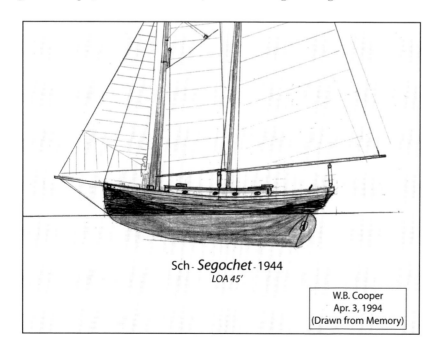

Sch - *Segochet* - 1944
LOA 45'

W.B. Cooper
Apr. 3, 1994
(Drawn from Memory)

At that time, in 1944, there were three yards building fishing draggers in Thomaston. Up the St. George River above the highway bridge was Gray's. Morse's Yard was right next to the Dunn & Elliot Wharf where we were laying, and a little farther down the river was Newbert & Wallace. Looking back, for me it was a most fascinating place. I could see the draggers on the ways at Morse's very clearly, hear the ring and song of the caulker's mallet in the morning, and smell the pungent smell of the green oak timbers and the delicious odor of the pine tar-based copper bottom paint. The ship's saw cutting out stock for frames was only 100 feet or so away. There was the "karma" of the time in the air that I don't feel in Thomaston today. It seems as if old Maine has passed away. I am thankful I knew it then.

Being from New York, I noticed right away the pleasant Maine dialect. I am unable to write "Downeast" dialect, but if I hear it today it is music to my ears. These people were Downeasters for generations and not from New Jersey, Ohio, or Chicago. Above all, compared to New York, the people were very friendly and that was probably because I had the privilege of having Captain Verge to show me around. Anyway, I thought Thomaston a fascinating place, and I loved every minute of it.

I remember going to Newbert & Wallace's Yard on a Saturday afternoon. Roy Wallace and Jim Newbert were the only ones working there. The yard had a dragger under construction in a shed, and Jim Newbert was working on the stern gland or stuffing box. Roy Wallace took me into the small office and showed me the blueprints, the first ones I had seen of a vessel. The designer of the dragger was Albert Condon. Thirty years later, I would work with his son Everett at Alan Vaitse's Yard in Mattapoisett. Everett Condon was born and raised in Thomaston.

Roy Wallace explained the launching ways and how the vessel would be lifted off the keel blocks with wedges. The Morse Shipyard was a busy place as they had three or four large draggers under construction at one time. I believe the owner in 1944 was Wilbur Morse (the Morse family seemed to use the names Charles, Wilbur, and Enos with each generation). I remember him very plainly as it was he who explained to me one morning how the tilting frame ship saw worked in cutting the bevels on the "futtocks" as he called them. I did not know what a "futtock" was, but Mr. Morse explained these pieces made up a sawn frame. In my mind's eye, I can still see the men cutting the oak pieces, about three inches thick, on the saw with the sawyer calling out the bevels in degrees, and another man turning the big hand wheel to tilt the frame of the band saw. The saw was out in the yard near the road in plain sight and I believe it was run by a gasoline engine.

Most of the men I saw working in Morse's Yard were well past middle age, in their sixties and seventies, and had been doing this work all their lives. Across the road from the yard, there was a flat piece of land where the spars, made from spruce logs, were gotten out. The tree or log was squared (four-sided) with large tree-width broad axes by two old sparmakers. The boss sparmaker told me he had gotten *Segochet*'s masts out of the woods in 1930 when snow was up to his waist.

The yards started work at 7:00 AM and knocked off at 4:00 PM. They had an hour for lunch. I don't remember that anyone worked Saturday afternoon. Delivery of the draggers really depended on when the diesel engines would arrive, and, it being war time, these engines could easily be delayed. All this ship-building activity was new to me, but as Captain Verge kept me busy during the weekdays, I did not have time to sightsee, except Saturday afternoon and Sunday.

Captain Verge had a little cottage on the St. George River a small distance from where we were laying, and he lived there while we were in Thomaston. I lived aboard the schooner and thought it was great fun. There was only the Shipmate coal stove for cooking and heat, and kerosene lamps for lighting. I slept very comfortably on a pipe berth, canvas bottom without a mattress, in the fo'c'sle before the mast. Captain Verge would arrive about 6:30 in the morning and get the stove going for the day, and we would have breakfast, usually eggs and fried salt pork. Some days he would make a pot of oatmeal with brown sugar and heavy cream. That was my favorite.

Early on I was warned about the coal gas from the Shipmate stove by all the men, and its deadly effects. As a rule, Captain Verge would burn off the gas in the afternoon before he went home, and then bank the stove for the night and open the draft vent. I would never touch it after that.

Across the road from the wharf was a little general store. I had never seen anything like it before, and was fascinated by the look and feel of the place. I realize now the store and its proprietor were right out of the nineteenth century. I would go there to buy a few groceries and the usually-stale cookies at times, and never saw anyone else in the store. It was as if time and activity had passed it by.

The man who owned and ran the store was Mr. Elliot. Guessing now, I would put him close to eighty years old if not more. One day when I was in the store, I gave him a $10 bill in payment. In 1944, when wages were forty or fifty cents an hour in the shipyards, a $10 bill was equivalent to a $100 bill today. Mr. Elliot could not change the bill from his little money box by the counter, so he told me to come with him to the office in the back of the store. When we arrived I was surprised to see, mounted on the walls, large half-models, about three or four feet long, of sailing ships which, I know now, were mostly schooners, probably three- or four-masters. These were builder's models.

There were also photographs of various sailing ships. Mr. Elliot, who hardly said two words to me generally, began talking when he saw my interest in the half-models. He told me the names of the vessels that were built from the models, and where each had been built: Thomaston, Rockland, Bath, Waldoboro. At that time, I did not realize that Mr. Elliot had owned a fleet of schooners or that he was the owner of the coal wharf at which *Segochet* was laying. It was only after I told Captain Verge about the half-models that I found out who the little old man was. In the past, he had been the largest ship owner in Thomaston.

I went with Captain Verge over to the riggers' and sailmakers' loft at the Morse Shipyard to get some hemp rope for the shroud lanyards on *Segochet*. Here again it was a step back in time. The rigger was about the same age as Captain Verge and had worked in the loft since he was a boy my age. There were prints on the walls of old three- and four-masted schooners, fishing schooners, barks, brigantines, etc., along with all the ship's gear that had accumulated through the years: large rope strap blocks, lignum vitae dead eyes, lizards, and other pieces of gear that were beyond my knowledge at the time. There was also, of course, the enticing smell of pine tar and hemp (the rigger told Captain Verge to put a little varnish in the pine tar on the dead eye lanyards, to stand up to the weather better).

The new dragger fitting out at the Dunn & Elliot coal wharf, just a short distance away from *Segochet*, was the *Catherine T.* of Nantucket. The hails of Gloucester, Nantucket, and New Bedford were the only names in the history book as far as I knew, but to see the ports printed on the sterns was a thrill I have never forgotten. *Catherine T.* soon left in early May for home and fishing, with everyone watching as she sailed down the St. George River, turned to starboard, and disappeared from view. She looked beautiful in her fresh coat of paint, hull green, bulwarks black, wheelhouse white, and spars and deck fittings buff. I saw her again in Woods Hole 14 years later, and she looked old and worn out from hard years of fishing.

Catherine T.'s place at the outfitting wharf was soon taken by a newly launched dragger named *Gladys and Mary* of Edgartown. I had no idea where Edgartown was, and, even after being told it was on Martha's Vineyard, it did not help because I did not know where Martha's Vineyard was! *Gladys and Mary* was launched on a Saturday morning and warped over to the outfitting wharf. She took on water all day and night to swell her up. Sunday evening one of the men from Morse's Yard came down to pump her out. For a bilge pump she had on deck a cast iron Edson Diaphragm pump activated by a long iron handle. After the pump was working, I was surprised by the color of the bilge water. It was a dark purple. The man who was working the pump told me it was from the tannic acid in the oak. Of course, I had never seen anything like that before. The pump worked easily with the long iron handle, and it got so that they would let me pump her out when she needed it. *Gladys and Mary* was still at the outfitting wharf when we left to sail to the Cape near the end of May. She was waiting for her diesel engine to be delivered.

Segochet was the only yacht lying in Thomaston at this time, and she looked pretty with gaff-rigged masts, topmasts, and a white bowsprit. On Saturday and Sunday, many people would come by to visit, especially if the tide was high when she would be near the top of the wharf. Tides in Thomaston were about ten feet.

Bound for Cape Cod

We left Thomaston the 24th of May, 1944, bound for Cape Cod, Falmouth Harbor we thought. Besides Captain Verge, the owner Mr. Peterson, and me, there was Bob Tilton, Bill Mullins of Falmouth, and one other man from Buzzards Bay whose name I don't recall. Before we left Thomaston, a painter from Morse's Yard painted large white identification numbers on *Segochet*'s bow, a requirement during the war years.

We sailed in the late afternoon with a fair wind down the St. George River, and then down the coast of Maine. It was the first time I had ever been under sail. I was cold on watch that night and also seasick. I remember thinking that maybe I did not want the life of a sailor after all. However, when I turned in I slept "like a log" and, when I awoke in the morning, the sun was shining brightly. We were making good time with the wind on the starboard quarter, with Boon Island Light and the Isles of Shoals in sight.

We reached the entrance to Gloucester Harbor in the early afternoon. We took in all sail and, as I sat on the bowsprit shrouds furling the jib, I realized where I was and thought about the great fishing schooners and especially of Rudyard Kipling's book, *Captains Courageous*. This was the harbor from which they sailed! It seemed to me at the time like a dream.

In war years, permission was needed to enter and leave harbors. We were met by a Coast Guard picket boat and, after receiving clearance, proceeded into the harbor. We anchored with all chain well into the harbor. We were all tired, and turned in early after supper.

The next morning was a beautiful May day with a southwest wind. Before we sailed, we had to get clearance from the Coast Guard to sail for the Cape Cod Canal. Captain Verge went to the Port Captain's office with *Segochet*'s papers to get the necessary clearance. *Segochet* had a beautiful round bottom dinghy about 12 feet long, which Captain Verge called a "Deer Island model." I used to row this boat on the St. George River and got so I could handle her very well, so I thought. I was pleased when Captain Verge told me I could row him to the wharf where the Port Captain's office was located. With him in the stern sheets and I rowing, we got underway. I was sure I was doing a good job.

Gloucester Harbor was a busy place with draggers everywhere unloading fish, and many other activities. We passed close by the schooner *Gertrude L. Thebaud,* which I found quite thrilling. Before he stepped out of the dinghy at the Port Captain's float, Captain Verge, instead of praising me for my performance as I had expected, said instead that I rowed like a "damn farmer" and he was ashamed to be seen in the dinghy with me.

On the return to *Segochet* he planned to give me lessons, especially on how to feather my oars "as a sailor would do." I learned later that the old-timers were very critical about the type of stroke one used and how the oars were feathered. They could tell the inexperienced or "farmer" right away. How times have changed. Whoever feathers their oars today? As far as my observations are concerned, almost everyone today rows like a "farmer."

We cleared Gloucester Harbor about mid-morning and soon entered Cape Cod Bay in a good SW wind and chop. This was not *Segochet*'s best point of sailing. We reached the Sandwich Coast Guard Station in the early evening and found the canal closed to small boat traffic for the night. Already I noticed that the weather was more pleasant and warmer than it had been in Maine. Bill Mullins and the man from Buzzards Bay left us at the canal that evening.

When morning came, Saturday the 27th of May, 1944, there was a lot of fog in the air. At 5 AM we got underway along with two other yachts, one named *Blitzen,* a famous racing yacht of the 1930s and 1940s, and proceeded through the Cape Cod Canal under power with a fair tide. As there was hardly a breath of air, we continued under power down Buzzards Bay. Finally the fog lifted enough for us to see the shore. Mr. Peterson pointed out a large building to me and said it was his "Cape Codder Hotel." Continuing to the SW, we soon came to the entrance of a small harbor, still shrouded in a light mist. Mr. Peterson said it was Quissett Harbor, where we would lay for a week or so before proceeding to our mooring in Falmouth Harbor.

Quissett Harbor

We picked up a mooring buoy in the inner harbor, and soon the mist began to clear. Although I could see houses and what looked like a small boatyard, there did not seem to be any activity. Even when we rowed ashore in the dinghy to the small wharf of the boatyard, we saw no one. After I returned to *Segochet,* I said to Captain Verge "This place is terrible, there is no one around." "Don't worry," said Captain Verge, "we will be in Falmouth Harbor soon enough."

Mr. Peterson had informed us before he left that if we went ashore, we should walk up the road by the harbor to the traffic light. That was the main road: left went to Falmouth, and a right turn would take us to Woods Hole. In the afternoon the sun was shining, and Captain Verge sent me ashore to get the lay of the land and to find out how far it was to "town." Since it was a Saturday afternoon, no one was working at the boatyard. As I walked up the road and came abreast of the first house, a boy was mowing the front lawn with a younger fellow hanging around, and watching them both was a pretty blonde girl. The two boys were Bob Metell and Bud Baker, respectively, and the girl was Cynthia Eldred.

There was the delicious smell of spring in the air, completely lacking in Maine which had not yet felt the full measure of the season. I kept going up toward the traffic light, and turned right there towards Woods Hole. We were used to walking in those days, so the distance to Woods Hole did not concern me at all. I saw very few people and hardly any cars. I reached the golf links and, when a sidewalk appeared, I knew the village was not far. I kept going as far as Sumner Street and then turned around to walk back to

Eldred Boatyard at Quissett Harbor, 1948. Owner Charlie Eldred built, maintained, and rented boats, tended moorings, and supplied yachts with gasoline, firewood, water, and ice. Photo by Edwin Gray.

Quissett. The main road in those days was only about two-thirds as wide as it is today. I hadn't been long on the return trip when two older ladies came by in a car and offered me a lift back to the Quissett four corners. When I got back to *Segochet* and told Captain Verge where Woods Hole lay, he said we'd go ashore in the evening and have our supper there.

Later Saturday afternoon the owner of the boatyard, Charlie Eldred, came out to change the mooring pennant. He had a large wooden skiff and he sculled it out with one long oar. I had never seen anyone scull before and was spellbound watching him.

After walking back to Woods Hole in the early evening, we found a small village, with three grocery stores, a drug store, a bar (The Rendezvous), and a restaurant (James Grill). This restaurant was where the Leeside [now Quick's Hole] Bar is today, across from the railroad station on one side and Cahoon's Fish Market on the other. We ate at James Grill, and the waitress was a very pretty girl about my own age, with a sweet smile. Captain Verge was very taken with her and said to me after we left, "If I were young again, that is the kind of girl I would like to have." The girl, as I found out later, was Louise Erskine. The Erskine family lived in Quissett, and the mother was a widow. Louise had five sisters. The family had originally come from Boothbay Harbor in Maine. Her mother's maiden name was Brewer and her brother, Malcolm Brewer, was a well-known and respected boat builder in Boothbay and Camden.

The next day, Sunday, Mr. Peterson came back and brought us a large amount of groceries and canned goods. Looking back, I remember Mr. Peterson (we never called him "Big Boy" as others did) as a gruff fellow who could lose his temper readily at times, but I also remember a nice, friendly man who treated me kindly. I also found his bark worse than his bite. Mr. Peterson asked me if I liked Quissett Harbor as he was considering keeping *Segochet* there. I told him it was rather quiet and lonesome. He said it could not be that bad for me, as he knew Charlie Eldred had two daughters about my age, and they lived in the house above the yard. I realized then that the girl I had seen the day before was one of the daughters, and later found out that they were named Judith and Cynthia. At that moment, a thought, or premonition if you will, flashed through my mind that I would marry Judith Eldred, whom I had never even seen. The thought was gone as quickly as it had come, and I never thought about it again for over two years.

Laying on a mooring near us was a small gaff-rigged sailboat which caught Captain Verge's eye. He said she looked like a "dandy little boat" to him. He asked Mr. Peterson what kind of boat she was and he thought it was a "Herreshoff". The little boat was actually a Herreshoff 12 1/2 footer, *Freedom,* owned at that time by S.W. Carey. She was painted with a white hull, varnished oak sheerstrake and combing, green bottom, and a typical Herreshoff tan deck. Fifty years later I would do a lot of work rebuilding *Freedom,* but, of course, I had no inkling of that in May of 1944.

Tuesday was May 30th, Memorial Day in the old days. We made *Segochet*'s colors at 8 AM, and tidied and smarted things up in general for the holiday, which included putting a "harbor furl" in the sails. In the mid-morning we saw one of the little Herreshoff yachts hoisting sail. It was a beautiful sunny day with a SW wind. Captain Verge had the binoculars trained on the gaff-rigged boat, admiring the sails, when he said to me, "There are two girls in that boat." At that time, I did not know how to sail, so I was quite impressed to see the little boat beating out of the harbor, tacking, with two girls aboard whom Captain Verge said were "sailing right smart." Remember, this was 1944. The Herreshoff 12 1/2 footer sailed up nearby and tacked right under *Segochet*'s stern. The crew of the little boat waved cheerfully and said they admired our schooner. The boat passed right close to our stern and I was able to read the name: *Pelican*. The girls, about 15 and 16 years old, were Dede and Bunny O'Sullivan. Quissett Harbor was getting more interesting all the time.

That afternoon, while Captain Verge was below, I was sitting in the cockpit of *Segochet* and just looking at the scenery and daydreaming in general. Suddenly when I glanced at the sandbar, a most interesting scene appeared before my eyes. I reached below the companionway hatch into the cabin and picked up the binoculars. "Well," I said out loud, "I think this is a pretty good place after all." Captain Verge, down in the cabin, heard me and asked what made me change my mind. A glance over to the sandbar, where I had been looking with the glasses, told him the answer. On the sandbar, sitting in the sun, were six pretty young girls about my age, four with blonde hair and two with light brown hair.

To my eyes, it was a most cheering sight. I found out later that two of the girls were Charlie Eldred's daughters, two were Baker sisters, cousins to the Eldreds, and two were Erskine sisters. I felt as if I had hit the jackpot! What I did not know at the time was that there were also many young sailors on the Coast Guard vessels stationed in Woods Hole, as well as Navy men from the Navy crashboats and subchasers. There was a lot of competition, even if one discounts all the young soldiers at Camp Edwards! Little did I realize that, from that time forward, my life would be changed forever.

Quissett Harbor turned out to be for me a virtual summer paradise, with more friendly people and pretty girls my age than I could have, in my wildest dreams, imagined. I thank God that, for some reason or other, we never went to Falmouth Harbor as originally planned.

After we had been in Quissett for a week or so, another schooner arrived and picked up a mooring near the sand bar. This schooner was a typical John Alden design of the 1930s, about 48 feet in length, with a bowsprit, a gaff foresail, and a jib-headed mainsail. Her crew consisted of a professional skipper and a boy. As we found out later, she was owned by a man who had made a lot of money during the war, but had never owned a yacht before. Her professional captain was a real Yankee sailor from Maine, named Bert Thron, about 76 years old at the time. The boy with him was the owner's nephew. I rarely saw the boy, did not know his name, and never had any companionship with him at all. Captain Thron said the boy hated life on the schooner. In a week or so he was gone.

WOODS HOLE, Mass., from the Rail Road Depot.

Above: *Late-1930s aerial view of Woods Hole, facing east. Woods Hole Oceanographic Institution (center); Marine Biological Laboratory (left); and Woods Hole Railroad Station and Steamship Dock (right). Photo courtesy WHOI Archives © Woods Hole Oceanographic Institution.*

Left: *Early view of Woods Hole Railroad Square. The James Grill is to the right and Cahoon's Fish Market is to the left. Undated postcard from archives of Woods Hole Historical Museum.*

15

Settling In

We soon settled into the routine of life living aboard a schooner moored in Quissett Harbor half a century ago. We turned out at 6 AM. At least I did. Both Captain Verge and Captain Thron were usually up well before dawn. Later I found out the reason. Both old-timers used the bowsprit shrouds as the head. The best time for this would be just before daylight before they could be visible to any onlookers ashore or afloat.

The first job in the morning was to wet down the pine decks with salt water. While Captain Verge did this, I rowed the dinghy ashore with our water jugs to draw fresh water necessary for the day from a tap on the wharf of the boatyard. We had a fresh water tank, but did not use the water. We saved that in case we should take off on a sail or a short cruise. After the decks had been wet down, we, using a small amount of fresh water, chamoised the dew off the deck house, hatches, and rails, and then in the dinghy we used the chamois on the topsides removing all traces of salt water. It would be about 7:30 AM now and time to get breakfast. All we had to cook on was the Shipmate coal stove. If it were a rainy nor'easter, the stove would be kept going all night. As the days grew warmer in June, the coal stove became too hot to use for cooking and too slow to get going for only breakfast. In this case we burned wood. I would take a canvas bag, open on each end, row ashore with a small hatchet and saw, and cut dead oak branches from the trees on the beach (where the Quissett Yacht Club sailing class gathers today), trees blown over during the 1938 hurricane. I did this job most afternoons, storing the wood and faggots in the canvas bag in the dinghy overnight. We used wood for breakfast and lunch, and wood and coal at night to cook supper. We also used it to heat enough water for washing dishes and ourselves in the evening.

Segochet had a deep, square copper sink in the galley just aft of the foremast. It was my job to wash the dishes, and, after I finished the breakfast dishes, I would polish the sink with Oxford Brass polish inside and out. The polished copper sink, contrasting with the well-blackened Shipmate stove, looked beautiful. We made up our berths, put every article in its place, "shipshape and Bristol fashion." We cleaned the lamp chimneys with newspaper, put the old paper in the stove, adjusted the wicks, and filled the lamps with kerosene, if necessary. The main cabin sole was riff grain fir (vertical), beautiful stock, that was well-scrubbed most every day.

All the preceding activity was accomplished usually by 10:30 A.M. After this time we did things just to keep us busy: take apart and grease one of the beautiful Merriman Bros. mainsheet blocks, smarten up on the deadeye lanyards, dry sails if there had been any rain the day or night before, sand and varnish the railcaps, never doing too big a job that might interfere with us getting underway quickly.

Charlie Eldred told Captain Verge that we could use one of his Beetlecats, *Seashell,* with a red sail so that Captain Verge could teach me to sail. We took him up on this offer, and spent many afternoons beating around and out of Quissett while Captain Verge explained the proper way to tack, all the proper commands, and the feel of the tiller when the boat was in harmony with her sails. We also sailed a larger open cockpit cat owned by Charlie Eldred, named *Coy.* Other afternoons, I rowed the dinghy many times under Captain Verge's critical eye and stop watch to the number 5 buoy and back, practicing my stroke and the proper way to feather the oars.

One morning, about 6:30 A.M., Arthur Weeks, who was lobstering out of Quissett, came alongside *Segochet* on his way in from hauling his traps, and passed Captain Verge a burlap bag. In this bag were a fresh mackerel and two lobsters. We had both the fish and the lobster for breakfast. At that time I did not know what a "short" lobster was!

Around the Cabin Lamp

Sometimes in the evenings, Captain Thron would row over to *Segochet* and ask permission to come aboard, which Captain Verge willingly granted. After they went below, Captain Verge would light one of the cabin lamps on the forward bulkhead of the main cabin. Both men would then take their places on the two settees, port and starboard, with their backs against the forward bulkhead. After they got their pipes lit and going, the yarns would begin.

Many evenings, instead of going ashore, I stayed on board to listen to these two old seafarers. In my mind's eye, I can still see, after all these years, *Segochet*'s old-fashioned cabin bathed in the soft light of the kerosene lamp and myself listening, enthralled, as Captain Thron in his reminiscing took us to China and Japan in a four-masted American bark in the 1880s, sixty some odd years ago. Captain Thron said, "The first time I sailed past Nobska (he pronounced it 'Nobskie', as it was at that time spelled Nobsque) was in 1880, bound for Yokohama in a bark commanded by my uncle. I was 12 years old and was a cabin boy. My uncle, the old bastard, made my life miserable. I swore to myself at that time that, when I grew up, I would kill him. The only thing that saved me on that voyage was the little kindness shown to me by my aunt, the captain's wife, who was sailing on the bark."

Captain Thron said, as a cabin boy, he was also the cook's helper. As helper, he got up at 4 AM and started the fire in the galley stove, which burned coal, to have ready for the cook who turned out at 6 AM. He also helped the cook in the galley, waited on the saloon table in the main cabin, and cleaned the officers' cabins. He scrubbed out the pots and pans when necessary, using ashes from the galley stove for grit, and washed the dishes from the main saloon. Sailors had their own tin plates, cups, and bowls which they washed themselves in salt water. His aunt saved him small tidbits from the cabin table. Captain Thron said, looking back sixty-plus years, "It was a terrible experience for a 12-year old. I don't know how I lived through it."

He sailed on that bark, with his uncle, going from cabin boy to deck boy. As deck boy, he had far less contact with his uncle. At age 16 he was made an ordinary seaman. He told us that the first words the "bucko mate" from Maine said to him as ordinary seaman were: "When I give you an order, I don't want to see you walk, I don't want to see you run, but when I give an order, goddamn you, fly!" Captain Thron, at 16, was light and nimble and could keep out of the mate's way, but some of the older fellows could not, and often received starting blows from wooden belaying pins (mates also had short lengths of rope with a knot worked in at one end, called 'starters'). He did not have happy memories from his days in downeast ships. Luckily his uncle died before he could kill him.

Captain Thron told us that on the bark he served in, all the spars, masts, and yards above the lower masts and doublings were finished bright, that is covered with tung oil and varnish. The sailors scraped the spars clean with their sheath knives—no scraper or sandpaper were used—and applied the varnish to the spars with their bare hands. The lower masts and yards were painted white.

Thinking back on that time, for me it was a wonderful experience, but I did not know enough to ask any decent questions of Captain Thron. Captain Thron had a good memory and could have told me many details about life on American sailing ships in the latter part of the nineteenth century. I knew that he sailed later in large yachts, both sail and steam, and even made a few trips in the large fishing schooners. He was, above all, a real deepwater American sailor of the late nineteenth and early twentieth centuries.

The two old men had some wonderful stories to tell, and I particularly remember the description each gave of his experiences in the "Portland Gale of 1898", and of their speculations as to what happened to the steamer *Portland* and where she might have gone down (it is the 100th anniversary of the loss of the *Portland* as I write these lines).

Captain Verge said he and a mate had been lobstering in dories while living in a shack on an island off the coast of Maine in November of 1898. They had planned to return to the mainland for Thanksgiving. There were few warnings of impending storms in those days. One relied on one's own prognostications, the barometer, and the look of the sky. Captain Verge said that "when it came on to snow from the northeast" before he and his mate had left the island to row to the mainland, they decided not to take the chance of getting lost while trying to row the dory, and stayed where they were. They were lucky. They made the right decision. The "Portland Gale" was a northeast snowstorm that combined with a hurricane and lasted about three days. There was a great loss of life along the New England coast, and the storm itself was an important topic of conversation among those with remembrance of it, the older generation when I was young. It received its name from the steamer *Portland* lost with all hands somewhere off Cape Ann.

The two men talked about other winter gales on the Grand Banks which each had endured, and spoke of the fact that "dories survived even when the vessel went down." When I asked how a dory could survive a gale, they said because a dory would slide off before a sea and therefore not ship the sea. Talk of hard sailing with a 'triple reef foresail' as told by the older men to each other kept me on edge as I tried to imagine the scene each would be describing. All this was spell-binding to me as a youth, and the setting in *Segochet*'s cabin with the glow of the oil lamp lent reality to the scene.

Captain Verge told me about his Friendship Sloop he had built by Wilbur Morse in 1900. She cost about $500 and he felt thrilled to have her. He fished in her, spring, summer, and fall off the Maine coast, handlining and lobstering. In the winter he would get a site on a schooner to fish the

Grand Banks. He sailed with Newfoundlanders and said they were a "hard bunch."

A few years before World War II, Captain Verge had been the professional skipper with Samuel Elliot Morrison when they retraced Columbus's voyage to the new world. Professor Morrison wrote about it in his book *The Admiral of the Ocean Sea*. Captain Verge had sailed over to Spain in the ketch *Mary Otis* with her owner and Dr. Morrison. *Mary Otis* was joined in the crossing by a schooner. The idea was that the two vessels would retrace Columbus's route to the new world. The passage to Spain and the return to the West Indies were made during the summer months.

Captain Verge said they made an attempt to follow Columbus's passage across in the NE trade winds, using Columbus's log, sailing in the beautiful blue waters with the trade winds giving them a fair wind day in and day out. This voyage impressed Captain Verge, for he had in his past life sailed in the gray-green waters of the cold North Atlantic. Captain Thron's comment was, after a few puffs to keep his pipe going, "Hell, that's flying fish weather" (a sailor's term for warm, pleasant weather, an 'easy life'). He also said that Columbus could not have failed to reach the West Indies with the steady fair wind of the NE trades. He felt that Columbus should have been given the most credit for finding his way back to home port, much of which was to weather.

Captain Verge was impressed with *Mary Otis*, a jib-headed rigged ketch of 45 feet, designed by Phillip L. Rhodes and built by Harvey Gamage in South Bristol, Maine, in the late 1930s. "One halyard to hoist and lower sail", he would say. "What ease compared to the hard handed gaff-rigged sails on this schooner" (referring to *Segochet*). Captain Thron agreed. "The Marconi rig is sure easy on us old-timers. Nothing beats it for quickly lowering sail in a squall. Just throw off the halyard and the sail comes down by the run." Thirty years later I would see *Mary Otis*, older and badly worn, in Allan Vaitse's yard in Mattapoisett, and at the time recalled the conversations of the two old seamen in the glow of the lamp in *Segochet*'s cabin.

Cruising in *Segochet*

As the month of June wore on, the weather became much more pleasant and we had more sailing. We left Quissett on a Saturday morning with Mr. Peterson and a few friends aboard. There was a good breeze from the SE and, as we were bound for Cuttyhunk, we could sail down in the lee of the islands, with no sea and the wind abeam. A "soldier's breeze", Captain Verge called it. As we sailed SW, the fresh SE wind would hit us with a few good blasts every now and then and the old *Segochet*, carrying full sail, would lay down pretty hard and bury her rail. We probably should have had a reef in the mainsail, but Mr. Peterson said he wanted to see what she could do. The other passengers were a bit nervous, but it did not bother me as I had never experienced this type of sailing and did not know any better.

Cuttyhunk Island, as I see it today, barely resembles the Cuttyhunk that existed in 1944. We took in the mainsail and jib outside the harbor, and sailed in through the channel by the Coast Guard station (then manned with lifeboat and all) under foresail alone. *Segochet* handled very well under this rig, and Captain Verge took her in very smartly to one of the few wharves in the harbor. There were very few people around. While Captain Verge and I furled the sails, Mr. Peterson and passengers went ashore to buy lobsters and look up his friend, Bob Tilton, one of the fishing guides on the island.

Mr. Peterson had brought a large pot with him from the hotel and I soon found out the reason for it. Captain Verge fired up the Shipmate stove and soon had a good fire going under the pot, into which he had put a quart or so of salt water. When Mr. Peterson returned he had with him a bushel basket of lobsters. We ate lobster until it came out of our ears, or so it seemed. After that session, where I ate my share and then some, I lost my taste for the meat which I am only now regaining after many years. I had lobster for breakfast, lunch, and supper many times that summer.

Mr. Russell Leonard, who owned a house at the south end of Shore Street in Falmouth and was the president of Pepperell Mills, the textile firm, seemed to have some interest in *Segochet* with John Peterson. He came to Quissett shortly after we arrived, when I picked him up in the dinghy and rowed him out to the schooner. He looked *Segochet* over thoroughly and had a conversation with Captain Verge. Unknown to me at the time was that Mr. Leonard was a first-class yachtsman and had owned some large schooners in the past. I remember him as a real gentleman.

A number of times Mr. Leonard would pick me up with his car when I went ashore to go shopping for some items we needed. He also brought supplies to us many times. I remember riding with him one day in his big black Cadillac down Shore Street, when he told me that troops had landed that morning in Normandy [June 6, 1944]. Mr. Leonard always brought on board with him his own Filipino steward, wearing a blue uniform with shiny gold buttons. This steward was a fabulous cook and I loved to help him down below when I could, since he would always give me some wonderful tidbits between meals. He was a very quiet man and rarely ever spoke a word.

One time, in July, Mr. Leonard had with him, as guests for a sail to Cuttyhunk, Governor Talmadge of Maryland and Walter George, a U.S. senator from Georgia. We had a very pleasant cruise to Cuttyhunk Island in beautiful weather. In the evening, after we returned to Quissett, I rowed the two guests ashore and then went back for Mr. Leonard. His steward was staying aboard to help clean up *Segochet*.

When Mr. Leonard got in the dinghy, he told Captain Verge he was going to keep me ashore for an hour or so. When we reached shore, Mr. Leonard asked me to come with him, and when we reached his car the governor and senator were sitting in the back seat. I got in front with Mr. Leonard. We went for a ride, down the back road to Woods Hole, around Nobska Light, along Surf Drive, to Falmouth Heights. I had no idea where we were going. The three men asked me many questions: where I was born, when and how far I had gone in school, how I came to be aboard *Segochet*, what I was interested in. I had not the slightest idea why these three distinguished men were so interested in my life. We finally arrived back in Quissett Harbor and Mr. Leonard drove around to the Quissett Harbor House and parked the car. After a few more questions, the senator asked me in his southern drawl, "Do you want to go to school, boy, because if you do, we will be willing to send you." I don't remember even considering my answer when I said, "No, I want to go to sea." Not another word was said about the matter.

When I came back to *Segochet*, Captain Verge asked me, "How did it go?" I told him about the questions I was asked and the final one, did I want to go to school? When Captain Verge found out I had said "no", that I wanted to go to sea, his face dropped. "You fool!" he said, "Those men were willing to send you through school, all the way. You passed up the opportunity of a lifetime."

Over the past 50 years, I thought over that incident many times, but really never regretted my answer. I went to sea instead of to school, and know in my heart that was the right choice for me, especially at that time. However, when I said, "I want to go to sea" I did not really know what I meant by that statement. In the summer of 1944, I was only living one day at a time, completely free from my confusing home life in Brooklyn, and also free from school which I had found rather boring. I had no inkling what the future had in store for me, but I was not going back to school if it could be helped. I had tasted freedom and I loved it.

Sometime, possibly near the end of July 1944, *Segochet* took a cruise to Nantucket Island. On board was Richard Tregaskis, a war correspondent, and his bride, who were to spend their honeymoon there. Mr. Tregaskis had been wounded in Italy and had a silver plate in his scalp. The year before, his book *Guadalcanal Diary* had been a best seller as well as a movie.

We sailed from Quissett with the newlywed couple in the morning and, after a pleasant sail through the Woods Hole passage with a SW wind, we arrived off Nantucket in the afternoon. Mr. Tregaskis did most of the steering and seemed to enjoy it very much. I always remembered what a nice young lady his bride was. When we arrived off Nantucket Harbor entrance, the steamer was just ahead of us. Quite often, in those days, small catboats with colored sails—red, green, blue, yellow—would come out to meet the steamers. It happened on this day, and Mrs. Tregaskis was thrilled at the sight of the little boats with their bright sails, called the 'rainbow fleet'. The steamer proceeded quickly through the channel and soon left *Segochet* astern surrounded by the small catboats. We sailed through the channel with all the little boats in company. We landed our newlyweds in Nantucket and sailed back to Quissett the following day.

Segochet is Sold

In early August, 1944, Mr. Peterson received an offer for *Segochet* and accepted it. With the prospective new owner aboard, we sailed around through the Woods Hole passage to Falmouth Inner Harbor, where *Segochet* was hauled on the railway of McDougall's yard. There she was surveyed and had her bottom painted. This was the first and only time I saw her out of the water. The new owner, a physician from Portland, Maine, hired Captain Verge as his professional captain and also asked me to stay on. *Segochet* was going to Portland which was going to be her homeport. I had no desire to return to Maine but preferred to stay around Quissett and Woods Hole, so declined the offer.

We returned to Quissett Harbor, where the sale was completed, papers signed, and, with Captain Verge and her new owner aboard, *Segochet* sailed out of Quissett for her new home. I accompanied Mr. Peterson in his power boat *Daydream* to escort *Segochet* out into Buzzards Bay, where she hoisted sail (the first time I had seen her under sail from another boat), set her course for the Cape Cod Canal, and soon disappeared out of my life. *Daydream,* which Mr. Peterson had owned for a few years, was a 65-foot raised deck power cruiser of a design very common in the late 1920s and 1930s. She was built in 1930 by the Gray Boat Company in Thomaston to an Albert Condon design. She was built for Charles and Anne Lindbergh for their honeymoon cruise.

I lived aboard *Daydream* for a while in early August, keeping her in shape generally. I was very happy and had no thought or concern for the morrow. About that time, the carnival came to town and set up on the vacant land behind the new theater on Scranton Avenue. While at the carnival one evening, I saw Bob Weeks, whose family were early settlers in Quissett. I told him that *Segochet* had been sold and returned to Maine. Bob was about my age, and that summer he working at the Woods Hole Oceanographic Institution on the schooner *Reliance.* His brother Bill was serving on the Oceanographic's *Anton Dohrn* in Provincetown on a Navy sonar project. He suggested I try to get a job at the Oceanographic, advice I did not take too seriously at the moment. Somehow, however, fate stepped in and, without much planning on my part, about one week later I found myself on a dock in Woods Hole looking at the world's largest ketch *Atlantis,* hired on as ordinary seaman at the princely wage of $85 per month, with room and board. A new period in my life began.

First Impressions

Woods Hole of early 1944 was much smaller than it is today but much more of a complete village. There were three grocery stores (the A & P, Tsiknas', and the Woods Hole Market, located where the Bank of Woods Hole is now), two drugstores (Daley's and Jim Lowey's Drug Store and Spa), Jock Lowey's hardware store and liquor store, a barber shop, and, in the middle of the village, a boat shop and marine railway owned by Oscar Hilton. The village also contained Sam Cahoon's Fish Market, a large operation in wholesale and retail, a restaurant (James Grill, where the [Quick's Hole Tavern] is today), and the local bar, the Rendezvous, where one could get a good dinner of fish and sea scallops.

To serve the people of the "Oceanographic" there was the "Mess", located in an old building on the land where the "Pie in the Sky" bakery is at present; three meals a day, five days a week were served there, with breakfast on Saturday morning. The Oceanographic Institution was certainly a lot smaller in area and in the number of people employed there, and consisted of the main laboratory and office building (Bigelow) and the shops and storage areas next door in the Penzance Garage. After a few months of working at the Oceanographic, one could get to know everyone from Director Iselin to the scientists, technicians, the men in the shops, the guards, to the maintenance man, Jim Salthouse, Sr.

Looking back about 60 years, I would best describe the Oceanographic Institution then, as seen through my eyes, as an "off the wall" operation which, in a way, made it interesting and fun to work there. At that time, I was never sure of the exact nature of the work done by the Oceanographic but it seemed to have a lot to do with explosives and underwater sound. Outside of Woods Hole, hardly anyone knew what oceanographic research

Aerial view of Woods Hole village (ca. 1935) facing SE. Mid-distance right is the U.S. Fish and Wildlife Service ("Fisheries") complex, with its square dock and boat basin configuration; mid-distance center is the Marine Biological Laboratory complex, bordering Eel Pond; farther distant, bordering Great Harbor, is the old MBL Club, the WHOI Bigelow Building, the Penzance Garage (with skylights) and the WHOI dock complex. Photo by Howard Wood, Woods Hole Historical Museum Archives.

consisted of, nor what an oceanographic research ship was. Today, in 2004, I look back with very fond memories of those times in Woods Hole, of all the nice people in the village and at the Institution, and especially of my first cruise in the ketch *Atlantis* to the Tongue of the Ocean, some 60 years ago.

Atlantis had returned from Lake Charles, Louisiana, about two weeks before that day in August 1944 when I walked down the Fisheries wharf to see her close up for the first time. John Churchill, Assistant to the Director, C.O. Iselin, had hired me the day before, after a few brief questions. I had an "Identification Card" issued by the Captain of the Port of Woods Hole, and it seemed that was all that was necessary. The Coast Guard yeoman who did all the work to issue that card to me was Yeoman First Class Bob Pratt (later the sexton of St. Barnabas Church in Falmouth). I remember that he always wore the undress blue uniform when he walked into the village. How simple everything was then!

Navy Crash Boat C39069 astern of R/V Atlantis. Several kinds of vessels operated by the U.S. Navy were based in Woods Hole during World War II. Photo courtesy of Nick and Susan Witzell.

Partial crew of Navy Crash Boat C39069 poses near the Candle House in Woods Hole. From left to right: Warren E. "Whitey" Witzell, George Emery, "Little Ben", "Chief" Lauder, and J.P. Mello. Whitey Witzell went on to a long career at WHOI as a Research Specialist in charge of the Electro-Mechanical Shop. Photo courtesy of Nick and Susan Witzell.

Above left: *Frank Glynn and girlfriend in front of Lowey's Drug Store and the Rendezvous Restaurant, where the* Atlantis *crew often went for a beer "or two". Photo from private collection.*

Above right: *Sailors in uniform were commonly seen on the streets of Woods Hole during World War II. Here two sailors pose on the Eel Pond drawbridge with local girls. Photo from private collection.*

John Churchill only asked me a few questions. The last was what experience I had had. I told him I had four months service on a 45-foot gaff-rigged schooner, as "the boy" under a yacht captain. "That will do," said Mr. Churchill, "report to the captain of *Atlantis*. You are hired as an ordinary seaman. Wages are $85 per month." I was really surprised when he sent me to *Atlantis*. I thought for sure I would be sent to one of the smaller boats.

I found out later there had been two other ordinary seamen in the two weeks preceding me, but they left because they did not like the old bo'sun and cared even less for the acting chief mate, Mr. Mandly. Mr. Mandly treated every ordinary seaman as he had been treated 50 years earlier in the 1890s when he was young.

Atlantis was laying port side-to the wharf, and the first thing that caught my eye as I walked toward the ship was the two whaleboats. This was the first time I had ever seen the real thing and thought they were beautiful. There was no one in sight on deck; the only activity was the sound of the exhaust of the single cylinder diesel generator. I might have looked aloft, but not yet with the eye of a seaman. Besides, there was too much on deck to

Above: R/V Atlantis *laying at the WHOI dock, with the steam ferry Nobska in the background, arriving on a morning run. The old MBL Club building is in the foreground center. To the left, with its cupola, is a new-looking Bigelow Building, WHOI's first base of operation, completed in 1931. Photo courtesy of Woods Hole Historical Museum.*

Left: *During the war, fences and security checkpoints appeared around Woods Hole. Here, second WHOI Director Columbus O'Donnell Iselin (tall man in center) enters the Bigelow checkpoint to the building and docks, with a guest. To their right are Kenneth McCasland and Security Guard Harry Handy. Photo courtesy WHOI Archives © Woods Hole Oceanographic Institution.*

The main dock at WHOI with some of the several vessels operated by the Institution during World War II. R/V Atlantis *lays on the outside of the dock with the smaller power vessel,* Anton Dohrn *off her bow. Bill Cooper crewed on both ships. The oldest WHOI boat is* Asterias, *seen here with her long bow pulpit. Photo by Claude Ronne © Woods Hole Oceanographic Institution.*

fascinate me. *Atlantis* was in every sense a deep-water ship, the type of which I'd never seen close up before.

Fifty years ago one could experience the feeling of a deep-water ship if one were to visit the Danish training ship *Danmark*, or *Horst Vessel* before she became *Eagle*, or most certainly the beautiful Portuguese bark *Sagres*, and *Atlantis*. What was it? It was the spars painted buff, the color so beloved by the old seamen, wooden decks—nothing like wooden decks—the teak cap rail on the bulwarks, the varnished teak wheelhouse, of practical and pleasing design, the varnished teak companionways and other bright work, the beautifully-formed ventilators with the bright red mouths, the ship's bell mounted at the base of the main-mast, the beautiful whaleboats with davits and rope boat falls, canvas buckets, hand-sewn with sennet work never seen today, the pleasing rhythmic beat of the single cylinder generator (one could sleep right alongside of it), the shrouds coated with white lead, terminating in turnbuckles covered in tailored canvas boots (we cut these off to adjust the rigging a few weeks later and they were never replaced), painted grey sailor's work, all the lines of rigging neatly coiled on the pin rails, her ensign proudly flying from the stern staff, not just an afterthought. All these things

 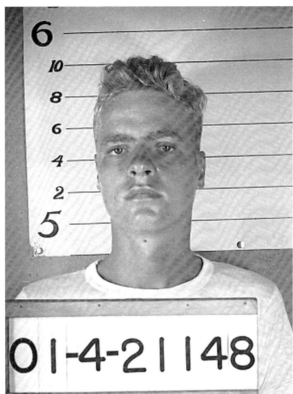

made up the components of a deep-water vessel. *Atlantis* looked and smelled the part, for even the men serving in her, although few in number, were all deep-water men. This is how I saw her, as a seventeen year old boy whose dreams of going to sea were about to be fulfilled.

After a while, Captain Lambert Knight arrived, took me aboard, and turned me over to the bo'sun. The mate, Mr. Mandly, was on vacation. The bo'sun wasted no time, but forthwith introduced me to a bucket of "soojee" [a mixture of detergent and hot water used for cleaning] and had me wash out the cold storage box in the galley. For lunch he took me up to the Oceanographic Mess to sign me in, but not before we first stopped at the Rendezvous, next to the Woods Hole drawbridge, where he ordered for us at the bar "one bottle Budweiser and a Coca Cola for the boy."

The bo'sun, Ernest Siversen, who had said very little to me prior to this, began to make small talk after he had a few sips of his beer. He spoke with an accent that was, at first, difficult for me to understand. His first bit of advice as we sat at the bar, something that I had never experienced before,

Above left: *John Churchill walks the main WHOI dock. Churchill was in charge of the wartime fleet and its crews. Seen in the background, center, is the MBL Crane Laboratory; to the right is the MBL Club building. Photo courtesy WHOI Archives © Woods Hole Oceanographic Institution.*

Above: *Employee I.D. photo of Bill Cooper. Cooper later discovered he was officially employed by the Navy, not by WHOI. Photo courtesy WHOI Archives © Woods Hole Oceanographic Institution..*

was to "never buy drinks for the house, and never accept drinks that way. Always go 'Dutch treat'." Although I did not realize it at that time, Ernest Siversen, a Swede, was my first introduction to that most excellent breed of seaman, the squarehead, and was himself a true old shell-back, a real Cape Horn sailor.

The Whaleboats

To my young eyes, the whaleboats were beautiful, and had much romance attached to them. They were the first whaleboat model I'd ever seen. I also liked the way they sailed and the handy, simple lug rig. Chief Engineer Backus told me that *Atlantis* originally carried dories. He said he had a conversation with Dr. Bigelow, then Director of the Oceanographic, about these dories at one time. Chief Backus did not think the dory a suitable life boat for *Atlantis*, which cruised well outside the normal shipping lanes. Dr. Bigelow agreed with him and the result was the two whaleboats ordered from Beetle.

These boats were built by the Charles Beetle Co. of New Bedford in the early 1930s, and, as the story goes, they were the last built to the old patterns before a fire at Beetle's yard destroyed all these patterns. The measurements, I believe, at this time, were: the Number 1 boat, 23 feet overall and the Number 2 boat, 28 feet overall. The Number 1 boat nestled inside the Number 2 boat.

These whaleboats were not of the usual whaleboat construction, which was smooth plane with batten seams similar to the construction in the Woods Hole Spritsail boat, *Spy*. They were all lapstrake or clinker planking. Except for this, all other details seemed to be the same as a regular whaleboat.

The smaller or Number 1 boat was rigged out with a centerboard and rudder (as were all whaleboats), and sloop-rigged with a standing lug mainsail and the jib set flying (not attached to a head stay). The mast in this boat was free-standing without head stay or shrouds. I had many pleasant sails in her. She had a number of canvas sand bags for shifting ballast, but they were rarely used or carried at any time I sailed in this boat.

The larger or Number 2 boat, which was nestled at the bottom, was ketch-rigged with standing lug sails and jib set flying. The mainsail in this boat was loose-footed, but the mizzen was rigged with a boom. This boat

could sail very fast with the wind free. I also believe this Number 2 boat was Captain Knight's favorite.

The whaleboats were painted Kirby's "French gray" inside and out, with varnished gunnels, chocks, and other brightwork. The bottoms in 1945 were painted Marblehead Antifouling Green (light green). The Number 1 boat had some really fancy sennet and coxcombing work for fender and gunnel guard. I always believed this work was done by the old whaleman, Henry Mandly, former second mate.

Captain Knight seemed to really appreciate these boats more than any

To Bill Cooper's young eyes, the whaleboats were beautiful, and had much romance attached to them. Photo by Jan Hahn © Woods Hole Oceanographic Institution.

other master I served under, and certainly more than the officers, with the exception of Henry Mandly. When work was slack, Mr. Mandly always would have us "mix up a bucket of soojee and wash out the whaleboats." We washed and cleaned them quite frequently.

Under Captain Knight's orders, I helped the bo'sun hand sew a new boat cover, as the previous one was beginning to wear out. We covered the boats in the fall and winter of 1945-1946, but I never saw the cover used again in my time on *Atlantis*.

Captain Knight told me one day, while sailing with him in the Number 1 boat in Woods Hole, that a model similar to the whaleboat with a shallow lead keel and centerboard would make an ideal cruiser for shoal water, such as in the Bahamas. Of such is the romance of boats.

I have seen a photo of the Number 1 being carried swung out in the davits, with the pudding boom in place, with *Atlantis* under full sail. We never carried the whaleboat swung out in davits under sail at any time I knew of. We did keep the whaleboat in davits with the pudding boom in place when at anchor or hove-to at sea. The whaleboats were lifeboats and as such, carried emergency containers of food and fresh water. Before 1945, the emergency water was carried in wooden water beakers made by Beetle and each boat also carried two wooden buckets.

The new second mate, who was 23 years old at the time, arrived on board shortly afterward, wearing the uniform of a Lieutenant Commander in the U.S. Maritime Service. We heard the captain tell the chief mate that the new officer had an "unlimited master's license, any tonnage, any ocean." Mr. Christopher, the new second mate, was a graduate of the Nantucket school ship before the war and had been sailing on merchant ships in the war zones for the past three and a half years. He said later that he wanted to make the Tongue of the Ocean Cruise on *Atlantis* for a vacation, a change from the life he had had in the past three years. Mr. Christopher (I don't remember his first name) wasted no time in getting into his duties. The chief mate assigned me to help him, and for a week or so I had some interesting jobs.

The first thing we did was to hoist the Number 1 whaleboat in the davits and swing it outboard to clear the Number 2 boat stowed underneath. He commenced to throw out of the whaleboats and on to the dock all the biscuit boxes, wooden water beakers, buckets and canvas-covered cases of emergency rations supplied by Beetle, the builder, as part of the gear of a whaleboat. This gear, left over from whaling days, did not meet Coast Guard

Opposite: Atlantis *glides away from the dock under power. The smaller power boat in the basin is Risk owned by Columbus Iselin and used to commute back and forth to his home fronting Lake Tashmoo on Martha's Vineyard. Photo courtesy WHOI Archives © Woods Hole Oceanographic Institution.*

wartime requirements for emergency equipment and stores in lifeboats. We replaced the hardtack biscuit boxes with emergency rations stored in metal cans, and the wooden water beakers with fresh water stored in quart size tin cans. The beautiful wooden buckets were replaced with galvanized iron pails. I asked Mr. Christopher if I could have a wooden bucket, which he allowed. I believe all the rest of the old gear went to the rubbish. I still have at this date (August 1996) that wooden bucket with the name *Atlantis* branded into the bottom.

I have always felt sad that officers and crew in the following years, through neglect or poor seamanship, were able to destroy the two beautiful Beetle whaleboats. These Beetle boats were so racked and damaged they had to be replaced in 1952.

Lake Charles, Louisiana

With America's entry into World War II, the Atlantic Ocean and Caribbean Sea became unsafe for U.S. ship operation. Nevertheless, Director Columbus Iselin was keen to promote the relevance of oceanography to national defense, through continued operation of an *Atlantis* research program. Early in 1942 it was decided to move *Atlantis* to the Gulf of Mexico, thought then to be safe from German U-boats, where she could continue work. The ship was moved south in short legs, sometimes operating at night without running lights. The first scientific cruise, out of Mobile, Alabama, set sail on April 11, 1942 under Chief Scientist Alfred Woodcock, a physical oceanographer. After three weeks at sea *Atlantis* put into Galveston, Texas, for fuel and supplies. While there they learned enemy submarines had been spotted in the Gulf of Mexico. This new threat, and associated spiraling maritime insurance rates, abruptly ended the planned research program at sea.

Galveston could not be considered a permanent refuge possibly because of its vulnerability to hurricane damage, dramatically demonstrated by the 1900 hurricane from which the city never fully recovered. After a few

months the decision was finally made to move *Atlantis* back to Woods Hole. She joined a Navy convoy but, because she was too slow under her own power, had to be towed by a Navy tug. Shortly after leaving Galveston, the seas started building and near Sabine Shoals the line parted. *Atlantis* drifted to a stop and anchored. The Navy tug returned, but too late to rejoin the convoy, and now a hurricane warning had been issued as well.

Atlantis was towed north to busy Port Arthur near the mouth of Sabine Lake, Texas, and later through the Lake Charles Deepwater Channel, an E-W dredged canal leading from the Sabine River to Lake Charles, Louisiana. She arrived on September 2, 1942 and would be docked there for nearly two years, awnings rigged, safe from submarines and hurricanes, but subject to peeling paint, blistering varnish, drying decks, and bottom fouling. Captain McMurray and most of the crew of 17 men left the ship, some joining the war effort. Remaining on board were Henry Mandly (in charge), Ernest Siversen, Harold Backus, and Hans Cook. Two local Cajun cooks were hired to man the galley.

The port of Lake Charles is located 120 miles east of Galveston on the coastal plain, 34 miles upstream from the Gulf of Mexico on the Calcasieu (Kalka-shoo') River, and two miles from the town center of Lake Charles (1940 population: about 20,000). Like the other significant Gulf settlements, Houston and Beaumont, Texas, Lake Charles is removed from the immediate coast because of the extensive, insect-ridden and flood-prone wetlands.

The earliest European settlers at Lake Charles arrived in 1781. The initial plantation economy was later dominated by lumber—longleaf yellow

Above left: Atlantis *often operated out of Galveston on cruises in the Gulf of Mexico. During 1942, through a series of war-related mishaps she was towed from Galveston to Port Arthur and then to Lake Charles, Louisiana, where she remained, essentially moth-balled, for nearly two years.*

Above right: Atlantis *alongside a deserted dock in Lake Charles, Louisiana, with a skeleton crew on board. Photo courtesy WHOI Archives © Woods Hole Oceanographic Institution.*

pine and bald cypress. Shallow draft schooners plied the tortuous Calcasieu River connecting shallow muddy lakes and bayous on its course to the sea, for trade with Texas and Mexico. This scale of commerce and the associated pace of life changed after the Civil War, when rice farming flourished and sulfur mining, using the new Frasch process, spurred construction of an east-west railroad connecting coastal Texas and Louisiana with New Orleans. In 1901 the Spindletop oil field at Beaumont initiated the transformation of Texas and southwest Louisiana to oil and petrochemical economies. The intracoastal waterway grew in stages to augment east-west transport of bulk cargoes by ship and barge. The growing agribusiness and chemicals industries prompted the development of maritime transportation infrastructure in the ports of Galveston/Houston, Port Arthur/Beaumont, and Lake Charles. By 1941 north-south deepwater shipping channels had been dredged, connecting these centers with the Gulf of Mexico and global ocean shipping lanes. Thus, by 1942 the port and town of Lake Charles provided the haven and Gulf access *Atlantis* needed to ride out the war years, although this had never been an express plan.

With Navy permission, *Atlantis* departed Lake Charles in July 1944, Lambert Knight in command, down the Calcasieu Ship Channel to the Gulf. Mates were Nels Nordquist and Henry Mandly. Backus and Cook continued in the engine room; Siversen was bo'sun and an assemblage of others filled out the deck crew, including AB Karl Johnson, who had sailed with Mr. Nordquist on *Manxman*, a large racing yacht out of Edgartown, Martha's Vineyard. After stops in New Orleans and Miami, the bedraggled ship arrived back at Woods Hole on July 28, 1944, shortly before Bill Cooper came on board as a newly-hired Ordinary Seaman.

Arthur Gaines

Sources:

Cullen, V., 2005. *Down to the Sea for Science*. Woods Hole Oceanographic Institution, Woods Hole, Mass. C&C Offset Printing Co., China. 174 pp.

Lane, B.L., 1959. *The Industrial Development of Lake Charles, Louisiana 1920-1950*. Thesis submitted in partial fulfillment of the requirements for the degree of Master of Arts. The Department of History, Graduate Faculty of the Louisiana State University and Agricultural and Mechanical College. [Transcribed by Leora White, 2008] McNeese State University.

Schlee, S. 1978. *On Almost Any Wind*. Cornell University Press, Ithaca and London. 301 pp.

John D. W. Churchill

John D.W. Churchill, variously identified as port captain and marine superintendent, was the Director's right-hand man. As arbitrator of disputes he was known as more likely to leave participants laughing than mad. Photo courtesy WHOI Archives © Woods Hole Oceanographic Institution.

From 1942 through 1946, John Churchill was in charge of the Oceanographic Institution's marine operations, including its growing wartime fleet of boats and ships and their crews. A long-time friend of Columbus Iselin, the second Director of the Institution, they had attended Harvard College together. In 1926, along with other classmates, Churchill sailed aboard *Chance*, a 72-foot schooner owned and captained by Iselin, on an oceanographic cruise exploring the coast of Labrador. Churchill served as engineer. In 1931 Churchill participated in the transatlantic maiden voyage, from Copenhagen, of the 143-foot ketch *Atlantis*, with Iselin as her first Captain.

In the summer of 1940 Churchill served among the scientific staff on five *Atlantis* cruises between Georges Bank and Galveston, Texas. As related by Cooper, he also stepped in as crew aboard *Atlantis* in later years, on occasions when there was a shortage of seamen.

Son of the American novelist Winston Churchill (not to be confused with the Prime Minister), whose books established the family fortune during the early 20th century, John was born in Boston. He grew up at Cornish, NH, under the influence of the Cornish Art Colony, an artists', writers', intellectual community (made most famous by the sculptor Augustus Saint-Gaudens) to which his parents belonged. Churchill studied architecture at MIT and Harvard College, and, prior to World War II he practiced architecture with the New York firm of Pennington, Lewis and Churchill. Upon leaving the Oceanographic in 1946 he resumed the practice of architecture. He was also associated with the engineering firm of Anderson-Nichols in Boston and with MIT's Lincoln Laboratory in Lexington.

Churchill built himself a summer home at Lambert's Cove on Martha's Vineyard, not far from Iselin's home at Lake Tashmoo, and they remained family friends. During his work at Woods Hole, Churchill and his wife Katharine resided on Millfield Street in the village.

John Churchill died in 1961, at age 58, after he was stricken while aboard his boat in Vineyard Haven Harbor, Martha's Vineyard. It is said that a sailing companion aboard that last sail went forward to pick up the mooring. The boat headed up and drifted to a stop. The friend picked up the buoy and made the pennant fast. When he turned back to report the mooring was secure John Churchill was dead--his last, perfect landing.

Arthur Gaines

Sources:
Cullen, V., 2005. Down to the Sea for Science. Woods Hole Oceanographic Institution, Woods Hole, Mass. C&C Offset Printing Co., China. 174 pp.
WHOI Archives. Unattributed newspaper clippings.

The Hurricane of 1944

2

SEPTEMBER 14, 1944, a month after I signed on aboard *Atlantis*, was a warm, hazy day, showing no sign of what the weather would be twelve hours later. On board *Atlantis*, we were in the process of renewing the mizzen standing rigging with the spar in place. The bo'sun and the mate, Mr. Mandly, were getting up a triangular staging to hoist aloft around the mizzen; the rigger could then splice the new wire around the mast. We disconnected the forward lower shrouds and the backstays. This left the mizzen with only aft lower shrouds and the upper shrouds holding the 103-foot spar in place.

For some time prior to this day, we had been setting up rigging on both the main and mizzen masts. At that time the main mast raked forward and the mizzen raked aft. In order to sight the rake of the masts, the captain would go over to the Steamship dock. *Atlantis* was laying at the old Fisheries dock (about where the new one is now), thus affording Captain Knight a broadside view.

He would then walk back to the Fisheries dock and tell the mate how much should be slacked off the turnbuckles, or taken up, one way or the other. There was more to this procedure than it would seem, as large crow-bars were required to move the turnbuckles. The turnbuckles were packed with a mixture of white lead and mutton tallow, covered with canvas boots, sewed on. The bars would slip in the grease when pressure was applied. This happened quite often, usually while a bar was in the mate's hands.

The sight of old Mandly as he pulled on the bar with a grunt, then slipped and rolled on the deck like a rubber ball, was enormously funny to me at the time (I kept this to myself, of course). On one particular instance, the mate slipped while tightening a turnbuckle, and hit the able seaman (AB), who was holding the other bar, opening up a small head wound. It makes me chuckle now to visualize the scene again; the old mate and bo'-sun examining the AB's head, moving it this way and that, mutton tallow and white lead spread over everything. Before they were through, his head and hair were covered with greasy fingerprints.

When we finally got things squared away, and the rake of both masts corrected to the captain's eye, we found that the main boom would not clear the mizzen mast. I can vaguely remember either Scotty Morrison or Henry Hodgkins cutting off the end of the main boom so it could clear. I assume they wanted the rake of the spars corrected before renewing the mizzen rigging.

About 9 AM Captain Knight came on board and told the mate that Columbus Iselin had heard that a hurricane might be coming up the coast. This was exciting news to me. At coffee time, Mr. Mandly informed us that we could have the day off tomorrow if we would stay on duty tonight. This was good news; there was no such thing as overtime, and even if we stayed up round the clock caring for the ship, we would not normally be entitled to the next day off.

At this time, we had a reduced crew on board. This included Henry Mandly, the mate, Ernest Siversen, the bo'sun, Hans Cook, the second engineer, one AB, a rigger, and myself—ordinary seaman, 17 years old. Also, of course, Lambert Knight, the captain.

We knocked off all other work with the news of the impending storm, and immediately embarked on the task of getting our whaleboats out of the Fisheries lagoon and hoisted aboard. This took some time to accomplish, as it entailed bracing the ship away from the dock so the boats could be worked in under the davits. We were laying port side-to and the boat davits were on that side.

The mate, Henry Mandly, a man then in his late sixties, had been one of the last whaling captains to sail out of New Bedford. He was very fond of these whaleboats (the last ones built on the original patterns by Beetle in New Bedford). Whenever there was a boat drill he was right on top of us. The commands would come fast and furious: "When I give an order, always repeat it after me, like a parrot!"

To brace the ship off from the dock and then hoist those boats aboard using "Norwegian steam" with just the three of us was hard. We had to take up a little on one fall at a time, with Mandly supervising and keeping the boat away from the ship's side. Captain Knight and the mate had discussed leaving the boats in the lagoon, but decided against it. I know now that if they had been left there, they would have been destroyed that night. The work on the boats was finally completed by mid-afternoon and we started on the job of securing *Atlantis* to the wharf.

We doubled up on all the dock lines and parceled (wrapped with canvas with half hitch rope-yarns) them in areas of apparent chafe. No one thought of allowing the lines to be rendered and slacked with the rising tide (I think this would have been impossible under the conditions of the storm). The idea that the tide would rise abnormally was never considered. I never heard it mentioned at all.

The mizzen halyard had been unroved during our work on the mizzen and was laying coiled up on deck. The captain suggested we use the wire of this halyard as an extra line out from the stern.

"Use the wire of the mizzen halyard?" asked the AB. "Why not?" said Mr. Mandly, "We would use the main topsail sheets to tie up a whale ship when I was young" (about 1900).

"Veil," said the bo'sun, "maybe ve should use the flag halyards too." Everyone laughed. They all thought the captain was overly cautious. We did not get out what the bo'sun called "the nine-inch insurance hawser" (actually 3-inch diameter manila rope) from the lazarette. "Ve keep dot for emergencies."

Captain Knight decided he wanted the 5/8-inch wire from the main trawl winch run out through the bow chocks and secured to the stone jetty. This idea irritated Chief Backus, as it required starting the main engine to run the generator necessary to turn the winch over.

The AB and I got the wire from the bow to the stone jetty. The AB sent me back to get some wire clamps. The mate took me down in the sail locker, where he searched and finally found two clamps. I could see they were marked 7/8-inch. When I got back to the stone jetty the AB looked at what I handed him and said, "Why in hell did he give you 7/8-inch" clamps for 5/8-inch wire?" He swore a few times, and then tightened the nuts down as much as he could. At that they hauled in on the winch and took the slack out of the wire. Neither the mate, the bo'sun, nor the captain examined the way in which the wire was made fast. They should have.

In the afternoon what little air there was dropped completely. The whole atmosphere seemed to take on an ominous yellow-purplish haze. The water looked as if it were covered with an oily slick. I did not notice at the time, but it was later said that, at Quissett, the tide dropped as if a plug were pulled from the bottom of the harbor.

At suppertime, we knocked off. The vessel was as secure as she was apparently going to be. Looking back, I would say we did not do enough. I can't remember removing the ventilator cowls and installing storm covers, nor did we check and close all the port lights (as I later discovered for myself). Neither did we place the canvas storm covers over the companionways. We did put the boat covers on and securely lash down Mr. Mandly's beloved whaleboats.

The bo'sun, looking around, said the only lines missing were the flag halyards and our clotheslines. The 9-inch insurance hawser lay securely coiled in the lazarette.

On board *Atlantis* for the coming night were to be: Captain Knight, Second Engineer Hans Cook, Bo'sun Ernest Siversen, one able seaman and myself, ordinary seaman. About 6 PM the *Saluda* arrived and tied up on our starboard side. *Saluda* was an 85-foot yawl-rigged yacht in Navy service, working out of the Underwater Sound Lab in New London. As I remember, she had been working on sonar ranging with the *Anton Dohrn*, out of Woods Hole that summer. She was typical of the mid-thirties design, with a double-planked mahogany hull. Her teak decks were well-scrubbed, her brass shone and, in general, she was kept ship-shape and Bristol fashion by her Navy crew. *Saluda*'s Floridian crew knew from experience what a hurricane could be like. They stripped all loose gear from deck and stored it below. Then extra lines were placed turn after turn around the main and mizzen booms lashing the sails down securely.

Sometime after supper, the sky clouded up and the wind came very lightly from the southeast with a light drizzle. The barometer was falling. Captain Knight said, if the glass fell at the rate of 1/10-inch per hour, that would be a sign the storm would hit us (I believe it finally fell something on the order of one inch in five hours, almost twice the above rate.).

About this time, a pretty girl in a yellow sou'wester and an oilskin coat came down on the dock and spoke to us for a few minutes about the impending storm. Her name was Nancy Sisson. The bo'sun said at the time that sailors considered yellow sou'westers to be unlucky and would never wear them. There was not much for us to do at this point, but stand by in the ever-increasing wind and rain. The excitement of the storm and the prospect of a day off tomorrow did much to keep me from being bored.

Ernest Siversen was bo'sun aboard Atlantis for many years, including during most of Cooper's time aboard the ship. He was an old-school Cape Horn sailor and he taught Bill the ethic and many of the skills of the professional seaman. Siversen was aboard Atlantis as she was driven under bare poles across Great Harbor by the 1944 hurricane force winds. Photo courtesy WHOI Archives © Woods Hole Oceanographic Institution.

Above: *Aerial view of the Fisheries and MBL buildings, showing waterfront damage from the 1944 hurricane. Later, the 1954 hurricane severely damaged the Fisheries buildings shown here, leading to construction of the present structures in 1960. During the early years Atlantis often used the northern (left) limb of the Fisheries pier and was tied alongside there when the 1944 hurricane struck. Photo courtesy of Woods Hole Historical Museum.*

Captain Lambert Knight

Lambert was born in New York in 1903, the son of a prominent physician, but moved as a young boy with his mother and grandmother to a family home on Martha's Vineyard, following his father's death. The house, on Main Street in Vineyard Haven, overlooks the harbor and Lambert was quickly captured by the water and the vessels that traveled on it.

Like several of the WHOI staff, Lambert Knight was a long-time friend of Columbus Iselin, with extensive experience under sail including aboard Atlantis *on her maiden voyage. Knight was hired in 1940 as captain of the Anton Dohrn,* and assigned later to bring Atlantis *back to Woods Hole from Lake Charles in 1944. Photo courtesy WHOI Archives © Woods Hole Oceano-graphic Institution.*

His earliest voyages into Vineyard Sound, in his small cat-rigged "pumpkin seed" sneakbox *Wild Duck*, were the beginning of a sea-going career that totaled thousands of sea miles and would bring him to many faraway places on a variety of interesting vessels. This included, among others, transatlantic voyages, a Cape Horn rounding on one of the famous "Grain Ships", and several Bermuda races.

His obituary in the *Vineyard Gazette* describes him: "A bear of a man physically, Lambert epitomized the oceangoing sailorman, skillful in sail handling, piloting, celestial navigation, ship handling, and yacht racing tactics, not to mention the arts of the boatswain. But above all, he was a gentleman in the true sense, full of kindness and quiet humor, and always willing to share his knowledge and skill with others."

In the 1920s and 30s he owned and sailed in *Alwilda*, a Crosby sloop, and *Pampano*, a Herreshoff Fish Class Sloop to which he added a small cabin for cruising. After a time at Princeton University he decided he preferred something different from academics and turned his attention and efforts to a career connected to the sea and outdoors.

In 1930, not knowing it would eventually have a major impact on his life, he signed on for the transatlantic delivery from Copenhagen of the newly constructed 143-foot. ketch *Atlantis*, and fell in love with her. A decade later he would serve a stint as her Captain.

Lambert crewed aboard the famous four-masted Barque *Parma* in 1932, owned and captained by the legendary Alan Villiers, from Australia around Cape Horn to England. The square rigged *Parma* measured 346-feet overall and carried 32,000 square feet of sail. Many consider the so-called "Grain Ships" to be the epitome of the evolution of square rigged ships. Like so many others, the ship encountered a winter gale while rounding Cape Horn and Captain Villiers credited Lambert, who produced a strong "electric torch from his kit", with helping to save the ship as the light aided the crew in shortening sail in very difficult conditions. Just as the famous Irving Johnson of Brigantine *Yankee* fame did on the *Peking*, Lambert brought along a movie camera and filmed during the voyage, a film he donated to Mystic Seaport in the 1970s as Johnson had done with his in the 60s. These two films provide the finest record in existence of these great ships underway.

Lambert Knight was affiliated with the John Alden Firm in Boston in the 1930s during which time he sailed on several of the famous Alden Malabar schooners in Bermuda races, and in 1935 was inducted into the Cruising Club of America. He also made several long passages, such as a cruise to the Azores and back on the 137-foot. Gloucester-type schooner yacht *Roseway*. Back on the Vineyard, Lambert made many trips aboard the well-known schooner *Alice Wentworth* with the storied Captain Zeb Tilton, including a record voyage from Vineyard Haven to Greenport, Long Island, downwind in a winter Northeaster.

Like sailors everywhere, Lambert never lost his interest in vessels and seamanship. He was especially interested in weather, and a prominent feature of the kitchen in his house was a large chart on which he had charted the track of all the big hurricanes from 1938 on. In the 60s and 70s, when he was not out tending his sloop *Pompano*, he could often be found sitting in his car parked halfway down the road leading to the town wharf at Owen Park, scanning the harbor with his binoculars.

While it is difficult to make a judgment about someone else's feelings, especially after they are gone, I think it is safe to say Lambert had a special bond with *Atlantis* beginning with his first voyage in her, had a passionate respect for the vessel's sailing qualities and seaworthiness, and greatly valued his time aboard her.

Mathew Stackpole

Adrift

About 8:30 PM we began to experience some heavy gusts of wind from the southeast, along with the heavy rain. This wind direction meant we would be laying broadside to the storm. It seemed to get very dark all of a sudden, and the wind began to blow with a howling shriek in the rigging. The rain seemed to be coming at us horizontally now. Tasting, we found that it was actually salt water. The sea coming in from the southeast was striking the stone jetty, being thrown in the air, and was driving against us. The harder the wind blew the more this salt water came on us like a deluge. The roar of the wind became so loud, it was impossible to talk or hear. *Atlantis* lay over at an angle of 20 degrees and remained very steady at that list. *Saluda*, on the other hand, would lay way over in the severe gusts, to about 45 degrees, and then come back again and crash into our bulwarks. The double-planked mahogany hull of *Saluda* began to cave in the steel bulwarks of *Atlantis*. The storm reached a violent velocity. *Saluda's* motion became so severe that her crew abandoned her, and came on board *Atlantis*. The impact of the two vessels was terrible, and the strain on *Atlantis* was such that we were ordered to cut *Saluda* adrift.

Her crew began to cut the mooring lines with their knives. This was a slow process, so the bo'sun got the fire axe and gave it to them. It was pitch-black, and we were under such a deluge of water, it seemed as if someone was spraying us with a large hose. The only light was given off by the deck lights on the starboard side of the upper laboratory. The man with the axe got as far forward as our main rigging. The bow line of *Saluda*, which passed through the chocks in the bulwarks of *Atlantis*, was forgotten. *Saluda* disappeared into the black of the night. Her crew felt sad, as they expected to find her wrecked on the beach in the morning.

About this time, the tide began to rise. The 1944 hurricane came in on a falling tide, so the height of the tidal wave was not as great as it could have been. It was said that the tide only went 4 1/2 feet above normal. However, in the light of what happened, it must have been higher.

An iron swing bridge connected the shore with the dock we were laying at. Sometime at the height of the storm, this bridge blew open. This action was afterward said to have cut the bow lines of the Coast Guard Cutter *Belafonte* (later *Albatross III*) and caused her to swing around and crash into the town dock. Captain Knight claimed later that this bridge also cut our stern lines. With that, *Atlantis* could move and move she did, with many of the lines lifting right off the bollards.

The dock could barely be seen with the help of the light in the deck laboratory. One of *Saluda*'s crew happened to be looking in that direction, when he noticed the dock passing by. He came round to the lee side of the deck lab and shouted to the bo'sun, "We are moving!" Without looking or checking, Ernest replied "It can't be!" We then heard the telegraph bell ring in the engine room. Ernest told me to go to the wheelhouse. When I arrived at the wheelhouse, the starboard door was open (hooked back) and the light was on. Captain Knight said, "Take the wheel, she is hard over to starboard!" I noticed the indicator of the engine room telegraph was on "stand by" but the engineer hadn't answered. I hadn't a chance to catch a second breath, before Captain Knight said, "Go find Hans and see why he doesn't acknowledge!" I ran down through the chart room and toward the engine room. I had just made the watertight door by the sail locker when I saw Hans Cook descending into the engine room. The ship still had a list, and I could see water in the starboard alleyway, between the officers' cabins and the fiddley. The water was coming out of the first and second mates' cabins. When I opened the door of the first mate's cabin, water was pouring in through the open ports. The scene looked like something out of a movie. All the books, papers, clothing, shoes, bedding and a wicker chair were afloat. I was tempted to run and tell somebody, but then decided I had first to close the ports and dog them. I must admit at the time as I waded into the water up to my waist, I was scared. I did not know enough to know if the ship was going to capsize or sink. It took all the courage I could muster to close and dog the port lights. When this was done, I stepped back out of the water, into the alleyway. I could see the water coming out of the second mate's door. Running forward a few steps, I found this door also unlocked and inside the cabin, the same scenario as in the other.

Going forward, I found the port lights also open in the officers' head and in the galley. All the other ports on the starboard side were closed. *Atlantis* seemed to be increasing her list to starboard now. I reported back to Captain Knight and told him what happened. He had just finished ringing up "finished with engines" and received the answering ring from Hans Cook. The main engine was never started.

Captain Knight said, "We broke loose from the dock and are sailing across Woods Hole Harbor under bare poles. I put the wheel hard over. We must be near Ram Island. Go tell Ernest to get an anchor out as soon as possible, and all hands to put on life jackets."

I ran forward and repeated the order to Ernest, who only said, "I think she's anchored already." There was nothing else for us to do but wait until morning.

The tide began to fall and the list of the ship increased. We would be heeling over to 45 degrees before it ended. At this degree of heel, it was impossible to walk on deck without holding on. We had ground out in seven feet of water, drawing seventeen feet.

The captain of *Saluda* and Captain Knight spent the rest of the night in the wheelhouse. We and *Saluda*'s crew sat on deck throughout the remainder of the storm under the lee of the whale boats with our feet on the sides of the engine room fiddley. Hans Cook moved out of his cabin on the port side and turned in for the rest of the night in the radio operator's cabin on the low starboard side. He never once put his head out during the whole storm.

Though the wind continued to blow and roar, it did not seem as bad to us. For one thing, we were not being constantly sprayed with salt water anymore. I was cold because I was soaking wet. About 2 AM I thought I saw some stars in the sky. This should mean the center of the storm was near us. Thirty-five years later, I would find out the center did indeed pass over the Cape.

It was still black as pitch out and we could not see anything outside the range of the one deck light. *Saluda*'s crew was lamenting the loss of their vessel and all their personal gear. Mostly, they feared shipwreckers would get to her before they did.

The scene that stands out in my memory is that of the bo'sun, Ernest, the old square rigger man, sitting on deck, wearing an old fashioned cork life jacket over his yellow oilskin jacket, staring off into the dark night. The deck light reflected off the wet black sou'wester against the background of the forward boat davit and the bow of the Number 1 whaleboat. With the ship listing over, I thought at the time, this is the way it must look when a vessel goes down at sea.

Sometime in the middle of that ferocious night, the Vineyard Sound Lightship did go down with all hands. I have often wondered what it must have been like for them at the end. With the approach of dawn, the inky blackness began to fade. The wind continued to blow hard. One of *Saluda*'s crew, staring into the night off our starboard bow, said he thought he saw something. Out of curiosity and also to try and find out where we were, Ernest sent me aft to tell Captain Knight. The captain had a powerful five-cell flash-light. He worked his way forward on the port side. The water was about a quarter the way up the deck, on the lower side. He shined the light in a direc-tion off the starboard bow and there was *Saluda*! She was held by the bow line that did not part and appeared to be floating upright in deep water. *Saluda's* crew cheered. She had been with us all the time. Unbelievable!

Sure enough, with the first light of dawn, we could see we were laying with our stern toward Ram Island, and the bow facing the Draper dock, right across the Gut of Canso. The wind began to moderate quite rapidly now. Ernest, the AB, and I got the port anchor rigged, with stock in, chain attached and landed on the rail ready to let go. This job was quite an oper-ation for the three of us, with the ship heeled over as she was. I couldn't understand why we needed an anchor ready with the ship hard aground. "For the insurance surveyor", the bo'sun said.

The wind had moderated enough so that the crew of the *Saluda* was able to get our dinghy off the top of the saloon house and launch it. In this way they were able to board her, and we soon could smell coffee perking and

On the evening the hurricane struck, the 85-foot yawl-rigged yacht Saluda, *operated by the Navy, tied up to* Atlantis. *At the height of the storm, both vessels broke free from the Fisheries dock and* Saluda's *lines were cut. To everyone's amazement, when dawn came the two vessels were still attached by a bow line, both hard aground near Ram Island in Great Harbor. Photo by Mary Curtis Cobb Thayer © Woods Hole Oceanographic Institution.*

bacon frying. It must have been 9 AM when a small boat came out from the Oceanographic with John Churchill and Chief Backus aboard. Before going ashore, Captain Knight told us to get everything removed that was of any value. This included the ship's bells, compasses, clocks, navigation lights, or basically everything that could be easily removed.

Now that all the excitement was over, I wanted, above all, my breakfast. I had a feeling we were to forego our day off. I could smell the bacon and coffee from *Saluda* and, being young, I was hungry! We never did get anything to eat until that night. Even *Saluda's* crew did not offer us anything! At the time, we did not realize that Woods Hole was not in any condition to offer breakfast to anyone. As we later found out, it was impossible to go from Woods Hole to Falmouth, with all the trees and telephone wires down. One was barely able to make it on foot along the main road.

About mid-morning, one of the Oceanographic boats hauled *Saluda* free; she waved good-bye to us and left, none the worse for the storm. It would be more than a month before *Atlantis* would be clear. Later we got some of our bedding from the fo'c'sle and placed the mattresses on the deck of the upper laboratory. The next day Captain Knight came back with the launch and asked the bo'sun and me to go ashore with him. We went in to the Fisheries dock, which was badly damaged. Many of the planks of the decking were missing and it was hazardous to walk on.

Captain Knight said he couldn't understand why the 5/8-inch trawl wire didn't hold, at least for a little while. He had found out, and he was going to show us. We reached the stone jetty, jumped on to the granite block, around which we had secured the trawl wire. There lying on the top of the block below, in a seam through which the wire had been passed, were the two wire clamps. It didn't seem possible the wire could have rendered and pulled out, leaving the clamps right there.

The captain picked up the clamps and asked me "Who gave these to you?" I answered, "Mr. Mandly." "Didn't you know these clamps were too big for the wire?" he asked me. I had a hard enough time knowing the difference between 6, 9, 12 thread or 21 or 27 thread in manila rope (all rope was identified by circumference or thread). I had no idea what size the wire was. I just took what the mate handed me. Lambert Knight was a kindly man, usually very pleasant (as seen through the eyes of a young ordinary seaman) but he was mad as hell that day. I am sure he believed if the wire clamps had been attached properly, *Atlantis* would have stayed there, head to the wind. All Ernest ever said (in an almost fatherly voice, unusual for him) "If you secure vire like this again, be sure you take a few round turns, to take the strain off the bitter end." A lesson in seamanship I have never forgotten.

Atlantis lay grounded out until early November. A salvage barge from Merritt, Chapman & Scott anchored in Great Harbor, and with a powerful steam winch, on a high tide, pulled her off.

A strange thing happened while we lay in the gutter. The tide running through scoured a hole around the ship, so that in a few weeks time, we remained upright at all times; a hole just large enough for the vessel to lie in.

Needless to say, the hurricane and the resultant grounding put an end to the job of renewing the standing rigging on the mizzen. I think one of the more interesting facts was that the spar stood throughout the storm, with only one half the shrouds still set up.

Although Saluda *could be hauled off the bar by a* WHOI *vessel that morning, it would be a few weeks before a salvage barge from Merritt, Chapman & Scott could free* Atlantis. *Photo courtesy* WHOI *Archives © Woods Hole Oceanographic Institution.*

Photo courtesy WHOI Archives © Woods Hole Oceanographic Institution.

Wider Impacts of the Hurricane

3

T
OD AY, those of us who are still alive in Quissett and Woods
Hole who were here in September of 1944 remember the "great
storm" and its fury, the worst by far in this area for the past 50
years. I've since learned of the other vessels that experienced that storm.

The *USS Warrington*, an 1800 ton destroyer, ran into the storm north of
the Bahamas Islands at 6 PM, Sept. 12th, and began to suffer about 11 PM,
or five hours later. The ship was feeling the full fury of the storm about 1 AM
on Sept. 13th, with wind of about 140 mph. She began to take in water
through the ventilation intakes, which the bilge pumps could not handle,
and finally capsized and foundered shortly after 11:30 AM, Sept. 13th.
Warrington had been caught in the grip of the storm for almost 18 hours.
Keep in mind that two most recent so-called hurricanes in this area,
"Gladys" and "Bob", passed by in only a few hours. Two hundred and forty
seven men were lost in the sinking of the *Warrington*. Unlike the three
destroyers lost in the Pacific typhoon of December 1944, *Warrington* had
75% of her fuel aboard, which gave her good stability but her deck had
cracked open near her gunnel and the water poured in.

From the Bahamas the storm continued north all day and night of
September 13th and 14th and, by 6 AM on the 14th, it was located about 60
miles south of Cape Hatteras, with the center offshore. It was about 9 AM
on the 14th when C.O. Iselin came over to the Fisheries wharf and informed
Captain Knight that there was a hurricane off Cape Hatteras and its course
was north (the storm had first been reported on Sept. 8th as approaching
and east of the Bahamas).

That morning of the 14th, north of Cape Hatteras, a small group of
ships were proceeding in convoy from the Atlantic to Norfolk. This convoy
consisted of a merchant ship *SS George Ade* being towed by another vessel
and escorted by two Coast Guard cutters, the *USCGC Jackson* and the

USCGC *Bedloe*. The *George Ade* had been torpedoed by a German submarine and had suffered considerable damage to her stern.

The hurricane winds drove the *George Ade* ashore on Hatteras without
loss of life, but the storm wrecked havoc with the two cutters. Both
foundered with heavy loss of life. The story I heard at the time was that both
vessels were hit many times by mountainous waves and that the *Jackson*
rolled completely over. I believe both were 125-foot class cutters and
because of the war time armament, depth charges and other ordnance, their
stability was reduced by a large amount.

Bedloe had 12 survivors out of a ship's company of 38. *Jackson* had 20
survivors out of a ship's company of 41. The sad fact was that the survivors
had to spend two days in life rafts and in the water before they were rescued
(part of the story I remember in 1944 was the men in the water suffered from
the stings of the Portuguese man-o-war).

The storm headed north all day of September 14th when, by 6 PM, its
center was about 40 miles east of the New Jersey coast and about 9 PM we
began to feel its effects in Woods Hole. A night of adventure was in store for
us in *Atlantis*. Fourteen miles to the southwest, the storm would take the
lives of 18 men when the Vineyard Sound Lightship Number 73 foundered
with all hands.

A few weeks later, when the tug and barge of Chapman, Meredith &
Scott, salvagers, arrived in Woods Hole to haul *Atlantis* off the beach, I
heard what happened to the Vineyard Sound lightship. The foreman of the
salvage crew was a big squarehead (a Swede). I heard him tell Captain
Knight and Chief Engineer Backus that, because of the big seas, the mooring chain sawed through the hawse pipe and right through to the water's
edge and the lightship filled with water. Before arriving in Woods Hole, the
salvage barge had found the wreck and sent a hard-hat diver down who discovered the cause of the sinking. Only two bodies out of 18 were ever found.
Lightship Number 73 had weathered numerous hurricanes in the past.
Lightship Number 86 (*Hens and Chickens*) was about four miles away, but it
survived the storm.

Gladys and Mary

Gladys and Mary, the big dragger I had seen launched at Morse's Yard in Thomaston, Maine, the previous May, had been fishing the week previous to September 14th, on Georges Bank. She was on her way into New Bedford that day, and at about 8 PM had reached the south side of the Vineyard. The weather during the day before the storm had been very pleasant, though there had been some ominous signs in the sky. Just how much the crew of *Gladys and Mary* knew of the approaching storm, I don't know. She did have a radio, so must have been aware of it. However, she was caught in the path of the storm, and was lucky to survive. What I now tell of the adventure her crew experienced, I learned from a man named "Foggy" Rogers of Sandwich, Massachusetts, who told me the story some 47 years ago. The crew of *Gladys and Mary* consisted of about eight men, of whom, "Foggy" said, four were squareheads. At first I could not understand the reason for the name "Foggy" but whenever he started to tell a yarn, his voice would become more like a fog horn with each word. "Foggy" said when they realized they could not make port in time, the captain decided that *Gladys and Mary* should heave-to. The seas moving ahead of the storm were building very rapidly and were getting very high at this time. Most of the crew had a great deal of experience and had fished for a number of years under winter conditions on Georges and the Grand Bank. Therefore they were not too concerned about the coming storm and were certainly not frightened. Perhaps this was because none of them had experienced a great Atlantic hurricane before with winds of over 100 mph and mountainous seas, especially with the wind in the SE quadrant.

After the vessel was hove-to, "Foggy" said they buttoned the *Gladys and Mary* up and lashed things down as best they could. They were not worried, at this time, as she was a new vessel. The squareheads in the fo'c'sle settled into a cribbage game, but soon it became difficult to hold the board in place as the vessel began to feel the force of the storm. The game ended. As the roar of the wind increased, a noise one never forgets once it is experienced, the seas began to build up with their tops being blown off by the wind. *Gladys and Mary* proceeded to roll down hard and the seas began to break aboard in continuous succession. "Foggy" said a peek out on to the deck showed it was pitch black and the shrieking wind sounded like "the fury of hell".

Below: Gladys and Mary, *which Bill had seen shortly after launching in Thomaston, Maine, rode out the hurricane south of Martha's Vineyard. Miraculously, she survived although she lost most of her superstructure and masts. Drawing by William B. Cooper.*

The *Gladys and Mary* rolled down further and further as she lay almost on her side. Sometime around 10 PM, she rolled over. It seemed to "Foggy" that it took forever, but she slowly rolled upright again. The storm was in its full fury, with the vessel being thrown down over and over and the sound of the sea crashing over her deck. "We lost the lights and were there in the dark holding on for dear life. We were being rolled down hard on the beam ends. It was all one could do just to hold on." It seemed to the men that *Gladys and Mary* rolled again, but they began to lose their sense of reality. "Foggy" said, "It was an absolute nightmare."

"What did you do?" I asked. "What the hell can you do?" was "Foggy's" answer. "I don't know how we could have been any closer to hell than we were that night. I believed that the vessel would founder at any time and we would all die together in the fo'c'sle. We started to pray, all of us."

Now one thing that was hard for me to visualize was a squarehead crew at prayer. They are good men, they are honest, fair and square and have

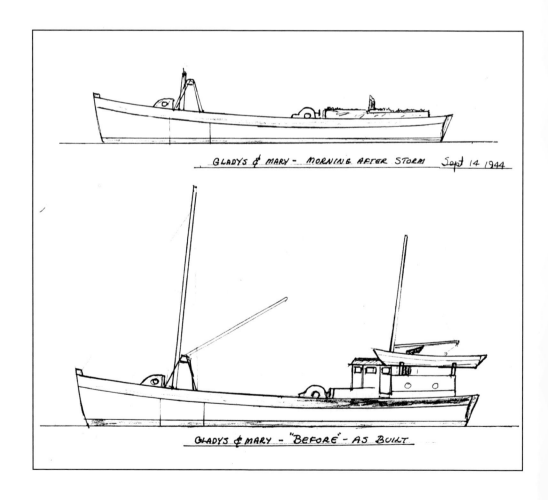

GLADYS & MARY - MORNING AFTER STORM   Sept 14 1944

GLADYS & MARY - "BEFORE" - AS BUILT

other virtues, but to be pious and pray, never! So I asked "Foggy" Rogers, "Can squareheads pray?"

He answered: "Can squareheads pray?" and, with his voice getting more like the sound of the foghorn, "You should have heard them praying out loud. They were calling on the Lord Jesus to save us from the terrible ordeal. Can squareheads pray? You bet your sweet life, they can pray when the time comes."

Well, the prayers of the crew must have had some effect. *Gladys and Mary* survived in a badly damaged condition. When the first light of day came, so the crew could chance a look out on deck, they were shocked at what they saw. The pilot house, dories, and mizzen-mast were gone, cleaned right off. They knew it was a miracle that she was still afloat. In a day or so she was towed to New Bedford, where the hatch to the fish hold was opened. They found the fish cargo had been churned into a slurry of fish, ice and water. The pieces of fish were so small that the whole mess was just pumped overboard.

The center of the hurricane continued on and passed near Boston that night and by 6 AM, September 15th, it was over the Penobscot Bay area of Maine, greatly diminished in strength. In its wake, the Great Atlantic Hurricane of September 9-15, 1944, took the lives of 312 seamen, a large number of them young boys, and most likely a few others we are not aware of.

Stern-quarter view of Atlantis *out of the water in a floating dry dock, showing her double-ended or "canoe" stern, and propeller. Photo courtesy WHOI Archives © Woods Hole Oceanographic Institution.*

Dry-docked at Electric Boat Yard

AFTER her grounding during the 1944 hurricane *Atlantis* had to be hauled and the hull examined for damage. She was to be hauled for a Lloyd's Insurance survey at the Electric Boat Company in Groton, Connecticut. The time was about mid-November 1944.

We left Woods Hole about 9 PM so as to be able to make a fair tide at the "Race" (the channel that is the navigable entrance to Long Island Sound). The tide at the Race runs about 4 to 5 knots, similar to Woods Hole. The night we left Woods Hole, it was dark, with a little wind and a November chill in the air. On board was the regular crew: Captain Knight, Acting Chief Mate Mandly, Chief Engineer Backus, Assistant Engineer Hans Cook, the bo'sun Ernest Siversen—and me, WBC, ordinary seaman. To make up for the lack of seamen, men were recruited from the other small vessels of the Institution, including Clarence Chase, Elmer Barstow and Bill Weeks. Captain Knight took one watch and Mandly the other. I was in Mandly's watch.

It was the first time I had steered *Atlantis* by compass. We steered using points. Mr. Mandly taught me to think of the compass card as the ship and I should steer so that the card remained on the lubber line. The ship steered very easily while under power, so I don't recall having any trouble keeping a straight course. Looking astern, I could see bioluminescence streaming from the propeller in a dead straight line in the wake.

While on lookout forward, it was pretty cold. Mandly told me to sit in the crew's companion way and gave me a talk about the advantages of growing a beard when going to sea in the winter time.

Watch below started about midnight. It seems to me now that when I came on deck again, it was daylight. We were near the entrance to Long Island Sound, and we passed easily thru the Race with a fair tide. Shortly after this a small "O" class submarine (a training sub, built in the 1920s) came up astern, quite close to the ship and wanted to know where our flag was. Mandly had me go to the wheelhouse and fetch the national ensign, which I hoisted on the ensign staff aft. That seemed to satisfy the men in the conning tower of the sub, and she soon steamed ahead of us and disappeared in the morning haze.

Later that morning, with the sun shining, we entered New London Harbor without a pilot and proceeded up the Thames River. Half way up the river, while most of the crew was sightseeing forward, we saw a blinker light flashing on the highway bridge ahead. Since none of us could read Morse code, we reported it to Chief Mate Mandly. He couldn't read Morse Code either, and said the "hell with it", and ordered us to ready the mooring lines at the proper locations on the deck. While the officers aft were trying to decide just where *Atlantis* was to moor, a Coast Guard picket boat came out from shore to challenge us as we had not responded to the flashing code signals on the bridge. This was wartime.

The Thames River shore on the Groton side seemed to be covered with submarines in various stages of construction. The base anti-corrosive paint was a dark pea green and the ones nearer to completion were painted gray. We had no means to communicate with shore in those days so we had to lie hove-to in the river until a tug from Electric Boat came out with instructions as to where we would berth. We finally tied up at the main fitting-out wharf which lay perpendicular to the river.

Electric Boat, at that time, was in the full round-the-clock wartime production of submarines. Why *Atlantis* was sent to that yard was a puzzle to everyone. The ship, being the largest sailing ketch in the world, with her tall masts, looked like a fish out of water among all the submarines.

The delivery crew left for home almost immediately, leaving Captain Knight, Mandly, Engineer Backus, Hans Cook, Ernest Siversen, and myself as the crew on her while in shipyard. We were to be paid $3.00 a day for subsistence or meals, which in 1944 would be equal to about $50 today (2006). Luckily there was a good restaurant right across the street from the main gate of the yard.

Electric Boat did not appear to me at the time to be an overly large shipyard, although the men there told us there was an annex further down the river, where the outfitting of the submarines was done. There were about four launching ways, under cover, where the submarine hulls were in vari-

ous stages of construction. On the northern side of the building ways was a large marine railway where we were to be hauled.

In November, Electric Boat was a very busy and noisy yard, with round-the-clock wartime production: welding flashes, flame cutting, and activities associated with building submarines. The number of the sub at the outfitting dock near us was SS 324 [*Blenny*]. There was a large sign board that could be seen when entering the main gate that contained the names of all the submarines built by the yard. A surprisingly large number had gold stars next to their names. When I asked what the stars meant, the gateman told me those were the subs lost in the war.

While lying at the wharf, *Atlantis* was hooked up with shore power electricity and steam, which meant our diesel generator did not have to run at all. We did not have to remain on watch at night. One morning, after being there a few days, we were informed that the ship was to be hauled out on the railway. The main engine was started and the bo'sun was ordered to take the wheel with the captain conning the ship. Mr. Mandly and I were the only ones to handle the line, a busy task for us. Luckily the hauling boss sent some men on board to help us and also to align the ship on the railway with rope tackle on each side rigged for that purpose.

I had a chance to watch *Atlantis* aligned on the cradle, with a board braced on the forward end of the cradle and her bow brought up to it (that was not exactly the way they did it in the Quissett boat yard), and the tackle to hold her in line fore and aft and athwartship on the cradle. The cradle and railway were used normally to haul submarines which drew a lot of water, so our ship fit on easily. Once out of water with her whole hull exposed, she looked very large to me and from the deck a long way down to the floor of the cradle (about 30 feet down—a long ladder), and on the floor of the cradle, a long way up to her rail.

As the work in the yard went on 24 hours a day, seven days a week, we, on board the ship, did not get much sleep. Being close to the building ways, I had a good chance to examine the submarines under construction, especially the one on the ways nearest to the railway. It just consisted of round cylinders. The pressure hull, as I remember, was about 3/4-inch thick steel. The sections looked like large tin cans with the top and bottoms cut out.

Unstepping the mast at Electric Boat

The spars—main and mizzen masts—were of hollow octagon construction, built with riff grain Douglas fir, knot-free (called "Oregon Pine" in Europe), glued up with casein glue. Casein glue required perfect joints as the glue itself lacked strength, compared with today's epoxies.

The main boom was about 57 feet long and quite heavy. The mizzen boom was 45 feet long and extended over the stern. The standing rigging, shrouds and stays was wire rope called plow steel construction and I believe it was galvanized. I never saw the standing rigging without coats of white lead and mutton tallow slush. All standing rigging on the upper ends were spliced with eyes around the masts. Originally the lower ends of the shrouds were spliced too, but this was changed to zinc sockets when the original shrouds and stays were changed on the mainmast in the late 1930s and on the mizzen in late 1944.

I recall the time the mizzen mast was hauled, using a crane barge which belonged to Merrill, Chapman & Scott, which came alongside. After the straps were attached to the mast, the yard riggers let go all the turnbuckles. The crane operator took a strain and nothing happened. The foreman signaled for more power, and with the power of steam we could feel the stern of the vessel beginning to rise. Holding the strain, the operator called the foreman over and said something to him. The foreman came over to where Captain Knight was standing and asked him: "How heavy is this goddamn mast?"

Captain Knight answered: "About two or three tons."

The foreman then said, "This crane has a strain of over thirteen tons on the spar. Could it be made fast in the step?"

The reason I could, as ordinary seaman, have time to observe all this is that we were down to a very short crew, and the mate, Mr. Mandly, was on vacation. There was no one around to harass me except the bo'sun, Ernest, and he was watching the whole operation, with the captain and me standing behind them.

The heel of the mast was checked out and no one could see why the spar was stuck in the step. The crane was very expensive and, to keep things moving, the rigging boss got a burner and they burned out the steel plate area around the mizzen mast step. When this was cut away, the spar came out quite easily and was laid down on the pier next to where we were laying.

While everyone, the boss rigger, Captain Knight, the bo'sun, and Chief Engineer Backus were studying the heel of the wooden mizzen in the steel step, trying to determine what was holding the two together, an old square-head rigger, summoned from the rigging loft, came up with a top maul (sledge hammer). "Ve'll fix this" he said, and gave the steel mast step one hard belt and, to everyone's amazement, off came the steel mast step from the heel of the mizzen mast. He looked at the inside of the step and said, "Yust a little Stockholm tar did the job." Stockholm tar (which we call pine tar) on the heel of a wooden mast held over thirteen tons of attachment to the steel step!

All of this was in a really strange setting, as we were laying in the Electric Boat shipyard, a sailing vessel in a yard which in late 1944 was engaged in full-time production, 24 hours a day, 7 days a week, building submarines for the war effort. Laying at the pier, we were surrounded by subs in the process of outfitting. One night, just after *Atlantis* had been hauled out on the large marine railway at Electric Boat, I had just climbed down the long ladder from the deck to the deck of the railway cradle when I noticed a man standing there dressed in the leather jacket and pants of a welder. I supposed he had come over from the building ways, next to the marine railway, where the round pressure hull of a submarine was under construction.

The welder had been looking at *Atlantis* when I approached, and said, "I know this ship, you are from Woods Hole." After a short conversation, during which I explained why the ship was hauled, he told me he was a welder at Electric Boat; submarine welders were the very best, and his name was Arthur Corey from East Falmouth. In later years, I was to know Arthur Corey as Shell Fish Warden, antique dealer, and Town Meeting member who sat behind me and kept me laughing with his many wonderful comments on the different people and events. Since he passed away a few years ago, I have missed him very much at Town Meeting.

During November of 1944, I had the opportunity of watching the Danish training ship *Danmark* passing up and down on the Thames River, New London, with cadets from the Coast Guard Academy. She was a pretty sight to behold, and even Ernest would stop and gaze at her as she passed by the docks of the yard. At a time when it seemed that every vessel was painted war-time gray, *Danmark* was painted in her peacetime colors, white hull, green waterline and buff spars. What a contrast to the war gray of the submarines and other Navy vessels, and what a beautiful sight she was in the soft light of the early evening. At this time (November, 1944), I got to know a cadet serving on the *Danmark* and had many conversations with him. His name was Nat Denman.

John Churchill's Driver's License

John Churchill came down to get me at New London to put me on the *Anton Dohrn* [a smaller power research vessel operated by the Institution] for a month or two while the *Atlantis* was laid up. He had a station wagon and with him he had the carpenter of the Oceanographic, Scotty Morrison. [Scotty Morrison was a fine carpenter. He spoke with a strong Scottish burr and lived over the food store in Woods Hole through the 1970s.] I sat in the back seat and those days we came home on the back roads of Connecticut. John Churchill was quite a wild man. He drove real fast and some place in the dark part of Connecticut a state trooper stopped us. He said, "You're going quite fast. Let me see your driver's license."

Churchill fished around and he pulled out his pass from the United States Navy, and he handed the state trooper that pass and said, "We're on

official business." The state trooper looked at the Navy pass and, it being wartime and there being a great deal of respect for that, he said to John—I can always remember because I heard him say it— "That's all right, John, just drive a little slower." After he left as we were driving away, Churchill turned to Scotty Morrison and said, "You know, Scotty, some day I've got to get a driver's license."

Churchill, that's exactly the way he was.

Atlantis, *under power, slogs through an uncomfortable sea. Photo courtesy WHOI Archives © Woods Hole Oceanographic Institution.*

Lambert Knight was captain of WHOI ships from 1940 through 1945 and captain of Atlantis for his last two years. Photo courtesy WHOI Archives © Woods Hole Oceanographic Institution.

Alongside at the Fisheries Dock

5

BACK IN Woods Hole about mid-March in 1945, a new chief mate and three new able seamen came aboard *Atlantis*. The chief mate was Nels Nordquist and, of the ABs, I can only remember one, Karl Johnson, a Swede. Both the mate and Karl were squareheads in their middle sixties. The other two new ABs were younger by 10 years or so. One of these was a French Canadian or "Frenchie" as they called him. The other was an Irishman who possessed the good nature and sense of humor of his breed. Neither of these stayed aboard to make the cruise.

They all came from a sailor's boarding house in Boston, recruited, along with the chief mate, by Captain Knight. Mr. Nordquist had been chief mate and Karl Johnson an AB in *Atlantis* when she came up from Lake Charles, Louisiana, in the summer of 1944. They had also been, respectively, mate and AB in the large racing yawl, *Manxman*, sailing out of Edgartown. *Manxman* had been built by Herreshoff's in 1926 with the name *Katoura* (# 1050). Rated as a 23 meter class, she was as large as a J-boat, being about 112 feet long.

They had been shipmates many times in large racing yachts, and both had served in the J-boat *Yankee* in the 1930s. They had made the cruise to England and return in her, as well as serving on her in all the racing she did over there. Mr. Nordquist was known by all the old sailors as "Long Nose Nels", to distinguish him from all the other "Nels" (we never called him that to his face).

Atlantis lay at the Fisheries wharf and as soon as the new men were settled aboard, we proceeded to rig her for the coming voyage to the "Tongue of the Ocean" in the Bahamas. As we had no cook or steward on board, at that time, we had all our meals at the Oceanographic mess. About this time, in late March of 1945, Bill Shannon, who was my age (18) and lived on the

Vineyard, was transferred from *Anton Dohrn* to *Atlantis*. He later served as a mess boy, but at this time, he worked on deck.

The bo'sun, Ernest Siversen, having had back trouble the previous winter, caused by a fall from the mizzen a few years before, was not on board at this time. I had helped the bo'sun unrig the running rigging and tackle in the late summer and fall of 1944 and had also helped stow the various pieces of gear away. The parts of the rigging were all tagged and easily identified when found.

The chief mate would ask: "Vere iss the main-topping lift pendant vires and yigs?" Bill Shannon and I would locate them, whether in the sail locker, forepeak or lazarette, and haul the gear on deck. All this gear—wire, ropes, blocks—was heavy and although the work was interesting and a lot of fun, Bill and I would be tired at the close of day. We would go to the Oceanographic mess for supper with the crew and then return to the ship. We were too tired to go ashore.

The older men and the chief mate, on the way back from the mess, would invariably drop into the Rendezvous and have a bottle or two of beer. They were usually back on board early enough to get in a few games of cribbage. Second Engineer Hans Cook, a Norwegian, would also visit the fo'c'sle in the evenings to join the cribbage game. He was a very good musician, who had been trained to play the violin at an early age, and had just acquired a banjo. He would play tunes with the banjo lying flat on the fo'c'sle table and could play all of Stephen Foster's songs by heart, as well as many other old tunes. But what he really liked most of all was to play cribbage. Many are the games I had to play with him when he had no other partners.

Chief Mate Nordquist would often come to the fo'c'sle. Smoking his cigar and sometimes with a glass of rum in hand, he would carry on his conversations about the next day's work or just tell stories, in spite of the cribbage players obvious obliviousness, and the bo'sun's only partial attention while reading his paper.

As I recall, in the time I served in *Atlantis,* Mr. Nordquist was the only mate to ever come to the fo'c'sle and chat with the men. Then, again, most of the men were his old shipmates. He was a cheerful, outgoing sort of man compared to the other squareheads, with a wonderful sense of humor. He was also the most competent officer I ever served under and a wonderful example to us "kids" (sailors and mess boys who he always called "chippies"). "Come, chippies, ve iss going to make a vire-rope splice in the main halyard."

"But, Mr. Nordquist, we don't know how to splice wire into rope."

"I know, dot iss vy you come and vatch me do it and help, so you can learn how."

Splicing wire to rope in the size of the main halyard (5/8-inch diameter wire to 1 1/2-inch diameter rope) was a very involved affair at this time in 1945 and there were few who could make such a splice. The wire rope—6 x 9 construction—was not preformed and would unlay very quickly if a seizing was not securing it at all times. The rope was spliced into the wire, but the wire was also spliced into the rope. Considerable skill here was required to do a neat job. I remember Mr. Nordquist, wearing his old-fashioned wire-rimmed glasses, telling us he considered the rope spliced into the wire as the strongest and most important part, and that it was not really necessary to splice the wire into the rope. Today we only splice the rope into the wire, which is much simpler.

One of the riggers at Merriman Bros., who had a hand in development of the modern wire-rope splice, where only the rope is spliced into the wire, was Herb Davidson. He had served as bo'sun on *Atlantis* in the latter part of 1945 and as second mate in the spring of 1946.

On one rainy evening in late March 1945, the subject of the seven-masted schooner came up. Seeing the chance, I asked Mr. Nordquist what the names of the masts and sails were in a seven-masted schooner. He answered: "I tink dey vas called after the days of the veek, Iss dot right, Ernest?" "Ya," was the answer, "beginning with Sunday." I then asked the chief mate what would the technical names of the mast and sails be? He thought a minute, "Veil, let's see, fore, main, mizzen, spanker, driver, pusher, yigger or vas it fore, main, mizzen, yigger, pusher, spanker and driver?"

The bo'sun, looking up momentarily from his newspaper, said to me: "Dot iss vy ve called dem after the days of the veek." What he meant is that no one was sure after fore, main and mizzen, what the correct order of the names for the mast and sails would be.

Second Mate Henry Mandly

Right after he came aboard *Atlantis* as chief mate, Mr. Nordquist informed the captain and John Churchill, the Port Captain, that he would not sail with Mr. Mandly, the present second mate. His reason was that Henry Mandly was an officer of the "old school"—inclined to be a "bucko" and the old sailors did not like him as he reminded them of the past. In addition, Mandly was not a sharp navigator, and since the chief mate did not navigate, they should have someone who could help take the burden of navigation off the shoulders of the captain. Anyway, that is what I heard the chief mate tell the older seamen at coffee time.

Henry Mandly was in his middle sixties when I served in *Atlantis* in 1944 and 1945. He was then acting chief mate. He was one of the last captains of a whaling vessel out of New Bedford. His father had been captain of a whale ship and Henry went to sea at a very early age, before the turn of the century in the 1890s. He had been second mate on the *Atlantis* in the 1930s and '40s and had been aboard and in charge of her while she lay in Lake Charles, Louisiana, for two years during the war. On the voyage up from Lake Charles, Mr. Mandly served as second mate under Nels Nordquist.

The bo'sun said he was an excellent seaman, and well able to handle a vessel under sail. Ernest Siversen was the bo'sun at that time and told me he would trust Mandly in any hard conditions at sea. His comment was, "Mr. Mandly would not hide under the mattress of his berth if things got tough." In 1945, Henry Mandly was an officer out of his time. He was, however, in the opinion of the bo'sun, "a superb seaman in sail." I liked old Mandly and knew his bark was worse than his bite, but was not sorry when he retired to a shore job.

I can still hear some of Mr. Mandly's comments and orders to Bill Shannon and me, 60 years later: "The trouble with you young fellows today (1945) is that you don't have any respect."

"Say 'Sir' when you speak to an officer."

"Repeat everything after me like a parrot, so I know you understand the order I've given."

"When you sight a ship, don't just say 'ship ho', sing it out as if you were sitting on the t'gallant yard so we can hear it on deck." With this he sung it out for us, "Saaail, Hoooooooo!"

"Learn to box the compass the right way. The course is not NNE a 1/2 East, it is NE by N a 1/2 N. You always work from the cardinal points and NNE is not a cardinal point" (who needs to know this today? Northeast by North a 1/2 North = 028 degrees).

"When you go to sea in the winter, you should grow a beard. It will keep your face warm in the brutally cold weather."

I used to watch Mr. Mandly practicing marlinspike seamanship, and now today am amazed how much he could remember. He did most of the

Boxing the Compass

New-School Course	Old-School Course	Azimuth Course
*North	*North	0
N 1/4 E	N 1/4 E	3
N 1/2 E	N 1/2 E	6
N 3/4 E	N 3/4 E	8
N by E	**N by E**	11
N by E 1/4 E	N by E 1/4 E	14
N by E 1/2 E	N by E 1/2 E	17
N by E 3/4 E	N by E 3/4 E	20
*North Northeast	North Northeast	23
NNE 1/4 E	NE by N 3/4 N	25
NNE 1/2 E	NE by N 1/2 N	28
NNE 3/4 E	NE by N 1/4 N	31
NE by N	**NE by N**	34
NE 3/4 N	NE 3/4 N	37
NE 1/2 N	NE 1/2 N	39
NE 1/4 N	NE 1/4 N	42
*Northeast	*Northeast	45
NE 1/4 E	NE 1/4 E	48
NE 1/2 E	NE 1/2 E	51
NE 3/4 E	NE 3/4 E	53
NE by E	**NE by E**	56
NE by E 1/4 E	NE by E 1/4 E	59
NE by E 1/2 E	NE by E 1/2 E	62
NE by E 3/4	NE by 3/4 E	65
*East Northeast	East Northeast	68
ENE1/4 E	E by N 3/4 N	70
ENE 1/2 E	E by N 1/2 N	73
ENE 3/4 E	E by N 1/4 N	76
E by N	**E by N**	79
E 3/4 N	E 3/4 N	82
E 1/2 N	E 1/2 N	84
E 1/4 N	E 1/4 N	87
*East	*East	90

*Cardinal points

Mate Henry Mandly was one of the last whaling captains out of New Bedford. Mariners of his school recognized only eight cardinal points of the compass, rather than 16. The courses steered aboard *Atlantis* were given as Mandly knew them over decades at sea. In the example Bill gives, 28 degrees expressed as "NNE 1/2 E" would incorrectly reference NNE, which old-time deep sea sailors did not consider a cardinal point. The old-school course aboard *Atlantis* for 28 degrees was given as "NE by N a 1/2 N", referencing NE, a cardinal point.

Source: Eldridge, 2014 p.223

beautiful fancy work, such as the rope-half hitched covers over the anchors and the sennet-worked fender and guards on Number 1 whaleboat.

I also loved to hear the stories he would tell at times about his whaling days. I think he must have been "one tough cookie" as master. One of the stories he told, which the late Captain Mysona also remembered hearing Mandly tell in the 1930s when Captain Mysona was mess boy aboard *Atlantis,* was how Mandly put two would-be mutineers in an empty oil cask with tops on and only the bung hole open for air. He said the men, who had threatened to kill him, were very subdued when they were released from the oil cask three days later, and he had no trouble with them the rest of the voyage. He also said that, to prevent the sailors from consuming too much fresh water, he would place a handful of tobacco in the water barrel to make the water unappetizing.

In his navigation he used logarithms and the old nautical tables, and relied mainly on the three L's of navigation: latitude, lookout and lead line. At that time in 1945, there was no LORAN, no Radar, and no GPS. All we had were magnetic compasses and a radio direction finder. The older seamen did not like Mr. Mandly, as he reminded them too much of the American "bucko mates" they had served under years before. He was also inclined to be tough on the younger sailors, and was after them every minute. But he always treated me fairly and, not only did I learn a lot from him, I actually grew to like and respect him.

In the chart room Mr. Christopher pulled out all the charts that we would need in the upcoming cruise and replaced them with the latest ones. Mr. Christopher was cheerful and pleasant, and, as a professional, he knew how ships were run. I liked working with him and even the squarehead bo'-sun and the ABs seemed to have a good word for him. He was certainly some different from the former second mate of the old school, Henry Mandly.

Near the middle of April, 1945, before we sailed for the Tongue of the Ocean, we were laying at the main Oceanographic dock, loading stores and gear. An elderly man came down the wharf, carrying his bag and in the uniform of a Lieutenant Commander of the U.S. Maritime Service. His uniform was resplendent with all the gold braid and ribbons for that time of the war.

The bo'sun, looking up from what we were doing, saw him at the gangway and ordered me to assist the "officer". I went to the gangway where the Commander told me he wished to see the captain. I picked up his bag and escorted him to the wheelhouse and to the captain's cabin. When I returned back to the job we were doing, the bo'sun asked me who the "officer" was. I told him he was our new steward. The bo'sun looked rather dumbfounded, and said: "A cook? A f—g cook? Why I thought he was an admiral!"

Salaries and Wages

When I was hired in August of 1944 and assigned to *Atlantis* as ordinary seaman, my wages were $85 per month, plus room and board. That was good money for an 18 year-old at that time. To get seamen for the Tongue of the Ocean Cruise in early 1945, the Oceanographic found it had to pay the going rate, which was $175 per month for able seamen and $125 per month for ordinary seamen. Also the wages for officers, both deck and engine, were much higher than the Oceanographic rates. Chief Backus and Second Engineer Hans Cook had a discussion with Captain Knight regarding the higher wages of the new officers. In the end it was settled that Chief Backus, Hans Cook, Ernest Siversen and I were considered permanent crew and therefore we were to be paid at a reduced rate. This reduced rate, however, increased my pay to $110 per month, which I considered pretty good.

The late Joe Goudreau was with the Falmouth Fire Department and, in 1945, was stationed in Woods Hole. He told me years later that his pay in 1945 was $28 per week, with which he had to support a family. I only write this to show how well we, the unmarried men, were paid on *Atlantis* during the war years, compared to the people who worked ashore. This was primarily due to the shortage of seamen.

Above: *On her first scientific cruise in three years, the research ketch Atlantis motored away from the dock in Woods Hole on April 23, 1945, bound for the "Tongue of the Ocean" in the Bahamas Islands. She flew her international signal recognition flag W-C-F-B from the upper starboard spreader, and the American flag at half-mast in honor of the death of President Roosevelt on April 12, 1945. Photo courtesy WHOI Archives © Woods Hole Oceanographic Institution.*

Once out in the Sound all hands turned to and with all sail set Atlantis easily held her "full and by" course. The wind was west of southwest, giving her a good slant down the Sound toward the Vineyard Sound Lightship. Photo courtesy WHOI Archives © Woods Hole Oceanographic Institution.

Tongue of the Ocean Cruise

6

O N   A   B E A U T I F U L   spring afternoon, April 23, 1945, the research ketch *Atlantis* left Woods Hole, bound out by way of Florida, for the "Tongue of the Ocean" in the Bahamas Islands to engage in a project in cooperation with the Navy on anti-submarine warfare. This was the first scientific cruise for *Atlantis* in three years, and my first voyage to sea.

The war in Europe was coming to a close. At this date, the Russian Army was fighting in Berlin and the Third Reich was in its final death throes. The Navy's sailing orders to the master of *Atlantis* were: sail south in sight of the coastline and carry navigation lights at night, as in peacetime, as to their knowledge, there were no U-boats near the East Coast.

The crew of the *Atlantis* at this time were: Captain Lambert Knight, First Mate Nels Nordquist (an old shellback about 65 years old), and Second Mate Mr. Christopher, holder of an unlimited masters license at age 23. Ernest Siversen (another old shellback) was bo'sun. The crew before the mast was a mixed lot with half of them WHOI technicians, two squarehead ABs, and me, ordinary seaman, age 18. At this time in 1945 seamen were hard to come by. Therefore it was decided that the three WHOI technicians (John Martin, Lennart Blomberg, and Hartley Cassidy) could serve in this capacity on the trip south. There was another man who slept in the fo'c'sle, a southerner ex-soldier, who served as the radio operator. Chief Harold Backus and Hans Cook were engineers. We had four squareheads including the chief mate, Nels Nordquist. At this time, we carried aboard a steward, cook, and two mess boys. The steward was an older man, well into his sixties. He was English or "Limey", as the older seamen called him, and this concerned them as the memory of anything British was "starvation and ease." Their fears would soon be allayed as the cook turned out to be absolutely first class, and took very good care of the men in the fo'c'sle. The two mess boys were Bob Metell and Bill Shannon, both my age.

In the scientific party, those that I well remember were: Paul Fye, Chief Scientist, Charles Wheeler, and last, but not least, the Navy's Liaison Officer, Lieutenant Paul Ferris Smith. There were also two electronic men whose names I cannot recall.

Complying with war time regulations, *Atlantis*, with her international signal recognition flag W-C-F-B flying from the upper starboard spreader and the national ensign flying at half mast in honor of President Franklin D. Roosevelt (who had died a few weeks previously), steamed past the entrance buoy of Woods Hole into Vineyard Sound.

The wind, as I remember, was west of southwest, which would give *Atlantis* a good slant down the Sound toward the Vineyard Sound Lightship. Captain Knight decided that he might as well start getting the crew worked up so ordered all sail set once we were out in the sound. All hands turned to and with all sail set, and the ship easily holding her "full and by" course, *Atlantis* started on her voyage down Vineyard Sound.

Because of the large number of green men, it was decided that we would run watch in watches of six hours on and six off. I was put in the second mate's watch with Ernest Siversen, the bo'sun, the old squarehead AB Karl Johnson, who was about 65 years old, and John Martin who was about 33 at

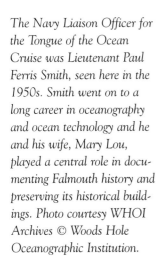

The Navy Liaison Officer for the Tongue of the Ocean Cruise was Lieutenant Paul Ferris Smith, seen here in the 1950s. Smith went on to a long career in oceanography and ocean technology and he and his wife, Mary Lou, played a central role in documenting Falmouth history and preserving its historical buildings. Photo courtesy WHOI Archives © Woods Hole Oceanographic Institution.

the time. Orders of the chief mate, with the Captain's consent, were that if any difficulty or problem arose while we were under sail, the second mate would step aside and command of the watch would go to the Able Seaman, Karl Johnson. Karl was picked because he spoke English clearer than the bo'sun and was not as likely to get frustrated and excited. I could understand the bo'sun's orders, but the others could not.

We sailed on towards the south coast of Long Island, taking in the main-sail before dark. Once south of Gay Head, *Atlantis* began to pitch in the head sea and shipped some water on the foredeck. The deck in the fo'c'sle and galley area began to leak.

Some fifty years later, I realized the cause of the leaks. The old bo'sun, Ernest Siversen, had been in the Marine Hospital in Vineyard Haven prior to *Atlantis* sailing in late April. Previously, Ernest had attended to wetting the decks down with salt water once a day, but he had been absent for two months or so. The winds of March and April tend to be dry, and the decks had not been receiving their daily wetting. I realize now the whole deck probably leaked, but since we only took water forward, the leaks that showed up first were in the fo'c'sle and galley. When I turned in at midnight, my upper berth was wet, so I spent the first night of the cruise in my oilskins.

New York

In the morning at 6 AM, we of the second mate's watch turned out and found the vessel under power, as there was little wind, and pitching into the swell off the south shore of Long Island. At that time we learned from the second mate that we were going to New York for repairs to the deck over the fo'c'sle. At 8 AM, we had the first breakfast for that trip. It consisted of boiled salt mackerel and boiled potatoes. The cook said that he thought it a proper meal for the men suffering from a mild case of seasick-ness (whatever that meant!). Those of us feeling a bit queasy before that breakfast would certainly be sick afterward! I only ate the potatoes, leaving the salt mackerel to the squarehead crew members.

About mid-afternoon, we passed Rockaway Point on Long Island and could clearly see the amusement park at Coney Island, then the lower bay, the entrance to New York Harbor, and the buoys of the Ambrose Channel. For me, it was very exciting. Though I had grown up in New York, I had never entered the harbor from the sea. I remember the different ships, naval and merchant, coming and going with flags flying and the Coast Guard picket boats checking all. We passed through the narrows between Fort Wadsworth and Fort Hamilton and, hugging the Brooklyn shore, went into a narrow inlet to the Erie Basin, which consisted then mainly of wharfs and shipyards. We moored alongside a T2 tanker (about 10,000 tons), which, to us at the time, seemed enormous. From the tanker's deck, *Atlantis* looked like a whale boat!

The next morning we moved alongside a fitting-out pier and the caulkers came aboard and started reefing out the pitch in the deck, even before we had a chance to rig an awning to help keep the drizzle off of them. I think this job took about two days. The mess boys and I wandered about the shipyard after work, having no desire to go any farther, as a peek out of the gate showed us what we took to be a tough neighborhood. I remember walking under the bottom of a freighter in the dry-dock, blocked about six feet high, the first time I had ever seen or done anything like that. We also examined a tanker with her bow completely holed and gutted. The night watchman told us she had been in a collision and had caught fire. He also said we should not be wandering at will around the shipyard without a pass from the front office.

On the afternoon of the third day, the work of caulking and paying the decks was completed. As we left the Erie Basin, I could see at a pier nearby, the hulk of the great French liner S.S. *Normandie.* It was a sad sight, all that remained of a beautiful ship, only ten years after her arrival in New York.

During this time, we passed very close to a Liberty Ship in light condition. More than half of her propeller was out of water and was turning very slowly. The pilot aboard the Liberty Ship called down to the pilot aboard *Atlantis:* "Where did you find that toy?" In my mind's eye, I can still see the name of that ship, gold letters on the black escutcheon board attached to the wheelhouse: *Louisa May Alcott.*

We steamed through New York's Upper Bay, very exciting with all the activities of those times, into the East River and moored at a pier near the Fulton Fish Market at the base of the Brooklyn Bridge. Early the next morning, with a clear sky and a NW wind in the offing, we left our berth in the East River with a New York pilot in command. We proceeded down the upper and lower bay and hove-to near the Ambrose Lightship to discharge our pilot. I heard him say to the captain as he went over the side to board the pilot boat, "Good luck and I wish I were going with you."

Southward Bound—All Sail Set

The captain ordered all sail set. On this voyage we carried a small power catboat as a launch, 16 to 18 feet in length, nestled on the starboard side and also a large pile of angle iron stock stored along the starboard bulwarks. Chief Mate Nordquist referred to the latter as a "pile of junk." None of this made life easy for us when setting and handling the mainsail. The northwest wind near the Ambrose Lightship increased to what the sailors called a "strong breeze" and, with the New Jersey shore creating a lee, the sea was comparatively smooth for a vessel of *Atlantis's* size.

For the next 10 hours or so we had the most exciting sail I ever experienced in my time on the ship. With the sheets started—wind on the quarter—*Atlantis* could sail fast and that she did when steadied on our course, south. She lay down so that her leeward rail (port) was level with the water. Most of the port lights on the port side showed green water when viewed from below. The unusually high bow wave caused a continuous roar that could be heard throughout the ship. We had, at that time, the taffrail log [a device towed from the aftermost rail, or taffrail, of ships to measure ship speed] streamed from the weather or starboard side. The log should have been streamed from the leeward side to get an accurate reading. Captain Knight did not think we should try to change the position of the log because there was too much strain on the line and rotor and we could have lost it.

I can still remember the governor wheel was spinning so fast it looked like an airplane propeller at full power. The reading from the log was 12.8 knots. While at the wheel, I heard the captain tell the second mate the reading was inaccurate, that we were going faster than that. Fifty-five years later I believe the captain was right. Our speed was probably closer to 15 knots, which was *Atlantis's* top speed.

In 1945, *Atlantis* was still equipped with the Burmeister-Wain controllable pitch propeller, the blades of which could be turned to align fore and aft or in "sailing position". The pitch of the propeller was controlled by a large hand wheel, located next to the clutch of the main engine. It took a large number of turns of the wheel to get the propeller blades from ahead pitch to sailing pitch. The fact that the propeller blades could be adjusted in this manner contributed greatly to the speed under sail that day.

We sailed past a Liberty Ship bound south in the same general direction as we were going. During my wheel watch that morning, the Navy Liaison

S.S. Normandie

The *S.S. Normandie* was built for the French Line Compagnie Générale Transatlantique in Saint-Nazaire, France. It was the most luxurious, largest and fastest passenger ship afloat at the time. She entered transatlantic service from Le Havre to New York in 1935 and set average speed records for the crossing in 1935 (29.98 knots) and 1937 (30.98 knots), for which she was twice awarded the Blue Riband. Her speed was attributed to her massive size, innovative hull shape and bulbous bow, which allowed a maximum speed up to 32 knots, at 70% of the power of comparable ships.

Her lavish and vast interiors, primarily directed to a first-class passenger complement (848 of the total capacity of 1,942) her Art Deco and Streamline Moderne-style appointments, and luxurious accommodations are described breathlessly in publicity releases. The 300-foot first-class dining room, with its crystal chandeliers and light columns, is compared with the Hall of Mirrors at the Palace of Versailles.

Normandie made 139 westbound transatlantic crossings before the outbreak of World War II. Upon the German invasion of Poland *Normandie* sought haven in New York where she was interned by the U.S. Government.

After the U.S. entered the war *Normandie* was taken by the U.S. government (under the "right of angary" in International Law) providing for conversion to a troop carrier, a process first estimated to take about one month.

While no doubt justified at the time, the transformation, which proceeded at a frantic pace, had a tragic quality, as gangs of workers armed with sledge hammers, pry bars and cutting torches swarmed aboard to attack the once-gracious facilities. After needed time extensions the process was terminated when fire started by a welding torch ignited kapok life jackets and spread throughout the ship, its elaborate fire-control system having been deactivated along the way. As fire crews on the dock poured tons of water into the inferno, the ship began to list.

The burned out, stripped and devastated wreckage of the once-grand S.S. Normandie as Cooper observed her in Erie Basin, Brooklyn, New York, in 1945. Photo courtesy of The Museum of the City of New York.

The ship's principal designer, Russian-born Vladimir Yourkevitch, happened to be in New York at the time and rushed to the scene. He pleaded to open the ship's seacocks to allow her to settle onto the shallow dockside bottom in an upright position. But Yourkevitch and his suggestion were rejected and early in the morning of February 10, 1944 the ship rolled onto her side. She lay there in the mud for over a year, her machinery and vast interior spaces flooded with murky harbor water.

Later, the ship was righted and moved to Todd Shipyard facilities at Erie Basin in Brooklyn to resume reclamation and conversion. It was there in April 1945 that Bill Cooper aboard *Atlantis* mourned the devastated wreckage. Eventually, after several attempts to salvage the hull were abandoned, *Normandie* was scrapped at Newark, New Jersey, in December 1948.

Arthur Gaines

Sources:
Ardman, H., 1985. *Normandie:Her Life and Times.* Franklin Watts, New York. 432 pp.
Maxtone-Graham, J. 1972. *The Only Way to Cross.* MacMillan, New York.
Kludas, A., 2000. *Record breakers of the North Atlantic, Blue Riband Liners 1838–1952.* Chatham, London

Photo courtesy WHOI Archives © Woods Hole Oceanographic Institution.

Officer, Lieutenant Paul Ferris Smith, came into the pilot house. He was excited and enthusiastic about the speed of the ship. As he was a Navy officer, I assumed he could steer as well as me. With the second mate's permission, I let Lieutenant Smith take the wheel.

He had never forgotten that moment, and speaks of it often. Many years later, I asked Paul what kind of boat or vessel he had sailed in before taking the wheel of *Atlantis* that day. His reply was "none."

No wonder he never forgot the experience. The first time at the wheel and in the world's largest ketch with all sail set, doing 15 knots, the whole ship and rigging vibrating because of the strain. In later years, when we had a Pitot log [the Pitot tube is a device developed by the French hydraulic engineer Henri Pitot in the 18th century to measure ship speed, now also used aboard aircraft], we found *Atlantis* could sail 11 to 11.5 knots under sail alone, and not make much of a fuss about it. The run down the Jersey coast that April day in 1945 was the most exciting sail I ever had in my four years on the *Atlantis*, and I never sailed faster until I sailed in a multi-hull many years later.

Coastwise navigation in 1945 was simple. It consisted of a magnetic compass, taffrail log, the fathometer and lookout. There was no LORAN, Radar or GPS for the officers to rely on. Compass bearings taken off shore objects would help determine speed and our distance from the shore.

We carried on at this speed until just before supper, at which time we were off the Delaware Capes and, at the suggestion of Chief Mate Nordquist, the captain agreed to take in the mainsail and not carry it after dark. The mate's comment was: "Yesus, captain, ve iss not carrying the mail!" With the strain of the mainsail off the vessel, she carried on pleasantly through the night.

U-boats

*A*tlantis' passage south—per Navy sailing orders—was to be along the East Coast, inside the Gulf Stream. We were to show navigation lights at night, as the chances at this stage of the war of any German U-boats being in the area was considered extremely unlikely. I found to my surprise, 50 years later, when reading the book "U.S. Destroyers" by Norman Friedman, that there were U-boats off the Atlantic coast in April of 1945. That month, six German submarines—equipped with the snorkels—left

Opposite: R/V Atlantis *in a fair wind on a reach, her optimal point of sail. Photo by Charles Spooner © Woods Hole Oceanographic Institution.*

U-858 surrendered on May 8, 1945 while off the East Coast of the U.S. On May 9 she was met by an armada of U.S. Naval vessels that took over operation of the submarine, replacing half her crew with American sailors. U-858 anchored in the Harbor of Refuge, Cape Henlopen, Delaware, on May 14 where the Captain signed official surrender papers and German prisoners were moved to nearby Ft. Miles. Photo courtesy of Captain and Mrs. Jerry Mason, USN (ret.)

U-Boats

Soon after *Atlantis* began operating in the Gulf of Mexico in April 1942, under chief scientist Alfred Woodcock, German submarines began attacks on shipping there. Of about 70 vessels sunk in the Gulf during the war, 56 American ships went down in May 1942 alone.

Some reports indicate Germany and Italy had long been buying crude oil from Mexico, and that German U-boats had been operating in the Gulf for years prior to U.S. entry into the war.

By July 1942 there were at least 10 German U-boats operating in the Gulf of Mexico, including the U-166 which had been laying mines off the entrance of the Mississippi River. On July 30 the submarine spotted the passenger freighter *Robert E. Lee*, converted to wartime use and painted gray, en route from Trinidad to New Orleans with a light cargo and 270 passengers. She was escorted by *Patrol Craft 566*, a short distance ahead.

The torpedo fired by the U-166 hit the starboard side of the ship and exploded near the engine room, sending the *Robert E. Lee* to the bottom 45 miles from Southwest Passage. Twenty five passengers were lost. The U-Boat surfaced soon afterwards and was itself sunk by the escort vessel which, racing back, launched depth charges. This was the sole U-boat sunk in the Gulf of Mexico. Both ships have since been found on the seafloor in 5000 feet of water, during pipeline surveys.

During *Atlantis'* return voyage to Woods Hole from Lake Charles, arriving on July 28, 1944, and her first cruise south to the Bahamas, departing April 23, 1945, it is now clear that U-boats were still operating along the East Coast of the United States—despite Navy assertions minimizing the risk. The surrender order—"cease hostilities and surrender to Allied forces"—from German Grand Admiral Karl Donitz (by then the President of the Reich, following Hitler's April 30th death) was radioed to the entire German U-boat fleet on May 4, 1945.

Possibly owing to communications failures, twelve U-boats continued operations until May 7. U-853 was sunk near Block Island, Rhode Island, on May 6 after torpedoing a collier. This was about two weeks after *Atlantis* had transited the area on her way to New York. Between May 14 and May 19 seven U-boats surrendered on the east coast of North America: four taken to Portsmouth, New Hampshire, and one to Lewes, Delaware. Of an estimated U-boat fleet of 375, 64 were at sea on May 4, 1945.

Despite Cooper's later belief that a U-boat would probably not have wasted a torpedo on *Atlantis*, U-boats were also armed with deck-mounted guns that could easily have dispatched *Atlantis* at little cost.

Arthur Gaines

Source:

Kingery, D., 2010. *In WW II, U-boats wreaked havoc in Gulf of Mexico*. American Press, Lake Charles, LA bases in Norway and were known to be approaching U.S. waters. This information was picked up by the British, who had previously broken the German Naval Code, ULTRA.

Between April 5th and April 22nd, 1945, two U.S. escort carriers and twelve destroyer escorts maintained a barrier patrol in the path deduced for the U-boats, based on the broken code. Number 1 U-boat was sighted by aircraft, when a puff of diesel smoke came from the snorkel, and was sunk by a destroyer escort. Number 2 U-boat was also sunk by a destroyer escort screening one of the escort carriers. Number 3 U-boat was apparently sunk about the same time. That left three U-boats that made it to the East coast area.

On May 5th, 1945, U-853 torpedoed a collier in Block Island Sound and was herself sunk by Navy destroyers and aircraft in the same area. The majority of U-853's crew was teenage boys. On May 14th, 1945, U-858 and U-805 surrendered off the East coast and entered U.S. ports.

As the day of April 27th, 1945 closed, *Atlantis* was sailing merrily on, lit up like a Christmas tree, approaching the entrance to the Chesapeake Bay and we, that is those of us in the fo'c'sle, knew nothing of the three German U-boats possibly lurking in the waters near us or in our path. I heard the second mate say casually to the captain in my wheel watch that evening, in regard to carrying our lights: "It may end soon, but the war is still on."

The next evening, when we were approaching Cape Hatteras, the wind had died out completely and the sea was now almost flat calm. While I was at the wheel, during my watch, Captain Knight said to me, "Your first time past Cape Hatteras and it is calm. The first time I sailed past Cape Horn, it was flat calm. I was disappointed, as I had heard so many stories about how rough it could get there. The next time I passed it, I was not disappointed. It blew with the fury of hell and at one time I was not sure if I would live to see the morning. Maybe Cape Hatteras will give you some excitement the next time."

From eleven o'clock to midnight, I had the bow lookout with Johnny Martin. Johnny was about 33 years old and was one of the WHOI technicians who were serving as a crew member on the voyage down to the Bahamas. He was a farmer and gardener by trade, and this was his first time on board a ship. He had been seasick and homesick for his wife and little girl the first few days, but this evening he was only homesick. Johnny had a good sense of humor and he got a big kick out of the squarehead sailors and the chief mate. Chief Mate Nordquist: "Yesus, Yohnny, when you makes dot line fast, you does it yust like a farmer!" "But, Mr. Nordquist, I am a farmer" was Johnny's reply.

I often thought it must have been very hard for Johnny to come aboard *Atlantis* as an ordinary seaman, not knowing exactly what everyone was talking about when handling the gear and having never steered a ship before, taking his turn at the wheel. In 1945, courses were given aboard the *Atlantis* in the points of the compass: "Steer, south by west, a quarter west." Johnny would always whisper to the man he was relieving: "What number is that?"

His work at the Woods Hole Oceanographic gave him an exemption from the draft—a "B" status. The previous year, the Army had been drafting men who were 35 years of age and had three or four children. "I could be worse off", Johnny would say, "I could be in the Army."

During the bow lookout, the night was hazy with some moonlight. Just before we were to call out the watch below, Johnny and I were staring off to starboard toward the Diamond Shoal Lightship. Suddenly two streaks appeared, one slightly ahead of the other, coming at us straight as a die, leaving a phosphorescent wake streaming out astern.

Torpedoes!

We both saw them at the same time and were both startled speechless, unable to say a word. In a split second, I only thought, "now I'll know what it is like to die."

Nothing happened.

After a few moments, we cautiously peeked over the rail, at the bow to see why there was no explosion. The answer to our torpedoes was porpoises, swimming with the ship, playing in the bow wave. It was a few minutes more before any words passed between us.

In retrospect, we knew a submarine would not waste a torpedo on *Atlantis*, much less two of them. Besides, there were no U-boats near the east coast, or were there? I turned in that night still shaken. Sixty years later, I can still see in my mind's eye those two thin streaks in the water coming at us at a terrific speed and waiting for the explosion I was sure would follow.

We did a lot of steaming the next few days as we had to work our way south. Off Savannah, we passed right through a large convoy going east, with naval escorts all around. Since we were under sail and power at the time, the second mate looked in the International Rules, and had us hoist the black "at anchor" ball to the lower starboard spreaders. This was the daytime signal for a vessel under sail and power in 1945.

Port Everglades

About May 1st, we were off Jacksonville, Florida and it began to get hot. We sailed down near the beach at Daytona and, with binoculars, could see the girls on the beach. For the mess boys and me, this was very exciting as we had never been so far from home before. We passed the sea buoy and entered Port Everglades in the late afternoon of May 2nd, 1945. Port Everglades contained both a Coast Guard and a Navy base, side by side. On the wharf where we lay was a large storage shed filled with sugar bags, a commodity that was rationed at home and, supposedly, in short supply. On the other side of the wharf lay an escort aircraft carrier (a baby flattop).

In Port Everglades, there was also a submarine training base, at which lay a manned Italian submarine flying the Italian flag, our former enemies. Outside the base gate, across the road, were orange groves. In fact it seemed to me there were orange groves along the road to Fort Lauderdale and from there all the way to Miami, unbelievably different from what the area must look like today. The mess boys, Bob Metell and Bill Shannon, and I went into Fort Lauderdale that evening. It lived up to my expectations, especially the park along the waterway. In later years, whenever I speak of Fort Lauderdale in 1945, I am told: "Don't go there now, remember it as it was." Of course, I would say the same about the Cape. If you knew Falmouth and Cape Cod in 1945, don't go there now. Keep it in your memory!

The next morning, we were working on adjusting the turnbuckles of the main rigging which had been stressed in the sail on the trip down. When it started to rain, the mate sent us to close the hatches and companionways and the port lights of the main saloon and deck laboratory. The rain came down in a deluge. Just as we got the last port light closed it stopped. We were completely soaked. I could see a big contractor's wheelbarrow on the wharf. It was full and the water was flowing over the sides. I couldn't believe it. The men working on the wharf told us that it was the first rain in three months.

Miami

At noon time, we were told we were going to Miami to the Coast Guard Inspection Office, that is, those of us who did not have Seaman's passports or "Z" papers. I think this included almost everyone except the second mate, Christopher, Assistant Engineer Hans Cook, the cook and the steward. Lieutenant Paul Ferris Smith procured a Navy truck and driver. He and the captain sat in the front seat and all the rest of us rode in the back like a load of cattle. It seems funny, now, when I think back on it. The truck dropped us off at the Coast Guard Inspection Office in Miami. Lieutenant Smith handled all the required formalities. We needed photos and birth certificates or a similar document. The processing of all the paper work, as I remember, took a long time. We were told after we received the necessary papers that we could stay in Miami and report back on board *Atlantis* late in the evening.

Neither Captain Knight nor the chief mate had in their possession any discharge papers from other ships, so to speed matters along, they were both issued "ordinary seaman" papers. Chief Backus, on the other hand, had a British license as chief engineer, diesel. This license was not accepted by the Coast Guard, so, much to his chagrin, he was issued a "wiper's ticket", the lowest rate in the engine room. The captain and the chief mate only laughed at their "ordinary seaman" ratings and did not take them seriously at all.

To my young eyes, accustomed to New York City, Miami of 1945 was a beautiful place. The two mess boys, Bob Metell and Bill Shannon, and I, being about the same age, stayed together and explored parts of the city and the ocean front. Toward supper time, we decided to take a bus back to Port Everglades. On boarding the bus, I noticed there were many Negroes at the back of the bus. At the time I did not associate this with segregation, although I am sure the realization was there. This was the first time I had ever been out of New York or New England. Now here we were in the South.

We sat in the front to make sure we got off at the right stop. This spot gave us the opportunity to observe everybody who boarded at the various stops. Many military and naval personnel got on and we could examine each one, sailor, private or officer, as to rank and campaign ribbons. This interested us at the time and we tried to identify the various ribbons for service in the Pacific, Africa, the Mediterranean, Italy, or Europe. I must note here that campaign ribbons were not in such abundant supply in 1945, as they seem to be today.

At one particular stop, as several people boarded, both military and civilian, an army officer waiting in line caught our attention, as he certainly stood out from the others. He was wearing a crisp khaki summer uniform and a cloth overseas cap. On this cap were the two bars of a captain. We were surprised by the number of campaign ribbons he was wearing, at a time when it was unusual to see more than two or three on any individual. This officer had ribbons from Africa, the Med, Italy and Europe and others which we could not easily identify. Even more surprising to us were the silver wings of a pilot above the ribbons.

While we were staring at him, almost dumfounded, we 18 year olds, sitting proud as punch with newly issued seamen's papers, in the front seats, the officer walked past us with his head held high and took his seat in the back of the bus. The captain, with the wings of a pilot, an officer and a gentleman, by act of Congress, and undoubtedly with war service overseas, was a Negro.

A young, white private came in after the officer and sat up front with us. I had lived in New York City during the war years, until mid-1943. New York, in those days, was awash with American service men from every branch of the services and every state in the Union. There were also soldiers and sailors from many allied nations: Britain, Canada, Denmark, Norway and Holland, among those I recall. I can even recall seeing Canadian Highlanders, in Grand Central Station, wearing the kilt. Although I had seen a few Negro Navy men, officers' stewards off Navy ships, I had never seen a Negro army enlisted man and certainly never a Negro officer! The white private, who looked to be one stage beyond a recruit, took his seat in the front while the decorated officer was required by the unconstitutional state law of Florida, to sit in the back of the bus along with people of his own race (I recalled this incident 40 years later when I found that, just because it is a state law, that does not necessarily make it legal under the Constitution. It took almost 100 years to overturn the unconstitutional law of the state of Florida.).

The Tuskegee Airmen

The black airman observed by Bill Cooper on the Miami bus in 1945 probably served with a group popularly known as the Tuskegee Airmen. The Tuskegee Airmen were the first African American military aviators in the United States armed forces. The Tuskegee program began officially in June 1941 at the Tuskegee Institute, with 47 officers and 429 enlisted men. Sadly, as Bill noted, during World War II African Americans, including the Tuskegee Airmen, were subjected to racial discrimination both within and outside the army, and in much of the federal government.

All black military pilots who trained in the United States trained at Moton Field and Tuskegee Army Air Field, located near Tuskegee, Alabama. Formally, they were the 332nd Fighter Group and the 477th Bombardment Group of the United States Army Air Forces. When the pilots of the 332nd Fighter Group painted the tails of their P-47, and later

Black Tuskegee Airmen in front of a P-40 training aircraft. In the course of World War II, individual pilots of the 332nd Fighter Group earned 96 Distinguished Flying Crosses. In all, 992 pilots were trained in Tuskegee from 1941 to 1946. Three hundred fifty-five were deployed overseas, 84 lost their lives, and 32 were captured as prisoners of war. Photo from U.S. Air Force.

P-51, aircraft red, the nickname "Red Tails" was coined. Bomber crews applied a more effusive, "Red-Tail Angels".

The budding flight program at Tuskegee, only a few months old at the time, received a publicity boost when First Lady Eleanor Roosevelt inspected it in March 1941, and flew with African American chief civilian instructor, C. Alfred "Chief" Anderson. Anderson, who had been flying since 1929 and was responsible for training thousands of rookie pilots, took his prestigious passenger on a half-hour flight in a Waco biplane,. After landing, she cheerfully announced, "Well, you can fly, all right." She went on to help provide for substantial funding for the Moton Field facility.

Their first combat mission, in July 1943, was for the 99th Fighter Squadron to attack the small strategic volcanic island of Pantelleria, north of Tunisia, to clear the sea lanes for the Allied invasion of Sicily. The surrender of the garrison of 11,121 Italians and 78 Germans due to air attack was the first of its kind. The 99th was moved to mainland Italy. By the end of February 1944, more graduates were ready for combat, and the all-black 332nd Fighter Group was sent overseas with three fighter squadrons to join the 99th Fighter Squadron in Italy.

On 24 March 1945, 43 P-51 Mustangs led by Colonel Benjamin O. Davis escorted B-17 bombers over 1,600 miles into Germany and back. Flying escort for the heavy bombers, the "Red-Tail Angels" earned an impressive combat record. The bombers' target, a Daimler-Benz tank factory in Berlin, was heavily defended by 25 Luftwaffe aircraft, including history's first jet fighter, the Messerschmitt Me 262. Pilots Charles Brantley, Earl Lane, and Roscoe Brown each shot down German jets over Berlin that day. For the mission, the 332nd Fighter Group earned a Distinguished Unit Citation.

After segregation in the military was officially ended in 1948 by President Harry S. Truman with Executive Order 9981, the veteran Tuskegee Airmen found themselves in high demand throughout the newly formed United States Air Force. Others taught in civilian flight schools, such as the black-owned Columbia Air Center in Maryland.

Benjamin O. Davis, Jr., the original commander of the 332nd Fighter Group became the first black general in the U.S. Air Force; and another

Tuskegee aviator, Lucius Theus, retired a major general after a 36-year career in the Air Force. Daniel "Chappie" James, Jr., who started his career in the early 1940s at Tuskegee, stayed on in what became the U.S. Air Force and flew missions in both Korea and Vietnam. In 1969, James was put in command of Wheelus Air Force Base outside of Tripoli, Libya, and was appointed a brigadier general by President Nixon.

The Congressional Gold Medal was collectively presented to approximately 300 Tuskegee Airmen or their widows, at the U.S. Capitol rotunda in Washington, D.C., by President George W. Bush in March 2007. The next year, the Tuskegee Airmen were invited to attend the inauguration of Barack Obama. Retired Tuskegee Airman Lt. William Broadwater, 82, summed up the feeling: "Now we feel like we've completed our mission."

Arthur Gaines

Sources:

Francis, C. E. and A. Case, 1997. *The Tuskegee Airmen: The Men Who Changed a Nation*.: Branden Books, Boston . 496 pp.

Homan, L. M. and T. Reilly, 2001. *Black Knights: The Story of the Tuskegee Airmen*. Pelican Publishing, Gretna, Louisiana.

Molony, C.J.C., F.C. Flynn, H.L. Davies and T.P. Gleave, 1973. *The Mediterranean and Middle East*, Volume V: *The Campaign in Sicily 1943 and The Campaign in Italy 3 September 1943 to 31 March 1944*. History of the Second World War (United Kingdom Military Series).: Naval & Military Press Uckfield, UK.

Moye, J. T., 2010. *Freedom Flyers: The Tuskeegee Airmen of World War II*. Oxford University Press (USA), New York.

National Museum of the United States Air Force Website.

Thole, L., 2002. *Segregated Skies*. Flypast No, 248, March 2002.

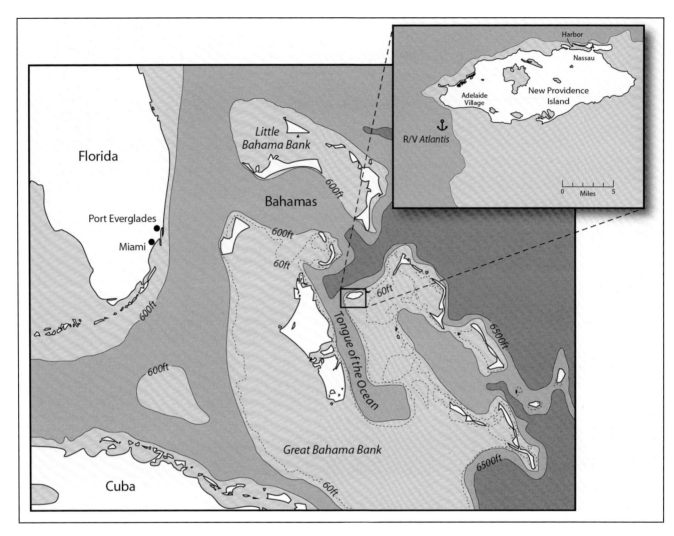

While the Great Bahama Bank averages only 14-feet in depth, the Tongue of the Ocean is an arm of the deep sea that penetrates far into the Bank. With its shelter from ocean swell, its crystal clear, deep water, and its proximity to logistical supply, the Tongue of the Ocean provided an ideal site for planned Navy research. Illustration by Jack Cook.

Bahamas Bound

A FEW DAYS LATER we left Port Everglades for the "Tongue of the Ocean", which was located between New Providence Island—on which Nassau was located—and Andros Island. This was in a partially sheltered area, and the water was unusually deep for the Bahamas. We anchored well offshore in the deep water [3/4 mile deep]. Our anchor was a 200 or 300 pound Danforth with a length of heavy chain, which in turn was attached to the 5/8-inch deep-sea trawl wire, which led through a fair lead block attached to the A-frame at the bow.

Our work, at this location, was to be in relation to undersea warfare and would include many depth charges being dropped, and other tests with model submarine sections and miniature explosions at deep depths. After we anchored, Chief Mate Nordquist told the captain that, since we were to be here a month or more, awnings should be rigged to help keep the decks protected from the sun and the cabins cooler below. We had no fans or any sort of air conditioning. The captain agreed, but also wanted our whale boats put in the water to keep them from drying out.

We rigged awnings over the fo'c'sle, galley and main saloon area, and launched both whale boats and rigged the boat boom to which the whale boats were attached. We also put overboard our motorized catboat—without a mast—and tied it astern. The weather was beautiful. The normal temperature was about 80 degrees or higher at noon. There seemed to always be a nice breeze to keep things cool in the evening hours. We went swimming over the side the first few days, but when we saw sharks around, we ceased that activity.

We were soon joined by the fleet tug *Navaho*. The fleet tugs were the largest seagoing tugs in the Navy, and had a diesel-electric propulsion system. The tugs also had a large Almon Johnson Automatic Towing Machine, which supposedly would enable the tug to tow a battleship at 13 knots [the

Almon Johnson towing machine was a newly invented shipboard device (patented in April 1945) for maintaining a constant tension on the tow line. This damped out surges from hull behavior of the tug and towed vessel and from ocean waves and swells. *Navaho* was the first Navy tug, of 70 built in that class, to have this equipment.]

After a week or so, *Navaho* left us. She was being transferred to the Pacific and was replaced by the fleet tug *Carib.* Soon, we were joined by the 301-foot frigate *Ashville* and other small craft. The *Ashville* was an American-built, British-designed ship. She had twin screws, powered by reciprocating steam engines, which made her very maneuverable. When she arrived on the scene in the Tongue of the Ocean, she was armed with a British Squid mortar forward that fired a depth charge out ahead. The Squid mortar reminded me of the pictures I had seen of a Civil War mortar.

The heavy ash can depth charges were usually dropped over the stern of the ship attacking a submarine, but the Squid enabled the ship to fire ahead when approaching a sub. Before the operation began, a floating target was attached about 300 feet astern of *Atlantis.* This was the target for the Squid depth charges fired by *Ashville.* Different instruments were hung from the target to measure the explosions, at various depths.

Normally *Ashville* would approach from astern of *Atlantis* at a good rate of speed, using radar to locate the target and then, when within range, would fire the Squid depth charge out ahead at the target. The depth charge was set to explode at a 600- and 800-foot depth. Immediately after *Ashville* fired the Squid, she turned hard to starboard, still at speed, and dropped a depth charge over the stern, which also exploded. The two depth charges exploding one behind the other would cause *Atlantis* to jump. Plates on the table in the crew's mess would jump up into the air and somersault before crashing down.

On the surface of the blue water, there appeared a blur caused by the shock wave. There would not be any high geyser of water as we had seen in the movies whenever the dropping of depth charges was shown. After about 30 seconds, the subsurface water would just bubble up—the gas bubbles coming to the surface. *Carib* would be standing by off to one side watching or filming the whole operation, as would the blimp overhead, if the weather permitted.

On the first run in, *Ashville's* radar operators picked up *Atlantis* and not the target with the result that the first Squid went into the water close to

Above: *The Navy provided the 301-foot frigate* Ashville *to help evaluate new technology in the deployment of depth charges. U.S. Navy photo.*

    Left: *The research program was also supported by the U.S. Navy 205-foot Cherokee-class fleet tug Carib (AT-82). U.S. Navy photo.*

our stern. When it exploded at a depth of 800 feet or so, it gave us one hell of a jolt—it was unbelievable!

    The reason for these tests, although no one ever said so, was that it appeared that the German U-boats were operating at greater depths than had previously been thought possible. The normal maximum depth for a U-boat was around 300 feet but the Germans were now going down as deep as 600 to 800 feet. World War II sonar was unreliable below 400 feet. The study was to ascertain the effect of explosions in the deep water. All this activity made life exciting for us and the best part was that it all ceased in the afternoon, which left us with pleasant evenings.

Hurricane Preparations

Because we were in the Bahamas with the approaching hurricane season, Captain Knight was apprehensive. Over a drink, one evening, he had a discussion with the captain of *Carib* about the situation, and they decided to rig *Atlantis* so she could be towed to safety by the fleet tug. What was required was a wire bridle rigged around and through *Atlantis'* anchor (chain) hawser pipes. The bridle was rigged in case it was necessary to quickly attach the tow wire from *Carib* at some future time. I heard Captain Knight tell the chief mate that the fleet tug could tow us to safety, if need be, to Nassau or Florida at 13 knots. This seemed to make Captain Knight quite happy as the hurricane of 1944 was still fresh in his mind.

Deck Work

While at anchor, the ship's crew worked constantly on *Atlantis'* gear. The deck work went very smoothly, as the older seamen understood what needed to be done and were good workers. The chief mate generally worked along with us, the only mate, in my time aboard, to do so. As he was always cheerful, it made for a very pleasant time.

Mr. Nordquist decided he did not like the "Dado brown" paint used on the ventilators, engine room fiddley hatches, and elsewhere. He changed the color to mast buff. The ventilator mouths were red, which conflicted with the mast buff, so they were painted a light blue instead. The cement waterways next to the bulwarks were changed from red to green. When the painting was completed, the two ABs said that *Atlantis* now looked like a Swedish ship.

One time there was a small job to do aloft on the mainmast. The general rule in *Atlantis*, at the time, was that the junior man was sent aloft. I was, by far, the junior man. As I started to climb into the bo'sun chair, Mr. Nordquist spoke to me in a quiet voice: "Ve let Karl do dis yob. He is old and to go aloft vill make him feel he is still useful. You are young and can go aloft lots of times in the years to come." Chief Mate Nordquist had an understanding heart.

The Galley Crew

The Tongue of the Ocean Cruise was the only cruise I'd made in *Atlantis* where we had a steward and cook, and two mess boys in the galley. On some cruises we had only one cook, or at other times a cook and helper, but never again a cook and a steward, at least not in my time.

The steward on this cruise was an elderly man who had spent a lot of time at sea. The fact that he was English did not sit too well with the squareheads in the crew, who thought of anything British as 'starvation and ease'. Chief Mate Nordquist in particular, was very apprehensive about having a "Limey steward". When the new cook, who was an American, arrived on board at Woods Hole shortly after the steward, their apprehensions were eased. The cook, a mulatto or "high yellow"—as the squareheads termed him—was a regular merchant service cook, skilled in the trade, with a lot of service under his belt. He had been a stateroom steward on passenger liners before the war, and was, as far as I am concerned, the best, by far, of any of the cooks I ever served with. The squarehead crew was pleased with him from the start.

I can't recall his name, but he was very intelligent, generally cheerful and a hard worker. He had studied for the priesthood and, when he turned to in the morning at 4:30 AM, he would sing the Mass in Latin while he prepared the vegetables and meats for the coming day. He was also spotlessly clean and had the mess boys scrub the yellow tiles of the galley sole every day after the noon dishes were done. The galley had never been so clean. He got on very well with the chief mate and the crew, who appreciated his talents and cleanliness. He thought the *Atlantis* galley very antiquated and the "cold box" as he termed it, inadequate. "How are we going to keep meat fresh in there in the tropics?" he had asked.

Compared to the cook, the steward, who seemed a nice enough fellow, looked like he was half-asleep most of the time. When he had the proper supplies, our cook served up wonderful meals and treated us in the crew's mess especially well. As the weeks wore on, the meat in our 1931 cold box began to turn bad. The cook did not want to serve it but the steward insisted there was nothing wrong with it, and that he would prepare and cook the meats. The cook swore the steward had lost his sense of smell! On those occasions, when he thought the meat was bad, before dinner at noon, the cook would come into the crew's mess and tell us: "Don't eat the meat today, boys."

No one warned the people in the main saloon, which was the steward's domain. I am surprised that many did not get sick, but the chief scientist,

Paul Fye, was one who did. My memory is of Dr. Fye, unconscious and suffering from ptomaine poisoning, lying on a stretcher, being loaded on to the 83-foot Coast Guard patrol boat, accompanied by Lieutenant Smith, destined for the British Naval Hospital on New Providence Island. Dr. Fye never returned again to *Atlantis* on that cruise.

It was a general agreement that the men in the Navy small boats could eat dinner in any ship they happened to be near at mess time. All the Navy boats came to *Atlantis*, regardless of where they were at noon, because of the good reputation of our cook. The Navy enlisted crews ate in the crew's mess on the ship.

The Underwater Light and Fishing

Chief Backus rigged up an underwater light, which he hung over the side of *Atlantis* at night. It was amazing to see the many kinds of fish that were attracted to the light. Most interesting were the barracuda, and I never tired of watching them swim in their natural habitat. They would swim very slowly toward the light and then, just as easily, swim backward, away from the light, as if they were mesmerized by it. Although there were other kinds of fish around the light, I never saw the barracuda make any kind of attack on them.

Second Engineer Hans Cook gave the Navy men in one of the motor whaleboats a couple of lures he had from the previous summer, when he fished for striped bass in Woods Hole. The men in the motor whale boat would troll with these lures as they traveled back and forth between different ships. One day they caught two barracuda and brought them to show to us on *Atlantis*. They were ugly looking things out of water. The question came up, were they good to eat? The bo'sun, Ernest Siversen, insisted they were very good to eat, because "He doesn't eat any yunk laying around. Everything he eats, he catches on the hoof."

Ashville on Collision Course

During one of the runs that *Ashville* made to fire the Squid at the target, something happened to her steering gear. After she made the hard starboard turn, she was not able to straighten out right away, and *Carib* was directly in her path, hove-to, and filming the shock waves of the explosions.

Ashville sounded four loud blasts with her steam siren—meaning "danger"—and luckily the men in the engine room crew were alert. They immediately put the reciprocating steam engines into full astern with full power which stopped her headway completely. If *Ashville* had had steam turbines, instead of the reciprocating engines, there almost certainly would have been a collision between the two Navy ships that day. Steam turbines are much slower to respond when changing direction, and the small astern turbine had not anywhere near the astern power that is found in the reciprocating engine. It was a close call, and it could have ended the project, then and there.

The 83-foot Coast Guard patrol boat would occasionally make trips to Nassau to pick up personnel and various supplies, which included liquor. The Navy ships were not allowed to have on board any liquor of any kind, therefore when the Naval officers wanted to purchase liquor, they would have it assigned to *Atlantis*. When party time came in the evenings, all the Naval officers that could be spared from their own ships came to *Atlantis* in their various launches and motor whaleboats. The parties took place in the main saloon and would last well into the night. The boat crews would be on deck forward drinking beer, and sometimes the officers would send up some hard stuff to them.

Since the ship was lying to at anchor, the watches of the regular crew were broken, with only one man on anchor watch from 6 PM to 6 AM. We were to take turns of one week each on anchor watch, and my turn came about the third week. There was always a great deal of activity starting about 8 AM, as the men would be working on deck, or worse, the depth charges would begin to explode. In a word, it was very hard to sleep in the fo'c'sle, at least for me anyway, after 8 AM. There were also many exciting events taking place—boats coming alongside, the movement of the various ships, and trips to other ships in our catboat launch.

During my week of anchor watch, one of the older ABs would take my place in the evening so that I could go to the movie shows on the aft deck of the *Ashville*. I did not sleep very much during my week on watch, and found it very hard to stay awake toward the early morning hours. It was also a strange feeling at times to realize that I was the only one awake on *Atlantis* as I made my rounds through the ship.

In the early morning, about 3:30 AM of my fifth day on this watch, my teeth, all of them, began to ache something awful. I had no idea what the trouble was, as the pain continued on through the morning. At 8: 30 or so

Above: *The 16-foot launch*
Lobster *proved useful in
moving personnel short distances among the assembled
fleet. A modified catboat, she
was probably built by Oscar
Hilton who ran a boat yard
in Eel Pond, Woods Hole,
and who was yet another
friend of Columbus Iselin.
She was transported on the
deck of* Atlantis. *Photo courtesy WHOI Archives ©
Woods Hole Oceanographic
Institution.*

Middle right: *Both of*
Atlantis' *whaleboats were
also deployed for a variety of
research and recreational purposes. Photo courtesy WHOI
Archives © Woods Hole
Oceanographic Institution.*

Bottom: *Chief Engineer
Harold Backus, an avid fish-
erman, displays his catch of a
dolphin fish. Photo courtesy
WHOI Archives © Woods
Hole Oceanographic
Institution.*

that morning, as I returned the keys to the second mate after winding the chronometers, I told him about my teeth aching. The second mate was supposed to be the ship's doctor. He told me he would look up in the ship's medical book what the reason might be. Shortly after, he said I was to report on board *Ashville* and see her doctor. When I boarded *Ashville*, a sailor, who was waiting for me, took me to the doctor. He asked me a few questions about the ache, and then asked: "How much sleep have you been getting?"

I told him I was on anchor watch that week and was not able to sleep in the daytime. He seemed to know right off that the problem was lack of sleep. He said he had seen it before many times. He gave me a note for Captain Knight and sent me on my way. When back on board *Atlantis*, I was taken off anchor watch, and the next morning, after a good night's sleep, my teeth were back to normal. I have never suffered from that again, in 60 years.

Ashore in Adelaide

The fishing vessels that were in the Tongue of the Ocean were small sailing vessels, of the native Bahamian sloop model. The only auxiliary power they had was a long oar, almost as long as the boats, with which the men would scull over the stern, whenever there was a calm. We would watch them scull, at times, for hours as they worked into some cove or harbor on the south side of New Providence Island.

At one time, during a quiet period, a native fishing boat came to *Atlantis* and sold us some Bahamian crawfish and red snappers. Captain Knight and the second mate, who were both probably bored with the operation and of laying to on the anchor, made arrangements with the fishermen to buy them some rum, and they would go ashore and have a party in the village shown on the chart as Adelaide, the following night.

The next day, the captain informed Chief Mate Nordquist that he was going ashore in the smaller Number 1 whaleboat for the evening. At the time, I don't think the chief mate liked the idea. He came to the fo'c'sle after supper and ordered me to take one of the mess boys with me and to go with the captain in the whaleboat. We were to stay with the whaleboat, and to be sure to bring the boat back after the party was over. He also said he would run the anchor light well up the forestay, so we could see it from the shore. I had sailed with the captain in the Number 1 whaleboat a number of times in Woods Hole Harbor the previous summer of 1944. I was well acquainted with the rig and its gear and handling. We originally had canvas bags filled with sand, which were used for shifting ballast to give the boat more stability. Captain Knight decided, after sailing in the boat a few times, that it had stability enough and the canvas sand-filled bags were discarded. He was very fond of *Atlantis*' whaleboats, and generally saw to it that they were well taken care of. On the way to shore that evening I recalled he had told me a year earlier in Woods Hole, while sailing with him in the Number 1 boat, that a model similar to the whaleboat with a shallow lead keel and centerboard would make an ideal cruiser for shoal waters of the Bahamas.

At this point in time, I don't remember anyone else in the whaleboat except Captain Knight, Second Mate Christopher, Bob Metell the mess boy, and myself. We left *Atlantis* and sailed for the shore with the captain at the tiller. The whaleboat had a compass, but without a light for it, so it would be of no use for the return trip. Only the anchor light aboard the ship would help us, if we could see it.

We sailed for a great distance over a shallow sandy bottom (though in the Bahamas, it could have been a lot deeper than it looked). Coming back out from shore that night, I found out it was not deep at all. In time we reached the shore near a collection of native huts that was called "Adelaide". When we approached the shore, a number of Bahamian natives came to the beach and helped pull the whaleboat ashore above the high tide line. It was the first time that Bob Metell and I had ever stepped on a foreign shore.

The fishermen's huts were a ways in from the beach at the end of a path, and were very simple buildings. The walls might have been coral and the roof, some kind of thatching. Bob Metell and I went with one fellow to his home which consisted of one room and, to our surprise, one bed. There were four or five kids inside and when we asked where they all slept, they got on the bed and lay down cross ways to show us.

The people all were very friendly and polite. The walls of the hut were papered with colored comic strips from the Sunday papers. There were many coconuts piled outside near the door, with the husks still on. The owner of the house offered us some coconut milk which we accepted, and with that he drew a machete—stored blade down through a crack in the floor—and, holding the coconut in his hand, cut away the husk with the machete to reveal the nut. He then punched a hole in the top of the nut and passed one to Bob and the other to me. Other native men soon arrived in the center of the so-called village, with the rum which they had purchased for the captain and the second mate.

Tiger Rum

The rum was in reused Coca Cola bottles and had a label which read "Tiger Rum". I think who ever sold it had a barrel of rum and used the coke bottles for distribution. The men, like most people that live in outlying districts, were very honest. They told the captain they had change from the money he had given them to buy the rum. The captain politely refused it and told them it was theirs to keep.

We had secured the whaleboat with the sea anchor warp to some strong bushes near the shore. I was satisfied she was safe enough for now and did not stay with the boat, in violation of the chief mate's orders, as I wanted to see what would happen at the party in the village. There was a sandy clearing off to one side with a circle of rocks in the middle, with a pile of wood there, the location of the fire.

When darkness fell, the fire was started and soon after, the man with the drum arrived. In the meantime, the captain and the second mate, along with some of the fishermen who had their coconuts with rum mixed in the milk, took their places around the circle of the fire. Bob Metell sat down in the circle with them. In time, the Bahamian belles arrived, and Bob and I were surprised to see the nicely pressed summer dresses they had on—their Sunday best—and with bare feet. The man with the drum held the drum over the fire to tighten the skin, he told us. He began to play a rhythm, and all the kids present jumped in the circle and began to dance. The dance they did was very similar to the kind of dancing one would see in the 1970s and 1980s. The difference was that the Bahamians had a natural rhythm and were much more graceful.

The older people eventually chased the kids out of the circle and a few of the older girls started to dance. The object seemed to be that one danced for a time and then picked someone in the circle to dance in front of. After a while the dancer and spectator changed places, and on it went until everyone around the circle had his or her chance to dance without too many people being in the circle at one time. Every now and then the dancing stopped when the skin on the drum stretched too much. Then the drummer would hold it over the fire to shrink it again. At the time the dancing was taking place, everyone except Bob Metell and I were drinking rum. The party was getting gayer and gayer.

I decided then the time had come when we would obey Mr. Nordquist's order and stay with the boat. Bob and I left the party, which was going great guns, and went down the path to the whaleboat. We decided to go to sleep in the boat, which would not be easy because there was no place to lie down except on the thwarts. We were, however, young and tired and soon settled in the boat covering ourselves with the lug mainsail. Before closing my eyes, I looked out to sea and could just barely make out the light that I supposed was *Atlantis'* anchor light.

We both fell asleep. We were awakened—God knows what time it was —by a great deal of singing and with a kerosene lantern shining in our eyes, and the whaleboat surrounded by a mass of black faces singing some hymn about a "lighthouse in the sky". Seeing the lighthouse—"Great Isaac"—off the western end of New Providence Island, I pointed to it and asked a man near me: "Is that the lighthouse in the sky?" "Yes" he answered, "the Lord's lighthouse for you and me."

We untied the sea anchor warp from the bush at the edge of the beach and all hands—it seemed like 25 men or so— picked up the whale boat and fleeted it down to the water. I never saw the second mate get into the boat but the captain got in, and then Bob and me. We soon had the sails set and, with the wind on the port beam, we began to sail offshore, with our Bahamian friends still singing and shouting "good-bye."

We found the water too shallow to either lower the centerboard or to ship the rudder. The captain asked me to steer out toward *Atlantis* and also asked me if I could see her light. I could barely see it, low down on the horizon. We had shipped the steering oar, and with that I steered out toward the ship. The second mate was completely passed out.

With the wind on the port beam, Captain Knight suggested I keep the light from *Atlantis* on the starboard side of the mast. Without the centerboard, we would be bound to make a great deal of leeway. We could tell the water was still shallow, as I could touch the bottom with the oar quite easily. Captain Knight stayed near me in the stern of the whaleboat as we sailed through the night. If he did doze off at times, he would awaken quickly if I asked him a question.

While still holding a course for *Atlantis'* anchor light, after what seemed a long time, we finally reached water deep enough to lower the centerboard and ship the rudder so I could now steer with the tiller. In time we could see *Atlantis* with her deck lights and all, and were soon alongside. Chief Mate Nordquist was on deck waiting for us. Bob Metell and I held the whaleboat in tight to the boarding ladder, as the captain and the second mate climbed aboard. We secured the whaleboat to the boat boom, and turned in, as the morning would come soon enough.

A week or so later, Captain Knight and the second mate took the small whaleboat to go ashore again in Adelaide. In the meanwhile, Director Iselin had come to Nassau and had been ferried out by the Coast Guard patrol boat and arrived on board *Atlantis*, unannounced. He was waiting aboard the ship when the captain returned later that afternoon in the whaleboat. "Hello, Lambert", Mr. Iselin said, to a startled Captain Knight.

Sometime in mid-June, we hoisted the whaleboats back on board and rigged in the boat boom. Some of the men forward hinted that the chief mate was taking away the temptation of going ashore in the whaleboat from the captain. I doubt that this was true, as very shortly after a Coast Guard 83-foot patrol boat came and lay along our port side, in place of the whaleboats.

Nassau

Sometime after we'd been anchored a month or so, it was decided that *Atlantis* could weigh anchor and spend a few days in Nassau. As we were preparing to get underway, I was given the job, along with Bob Metell, to take the catboat launch over to the *Carib* where it would be hoisted aboard and stored on her after deck. *Atlantis* had left and was underway before we had the launch secured on board *Carib*. Even though she had a good start and 15 knot speed, we soon passed her by and were docked in Nassau a good two hours before *Atlantis* arrived.

With the war in Europe just ending, in that early summer of 1945, Nassau was devoid of tourists. However there was still a lot of activity. A great many of the buildings were painted in bright colors such as the yellow and white trim of the government house and others in dark pink with white trim, which gave the area a light cheerful look. The British Colonial Hotel was headquarters of the West India Regiment. There were black troops of the West Indian Regiment, RAF types and Royal Navy men everywhere, along with the crews of the Navy ships and also our crew when we went ashore.

The main business area of Nassau did not seem that large to me at first, but like other places, grew larger the better we came to know it. There were many horse-drawn carriages and wagons. The aroma of horse manure and urine filled the air on the main street, accentuated by the heat. Because we did not drink, the mess boys and I did not get to see any of the bars or night life. We went to a movie instead, and were introduced to the custom of the playing of "God Save the King" with the audience standing at attention, and singing the words of the song before the movie began.

In the evening, after supper, one of the Bahamian boys came to the ship where she lay at the wharf and asked if he could empty our garbage cans. We passed them two cans, which they took down the wharf and around the corner of the shed. In due time, they brought the cans back empty and washed out nice and clean. I told Bob Metell he should pay them something, and he offered them two shillings (in 1945, 40 cents). The Bahamians refused to take the money, saying if we gave them the garbage that was enough.

The next evening, after we let the Bahamians take the garbage, Bob and I waited for them to get out of sight before we followed them down the wharf. When we came to the end of the shed, we carefully peeked around the corner and watched the boys dump out the cans and carefully pick the contents over for edible food which they placed in a bucket. Now that is poverty! After that, for the next two days, the mess boys made sure, with the cook's help, that there was extra food sneaked out of the galley and tucked in with the garbage.

Carib Comes Alongside

While anchored on station, Chief Mate Nordquist did not approve of *Carib* coming alongside to give us water, at that particular time. It was too rough for this kind of a transfer, as it would take two hours at the very least, to fill our tanks.

When his advice was ignored by Captain Knight, Mr. Nordquist said he relinquished all responsibility and went below to his cabin, leaving the captain in charge on deck. There was a good swell running at the time, as *Carib* came slowly up from astern on *Atlantis'* starboard side. When alongside, the mooring lines were passed from *Carib* and made fast on *Atlantis'* mooring bollards. Once stopped, *Carib* began to roll and her rolling was different from the roll of *Atlantis*. Though she was not much longer than *Atlantis*, she was of much greater displacement (weight). She rolled down and struck us hard a few times and, when rolling in the opposite direction, one of her mooring lines, fastened to the main sheet bronze bollard, put such a strain on that piece of hardware that the bollard ripped right out of the deck and shot out over the side like a cannon ball, and crashed into the hull of *Carib* before sinking into the sea.

I was standing a few feet aft of the mainsheet bollard at the time, and saw the whole process. *Carib* then rolled again toward *Atlantis* and hit us a real hard blow, bending in the bulwark and smashing the teak rail. The last crash must have sounded to the chief mate, in his cabin on the starboard side, as if he were inside a bass drum.

Mr. Nordquist suddenly appeared on deck, and, completely ignoring the captain and second mate, ordered all the mooring lines of the tug to be let go, and those that could not be released to be cut with the boat's fire axes. This order was promptly obeyed. *Carib*'s captain, in a higher position on her bridge and seeing the action below on *Atlantis*, ordered seven revolutions ahead. Slowly *Carib* pulled ahead and clear. As she passed, we could see her large propeller turning slowly in the beautiful, clear water.

I believe we later did receive fresh water from *Carib*, but that was in the quiet of Nassau Harbor. *Carib* smashed in the steel bulwarks in almost the same area that the Navy yawl Saluda damaged them in the hurricane of 1944.

Sixty Cents a Carton

Because *Atlantis* was considered a merchant ship, working for the Navy on foreign service, we were allowed a sea store. Included in the sea store were cigarettes, which the U.S. government supplied at a tax exempt cost of six cents a pack, or sixty cents a carton, for the best brands. The better brands, such as Camels and Lucky Strike, were scarce at home and the cigarettes that were available there were the poorer brands.

We were allowed a ration of one carton a week, per man. As I did not smoke, the second mate, who was in charge of the sea stores, did not want to allow me my ration. Captain Knight intervened, and said it did not matter what use I had for the cigarette ration, I was entitled to my share. I sold my ration to the other men in the fo'c'sle and also brought some home to people in Quissett and Woods Hole. This action was probably against the law, as these cigarettes were supposed to be consumed outside the United States. Out of the ten men before the mast, which included the two mess boys, the bo'sun and I were the only ones who did not smoke. The bo'sun however, used Copenhagen snuff.

At the time I am writing this narrative, the U.S. government is engaged in a lawsuit against the tobacco companies, claiming that the cigarette companies misled the public for at least sixty years about the dangers of cigarette smoking. What a hypocritical joke! That same government made cigarettes readily available to all service men and others during the war years, at a greatly reduced price that encouraged smoking!

I was only 18 years old at the time, but I knew as well as most everyone did, that cigarette smoking was an unhealthy habit to get into. Cigarettes were called "coffin nails" at the time, and, when lighting one, the phrase "here goes another nail in my coffin" was often quoted. People smoked and do smoke cigarettes because they are a drug of sorts, and were and are habit-forming. The young ones took it up because it was considered "sophisticated" or "smart" (or "cool" as they say today). In my opinion, whatever ills that smokers suffered in later years, they brought on themselves.

Submarine Model Sections

A great deal of time was spent by the technicians, especially Charlie Wheeler and John Martin, testing and photographing the submarine model sections, which were lowered over the side into deep water on the hydrographic winch wire. The cylinder model sections were about the size of round gallon paint cans, closed on the ends. Steel ribs were welded on the outside as it would be in an actual submarine (about 1/32 scale).

The model sections were mounted on one end of a steel frame, 6 to 8 feet long with a small explosive charge and a camera attached to the other end. The steel frame, together with the model, the explosive charge and camera, were lowered over the side to a predetermined depth, whereupon the camera was started and the charge detonated. Sometimes the model would be completely crushed (imploded). At other times, it would appear to be completely intact, and at other times, only slightly damaged. The purpose seemed to be to determine how close the depth charge had to be in deep water to damage the submarine.

Chief Engineer Backus had a special interest in the anti-submarine warfare operation, as he was the only man aboard *Atlantis* who had ever served in submarines. He had joined the British Navy in 1914, at the start of World War I. He was commissioned as an engineering officer, diesel, and assigned to a British E-class submarine. In the submarine he saw action in the Gallipoli campaign at the Straits of the Dardanelles in 1915.

In the previous year, I had heard him give details of the parts played by the E-Class submarines, but unfortunately cannot remember the number of the sub he served on. He said that submarine officers were considered and treated as second class people by the other officers of the Royal Navy. A lot of that had to do with the stench of diesel oil that permeated their uniforms as well as everything else on the submarine in those days.

When *Atlantis* was at Electric Boat Company yard in Groton, in the fall of 1944, we had the opportunity to examine American submarines under construction, just before commissioning. Chief Backus was amazed at how large and luxurious these subs were, compared to the E-Class boats he had served on.

Homeward Bound

Toward the end of June, we learned that, because the cables attached to the measuring instruments had tangled themselves up, the project was to be terminated and we were to sail for home. This news made my watch partner, John Martin, very happy. One fellow of the scientific party had a pile of angle irons and other stock stored on the starboard side, amidships, next to the bulwarks. This pile of "yunk", as the chief mate called it, was right next to the main preventer backstay, tackle and gig, and we found it to be a considerable nuisance. In addition, it was rusting and staining the general area of the bulwarks and deck.

While getting ready to sail home, the chief mate wanted to get rid of all the unused angle irons and such. The scientist, whose project owned the iron, wanted to take it home as it was "worth money". The chief mate asked him "how much money?" "About forty dollars" was the answer. Chief Mate Nordquist went directly below to his cabin and soon returned with the forty dollars, and immediately gave the order: "Over the side with dis yunk, boys."

Before leaving for home, we went once more into the port of Nassau for a few days, our second visit. In Nassau, we put the catboat over the side, and the mess boys and I made a number of trips taking people from *Atlantis* farther up into the harbor. We landed at a pier on the outer side of the harbor where everyone but the mess boys and I went ashore. The place was called Paradise Island, and was mostly beach at that time. The water of the harbor at the pier was crystal clear, with a sandy bottom. Although at first we guessed the water depth to be about six feet, none of us could reach bottom in our attempts to dive down to it.

A new cleat for the main sheet, to replace the bronze bollard lost overboard when *Carib* came alongside, was installed during this time in Nassau. For the voyage home, the watches were set at 4 hours on and 8 hours off, which was much more pleasant than the 6 and 6 we stood on the trip down.

Leaving Nassau, on June 25th, 1945, we had a few days of pleasant sailing, after which time we reached Bermuda. While laying off the harbor of St. George, hove-to, waiting for the pilot to come out and guide us in to port, Chief Mate Nordquist informed us, "Dis place iss yust like Limeyland, boys, so don't get into trouble. If you do, you goes to yail and you stay there, no matter who you are."

Bermuda in mid-1945, without tourists, looked to my young eyes like paradise, as we entered through the gut into the picturesque harbor of St. George. The only vessels in harbor were some Royal Navy sub-chasers, whose officers were in tropical dress uniforms, white knee-length shorts and white stockings. British naval officers, unlike our chief mate, did not do any manual work, so could keep very neat and proper.

Shortly after clearing Bermuda, we ran into an unusually short, high swell in the area of Cape Hatteras, caused, it was said, by seas left over from a northeast gale a few days before. The sea from the northeast was flowing against the Gulf Stream current going north. Sitting in the bow of *Atlantis* when she rose on a swell was like sitting on the top of a steep hill and looking down to the stern. We estimated, at the time, that the swells were forty to fifty feet high. There were no breaking crests on the swells, so we did not ship any water aboard. During my wheel watch, Captain Knight said to me, "This gives you some idea of the size of the seas that can be encountered off Cape Hatteras in a northeast gale."

Fog and Noman's Land

Late one afternoon, when we were a few days out of Bermuda, the water changed color from indigo blue to a grayish-green. We were out of the Gulf Stream and the air, which had been pleasantly warm, now had a bit of a chill. We had had three days of very heavy overcast, so bad that neither the captain nor the second mate, a superb navigator, could take a sight with the sextant. As we were approaching Nantucket Shoals a thick fog set in. By dead reckoning they thought we were off the island of Noman's

Each departure or return of the ship was celebrated by family, friends, and WHOI employees. Single crew members had their eyes out for pretty girls of Woods Hole and Quissett. Photo courtesy WHOI Archives © Woods Hole Oceanographic Institution.

Land. I give Captain Knight credit for realizing the fact that most of the time you are not where you think you are. With thick fog and night coming on, he decided to anchor, since we were well on soundings.

The air-powered fog horn was constantly blowing, making it difficult for the watches below to get their sleep. Sometime after midnight on the chief mate's watch, the ship stopped and we were anchored with the anchor and trawl wire that had been used in the Tongue of the Ocean. It was dead quiet after that, as I don't remember the bell being struck, as required by law for a ship at anchor.

When I went on watch in the morning at 8 AM, it was still foggy, but we could see a glimmer of sunlight high in the sky. Chief Backus had set a fish line with a large baited hook over the stern, hoping to catch a tuna or perhaps even a swordfish. In a short time the bait was taken and the fish hooked, but when the chief started to haul the line in he found to his surprise the creature was heavy and he needed help to haul it in. Near the surface the catch turned out to be a large hammerhead shark.

That was the last thing the chief wanted, so in order to retrieve his hook he went below and returned with a shotgun. He fired twice at the shark and whether he killed it or not, I don't recall. Right after the second discharge from the shot gun, we heard the engine of a power boat start and approach us from the starboard bow, and come alongside. They were swordfishing and we had not seen them before. The boat was owned by Bill Hand, a well-known naval architect and, incidentally, a friend of Captain Knight. Mr. Hand gave us a bearing for the Noman's hooter, which was a short distance off our starboard bow. Chief Backus had the engine watch, so before he went to the engine room he had to cut his fish line free, shark and all.

The anchor was hove in and landed on deck, and we proceeded to the direction of the buoy. Once the buoy was sighted, and a course set for the Vineyard Sound Light Ship, the fog had mostly lifted.

I only relate this to show that we could have just as easily been on the back side of Nantucket and if we had gone aground there, it could have been serious. Navigation off the coast in summer time is child's play compared to what it can be in the winter, especially in a NE snowstorm. Captain Knight said that most vessels are wrecked because the vessel is not where the master or mates think it is. In 1945, only the Navy had LORAN and Radar. Most merchant ships had, at least, a gyro compass.

The mess boys and I were surprised to see how muddy the water off Vineyard Sound looked after the beautiful clear waters of the Bahamas. We arrived home in the afternoon of July 4th, 1945, on a beautiful summer day, with lots of people to greet us, including the pretty young girls of Woods Hole and Quissett.

United States Navy Employees

Back in Woods Hole we found out that those of us in the ship's crew had been U.S. Navy employees since we sailed from Woods Hole. At that time, all the crew had been called aft and the captain passed out our Navy I.D. cards, which contained our pictures. We had to sign for the cards. The chief mate's comment, when he saw his photograph on the I.D. card, was "Dat face belongs in Hollywood." The I.D. cards were collected from us after we returned to Woods Hole by Madeline Broadbent.

So ended my first cruise on *Atlantis*, which was made in "flying fish weather", as the old sailors said. Never once did I have to wear my oilskins in two months, and the scientific work done was most interesting and exciting, especially for the mess boys and me. Also, we had three months' pay waiting for us.

Altantis' whaleboats were replaced in 1952 by Len Broadhurst, working at East Marine at the head of Falmouth Harbor. The work was so close to the original Charles Beetle whaleboats, built in 1933, that it was difficult to tell the new boats from the old. Photo by Edwin Grey © Woods Hole Oceanographic Institution.

The New England Whaleboat

The original builder's invoice for *Atlantis* listed two dories among other gear provided for the ship. According to Cooper, Chief Engineer Harold Backus urged then-Director Henry Bigelow to replace the dories with whaleboats, which he said were better-suited for lifeboats. Bigelow agreed.

The whaleboats that first caught Cooper's attention in 1944 were built by Charles Beetle of New Bedford. His father, James, had started in the trade in the 1820s and in the span of his career built hundreds of boats while perfecting the type with many innovations. Charles, working alongside his father and subsequently on his own, mastered the technique and provided features that made the Beetle whaleboat one of the best.

When the whaling industry left New Bedford in the early 20th century, Beetle's business slowed to a trickle. Building two boats for the Woods Hole Oceanographic's research ketch was emblematic of the new customer for a waning art. The boats built for *Atlantis* were 28- and 23- feet, respectively, and had much of the equipment found in a working whaleboat: one long oar per man, a rudder hung on the stern, stowable sailing rig, and the reliable cedar bucket.

The New England whaleboat is very likely a direct descendant of the Norse longship. The similarities are striking: double-ended, clinker or lap strake planking where the planking edges overlap, open or un-decked, and handy and fast under both sail and oar. The course of the heritage from longship to whaleboat seems clear: Scandinavia, England, America, and then spreading across the globe. Although there were boats built specifically for whaling in Europe it was in New Bedford, Massachusetts, where the type was perfected.

The American boats had a hull shape established by the English but some say influenced by native birch bark canoes. Light cedar planking and steam bent oak frames (New England white oak being the best in the world for the purpose) made the boats light enough to move by hand yet durable in the task of hunting whales. Originally pulled up on a beach and eventually taken to sea hung on davits, the whaleboat had to withstand long periods of being dry yet be ready to go in the water and be watertight on short notice. Lapstrake planking was the traditional solution as when the planks dried out the seams didn't open up.

The disadvantage to this construction is it offers slightly more resistance at slow speeds, is difficult to repair, but most importantly it's noisier, especially from underwater, and boats thus built had a greater tendency to "gally", or frighten, the whales. It was Beetle who started building his boats smooth planked with seam battens to solve the problem of keeping the planking tight when dry, with the added benefit of a quieter flow over the hull. Contrary to popular impression, in later years much of the pursuit of whales was done under sail. If there were a breeze, larger faster whales could be chased down for a longer period of time without tiring the crew, and with the added benefit of no oars disturbing the water.

Since *Atlantis* was not going to be chasing whales Beetle built her boats with lapstrake planking, going back to the previous method. Not only was there no disadvantage in service, the older planking technique was probably easier, quicker and cheaper.

Douglas Cooper

Atlantis *was built in 1930 in Copenhagen, Denmark, at the Burmeister & Wain Shipyard, which won the bid for her construction. Columbus Iselin, later Director of WHOI, was the first captain, and several of the crew on the maiden voyage to Woods Hole were people Cooper came to know during his years aboard* Atlantis. *Photo courtesy WHOI Archives © Woods Hole Oceanographic Institution.*

Atlantis: The Ship and Shipboard Life

8

T HE KETCH *Atlantis*, the original seagoing research vessel of the Woods Hole Oceanographic Institution, was built in 1930 with a grant set up by the Rockefeller Foundation. *Atlantis* was designed by the Boston firm of Owen & Minot, Naval Architects and Marine Engineers. This was at the request of Henry Bigelow, the first director of the Institution.

George Owen was a professor of naval architecture at the Massachusetts Institute of Technology (MIT). I believe one of his students long associated with WHOI, and formerly of Quissett, was Frank Mather. Another student was Fred Huntington, a native of Chilmark. Fred Huntington was the naval architect at Luders Marine Construction Company when I went there as a marine draftsman in 1952.

Fred Huntington told me George Owen had been a draftsman at Herreshoff's, and also that he was rather casual about calculations, considering he was a professor of naval architecture. Fred, however, liked Professor Owen very much and liked his designs. Without doubt, *Atlantis* was a very nice design and really a "sweet vessel", as Dr. Bigelow is reported to have said.

Atlantis' general dimensions are:

        Length overall—142 feet 9 inches.

        Beam overall—28 feet

        Draft—16 feet (later 17 feet)

        Displacement—

                originally 364 tons;

                changed to 407 tons

        Displacement/length ratio—352

        Ketch rig, sail area—6,957 square feet

        Fuel—21 tons

        Fresh water—31 tons

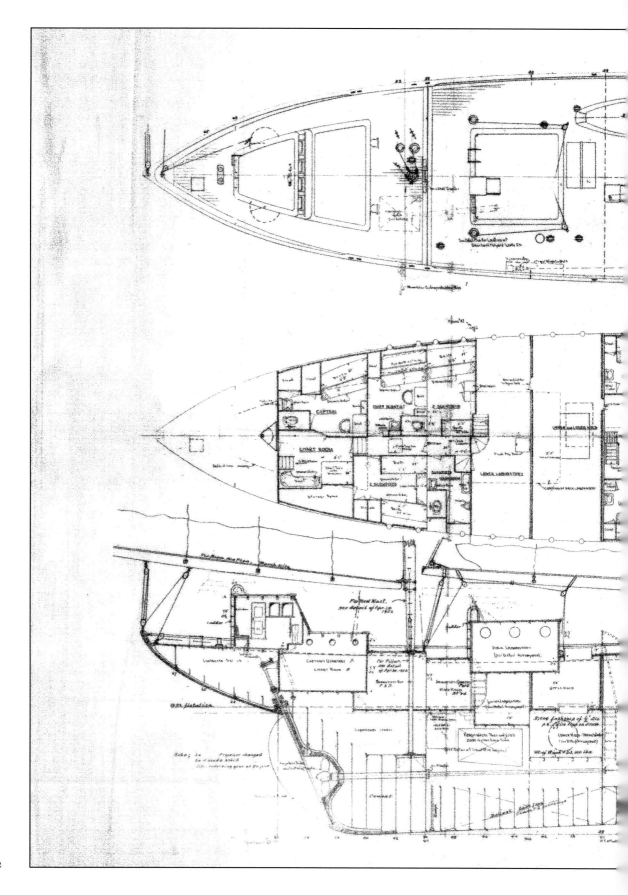

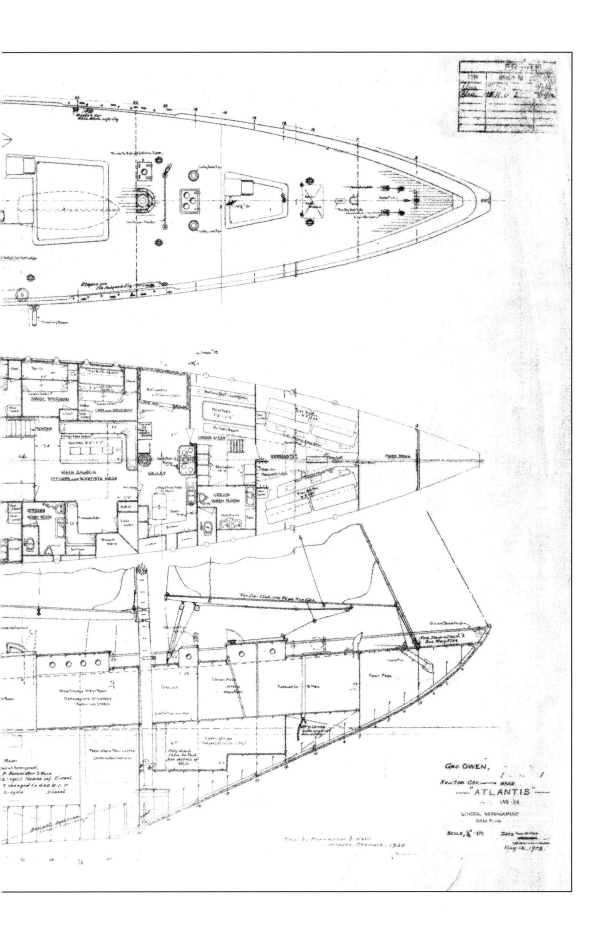

Geo. OWEN,
Newton Ctr. Mass
"ATLANTIS"
140-36
GENERAL ARRANGEMENT
DECK PLAN
SCALE, ⅛" = 1ft.

She was built by Burmeister-Wain Ltd, of Copenhagen, Denmark as hull # 596. Supposedly, the estimated price was $175,000.00, but the actual cost was $218,647.00, a normal overrun. This price in today's dollars (1996) would be about four million—not a cheap ship. Burmeister-Wain as ship and engine builders, was second to none, and the Oceanographic got its money's worth, as *Atlantis'* construction and fittings were the equal of any yacht. She stood up very well in service. It was originally planned to christen her *Penikese*, but Dr. Alexander Forbes, of Harvard Medical School and a trustee of WHOI, must have had a bit of romance in his soul. He transferred from his schooner yacht the name *Atlantis* to the new vessel.

The Hull

The hull was double-ended with an over-hanging or canoe stern, as it was called. This type of stern seemed to be very popular in the 1930s. The beam was not too great for the length and she was, by all counts, a splendid sea boat, if not driven too hard. *Atlantis* was built during the time when there was still some art and pride in steel ship building, and before the wide use of electric arc welding. The steel plates forming the hull, riveted to the angle iron frames, were laid off in fair lines on a wooden half-model (plating model), and faired in to be pleasing to the eye. The line of the plating, called "one on and one off", showed up as shadow lines on the hull. The builder took great pains and pride to make these plating lines fair. Today with electric welding, the hull plating is thrown in anywhere, pieced here and there as required, without any concern for plating lines (In my opinion, most of the ships built today are so ugly it doesn't really matter).

The rivets used to hold the plates to the frames were flush on the outside of the hull, with the rounded heads inside. The steel of the hull plating was top quality "crown steel, same as used in British cruisers", Chief Backus was proud to say. The plates were hand-hammered fair after being installed. Without question, *Atlantis* was built as well and with as much care as would be any yacht and equal to any work done on the famous J-boats.

Rig and Sails

Atlantis was ketch-rigged, in fact; at the time of her building, she was the largest ketch in the world. The sail area was divided into four sails: jib of 982 square feet, forestaysail (called jumbo) of 775 square feet,

The main mast, seen here at the Burmeister & Wain yard, was 154 feet long. It was of hollow octagon construction (eight pieces), rounded on the outside, built with knot-free riff grain Douglas fir and glued up with casein glue. Later, the mast was shortened by about 20-feet. Photo courtesy WHOI Archives © Woods Hole Oceanographic Institution.

mainsail of 3,280 square feet, and mizzen of 1,920 square feet. The mizzen was about 2/3 the size of the mainsail, but was easily less than half the work to handle, set, take in, tack or jibe around.

The ketch is, without doubt, one of the best rigs to heave-to, and can also set many different sail combinations. This is probably the reason *Atlantis* was designed as a ketch. Although reefing gear was installed on the main and mizzen, we never reefed sails at any time that I served in her. We set trysails instead, if, for any reason, the need to carry less sail arose.

The old sailors that I served with could not see any reason for such a large mainsail in a research ship that would be used summer and winter with a small crew. A watch consisted of an officer and two men, one of whom always had to be at the wheel. They thought *Atlantis* should have been a three-masted schooner instead of a ketch, with masts and sails the size of the mizzen. She certainly would have been much easier to handle with that rig.

Atlantis was always hove-to with mizzen sheeted in hard, helm turned to weather, and the forestaysail (jumbo) hauled tight to weather to offset the thrust of the rudder. In real bad weather, she would be hove-to under the mizzen trysail only, with the helm to weather. If it were blowing "as hard as ever it could blow", she would be hove-to under bare poles and helm to weather. Under these conditions, she would lay about 45° to just short of 90 degrees to wind and sea (4 to 7 points). She could ride out most anything like a duck. We always felt pretty safe whenever hove-to, as *Atlantis* seemed to rise to an oncoming sea, and rarely, if ever, took any water on board.

Spars and Rigging

All the spars were made of wood. The main mast, which rose about 138 feet above the deck (it was 154 feet long), and the mizzen (119 feet long), which was 109 feet above the deck, were of hollow octagon construction (eight pieces), rounded on the outside. They were built with riff grain Douglas fir, knot free (called in Europe 'Oregon pine'), and glued up with casein glue. Casein glue required perfect joints as the glue itself lacked strength, compared to the epoxy glues used today, where the seam could be a quarter inch wide without harm.

The main boom was about 57 feet long and quite heavy. The mizzen boom was 45 feet long and extended well over the stern. The standing rigging, shrouds and stays were wire rope called plow steel construction. We always kept this wire covered with a mixture of white lead and mutton tallow—called "slush"— to prevent corrosion. This seemed to work very well.

All standing rigging on the upper ends had eyes spliced around the masts. Originally the lower ends of the shrouds were spliced eyes too, but this was changed to zinc sockets when the original shrouds and stays were changed on the main-mast in the late 1930s, and on the mizzen in 1944.

A twenty dollar US gold piece (1 oz.) was to have been placed under the heel of the main-mast at the time the spars were first stepped. When the main mast was removed in the late 1930s, Director Iselin told the bo'sun, Ernest Siversen, to look for that gold piece and retrieve it. All Ernest found was a Danish krone worth about 20 cents. Someone, probably the boss rigger, had swapped the 20 dollar gold piece for the Danish krone. Ernest said that Iselin was furious.

Rigging and Hardware

All of *Atlantis'* rigging hardware and fittings were of galvanized steel or bronze, and first class in design and construction. *Atlantis* was rigged in all her hardware and gear as a typical large yacht of 1930s. The custom designed and made hardware was of high quality—as good in construction as any done by the Herreshoffs—and the blocks, if not Merriman Bros., were very similar in design and quality. Whenever he referred to the gear, the bo'sun would say, "Dis iss no yunk, dis iss first class stuff." I believe George Owen had a hand in the design of the hardware, as is shown in the original blue prints. His time spent in the Herreshoff's drafting room would have well-prepared him for this job. Added to this, Burmeister-Wain was capable of making anything.

Engine and Propeller

Atlantis' main propulsion engine was a Burmeister-Wain-built diesel engine rated at 250 HP at 350 revolutions per minute. This was a low speed, high torque engine. It had a steady but quiet rhythm that was very gentle on one's senses. A 250 HP diesel of today certainly could not equate the 250 HP of that diesel. The old Burmeister-Wain engine had the torque or real power to turn the large controllable-pitch propeller. At that time of her building, *Atlantis* had a Burmeister-Wain controllable-pitch propeller, in 1930 unheard of in the United States, but quite common in Scandinavia. The propeller had three blades and could be placed with the blades in a fore and aft position to give little resistance when sailing. The engine had a clutch for "in" and "out" of gear only. The pitch of the propeller controlled the ahead and astern and sailing positions. There was a large hand wheel just aft of the clutch casing, which was turned to set the pitch of the propeller. This controllable-pitch propeller was twenty years ahead of its time in the U.S. The propeller was lost in 1949 and [the original model was] never replaced.

When making a plankton tow, for instance, the engine could be run at normal speed and the pitch of the propeller could be reduced so that the

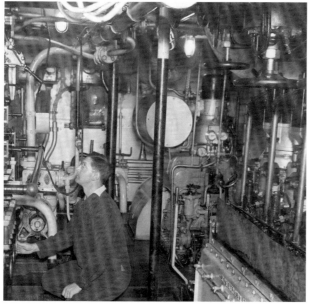

Above: *Chief Engineer Harold Backus in the engine room. As one of the original Atlantis officers, Backus (a British national) had been in Copenhagen while the ship was built and remained chief engineer for 22 years. His predilection was to paint green any surface in the engine room that was not hot or polished. Photo courtesy WHOI Archives © Woods Hole Oceanographic Institution.*

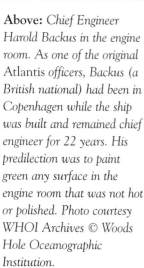

Above right: *The galley aboard* Atlantis. *Photo courtesy WHOI Archives © Woods Hole Oceanographic Institution.*

speed of *Atlantis* would only be 1 knot to 1 1/2 knots, ahead. This would not be possible with a normal propeller, as it is not practical to run a diesel at so slow a speed.

The ship's service generator was a single cylinder Burmeister-Wain diesel that ran comparatively quiet and at slow revolutions, again compared with the modern diesels. The single cylinder diesel generator was started by hand. The electrical ship's service in *Atlantis* was 110 volts DC. The engine room was not crowded at all in 1945. The engines were painted a dark green. This color contrasted with all the polished copper and brass fittings and made the engines seem, in my eyes, to be large pieces of jewelry.

The main engine and propeller pitch control were controlled by the engineer in the engine room. He would receive the order for ahead, astern, full, half or stop by engine room to wheelhouse telegraph or "enunciator". Speed under the Burmeister-Wain diesel was about 6.5 knots, sometimes a little more. Chief Backus once told me that, with mizzen and jibs set and drawing, and the main engine running at normal speed, fuel consumption was cut in half.

Deckhouse, Wheelhouse and Winches

Aft of the engine room was the main winch room. In here was the Lidgerwood main trawl winch with about 5 miles of 5/8-inch wire cable. It took the main engine generator to run the winch, which was used for deep-sea trawling and anchoring. The hydrographic winch was located on the poop deck, starboard side, abreast of the mizzen mast. This winch, with its bronze gypsy head, was also made by Lidgerwood. It was powered by a large electric motor, with 110 volts DC, and had full torque at all speeds. It also had direct reverse, and the various speeds were attained with a throttle control similar to that of a trolley car. Fifty years ago, this was a superb winch.

The anchor windlass was an old hand operated affair—"Norwegian steam" the sailors called it—and was bought by C.O. Iselin from an old ship in Sweden, so the story went. We hated to operate this machine, as it was one stroke and only one link of chain would come in. It could take more than an hour to raise the anchor. Chief Mate Nordquist said, "Dot ting vas old ven I vas a kid 50 years ago." It must have been about 100 years old when installed [an electric motor was added in the early 1950s].

The halyard winch for the jibs was also electric, and was located low down at the base of the mainmast (it was moved up on deck in late 1947). The halyards led through tubes to this winch, and strange as it may seem, we never had any trouble with this arrangement. The main and mizzen halyards were handled by the gypsy head on the hydrographic winch. We also used this winch to trim the main and mizzen sheets. As I said previously, this particular winch was a superb machine that was not surpassed until the introduction of the hydraulic winches.

Atlantis' wheelhouse, in design and construction, was a beautiful piece of work. It was also very practical for the type of vessel and service that she did. The wheel, engine controls, and entrance to the chart room were all protected from the elements and the sea. It also was a real godsend to the helmsmen in the wintertime. I, for one, cannot imagine how the men at the wheel survived at an open wheel in the old days in the brutal winter conditions sometimes found at sea. The watch officer would invariably stand his watch in the lee of the wheelhouse. Chief Engineer Backus told us that the wheelhouse had a steel frame which was riveted to the deck beams aft. This gave it a great deal of strength. The steel frame was then covered with wood—teak. It was of panel construction and well-proportioned. It never seemed to suffer any damage, although *Atlantis* was not the type of vessel to ship a dangerous sea.

The main deck was wood, riff grain Douglas fir. It was laid in square nar-row pieces, about 2 inches square in section. These were bolted thru the steel deck beams, well secured. The seams were caulked with cotton and then oakum, and payed with regular tar pitch. In the hot tropic sun, this pitch could boil out.

The decks never leaked, to my knowledge, except when they were allowed to dry out. The old bo'sun told me decks have to be wet most every day, if possible, with salt water, and then you would never have rot and the deck would never leak. When I was young, the old-timers in Maine wet the decks with salt water every morning, even if the decks were painted.

The deck houses, such as the upper deck lab, engine room fiddley, saloon house, and the house over the crew's mess, were all steel and, except for the engine room fiddley, had beautiful teak trim. All the companionways were of teak, beautiful in design and construction. All the port lights, hard-ware, and fittings were of bronze.

The Taffrail or Patent log

Speed was measured by the distance run in an hour, which was recorded by the patent log. The patent log or recording device was a round cylinder about 5 inches in diameter and perhaps 4 inches long. The face had two or three dials that read off in knots and tenths of knots. Attached to the log itself, with a piece of sennet- and coxcombing- served rope, tarred to make it stiff, was a large iron wheel, about 8 or 9 inches in diameter, called the "governor", to which was attached the log line itself.

The log line was a tightly braided rope, similar to a sash cord, but larg-er in diameter, about 50 fathoms (300 feet) in length, to which was attached the rotor. An old saying went "that ship passed close enough astern to cut our log line". The rotor was a metal device tapered to a sharp point forward, where the log line attached, going back to form four metal fins with a spiral shape which measured about 4 inches in diameter. The patent log itself was mounted into slotted bronze castings on both port and starboard bulwark rails just aft of the wheelhouse door.

As the vessel moved through the water, the rotor was twisted or turned.

This turning was transferred back to the log line and through the governor, which acted as a flywheel, to the recording patent log. The short name for this whole piece of equipment—log, governor, log line and rotor—was the "taffrail log". The registered distance was recorded every hour in the ship's log.

If *Atlantis* was moving at a slow speed or if she was bucking a head sea, the governor would spin quite slowly. The greater the speed, however, the faster the governor would spin so that at 10 or 11 knots it would be fairly humming. If the leeward wheelhouse door was open, the man at the wheel could easily see and hear the log. The mental game would be to try and guess the exact speed that *Atlantis* was making by listening to the spinning governor. The rotor was hauled aboard at least at the change of every watch, and

Eldridge and the Spherical Compass

Atlantis' wheelhouse configuration. Forward of the wheel is the Kelvin-White spherical compass. The small bell rope between the wheelhouse windows activated a bell outside the wheelhouse, with which the man standing wheel watch would signal the time. Some captains required the bow watch to repeat that time signal from a bell located forward. The telegraph used to signal the engine room stands to the right of the wheel. Photo courtesy WHOI Archives © Woods Hole Oceanographic Institution.

The marriage of Wilfrid O. White and Ruth Eldridge at the turn of the 20th century united two families of celebrated nautical prowess. *The Eldridge Tide and Pilot Book,* with its familiar yellow cover, has been known simply as "Eldridge" to generations of yachtsmen and mariners. Providing information on tides, currents and on other practical nautical and celestial matters from Florida to Maine (including Bermuda) it is the pilot's bible.

The following is taken from the history given by Robert Eldridge White, Jr., and his wife, Linda Foster White, 4th generation publishers, in their 140th annual edition: "In 1854 George Eldridge of Chatham, a celebrated cartographer, published Eldridge's *Pilot for Vineyard Sound and Monomoy Shoals.* The book had 32 pages, a grey paper cover and no recorded price. Its pages were devoted to 'Dangers,' embellished with his personal observations, and to Compass Courses and Distances, etc. This volume was the precursor of the *Tide and Pilot Book,* which followed 21 years later."

"In 1870 George Eldridge published another small book, called the

Compass Test' and asked his son, George W. Eldridge, to go to Vineyard Haven [Martha's Vineyard] and sell it for him, along with the charts he produced." ". . . Vineyard Haven was at that time an important harbor for large vessels. The number of ships passing through Vineyard and Nantucket Sounds was second only to those plying the English Channel. As the ships came into the harbor (frequently as many as 100 schooners would anchor to await a fair current), George W. would go out to them in his catboat to sell his father's charts and the 'Compass Test.' He was constantly asked by mariners what time the current turned to run East or West in the Sound. He then began making observations, and one day, while in the ship chandlery of Charles Holmes [the original name for Vineyard Haven was "Holmes Hole"], made the first draft of a current table. Shortly after, with the help of his father, he worked out the tables for places other than Vineyard Sound, and in 1875 the first *Tide Book* was published. It did not take long for mariners to realize the value of this information, and it soon became an indispensable book to all who sailed the Atlantic Coast from New York east."

In 1910 Captain George W. Eldridge transferred the management of the book to the next generation of his family, and upon his death in 1914 his son-in-law Wilfrid O. White, became publisher. Wilfrid O. White, born in Melbourne, Australia, came to the United States in 1898. White travelled to Glasgow in 1904 to study with Lord Kelvin, of compass fame, in order to become certified as a compass adjuster. Born William Thomson (1824-1907) in Belfast, Ireland, Lord Kelvin (referring to the nearby Scottish river Kelvin) held a position of Professor of Natural Philosophy at the University of Glasgow. His theoretical and applied accomplishments in mathematics, physics, geology and engineering were legendary and remain at the foundation of modern science and engineering. Between 1870 and his death in 1907 Lord Kelvin worked on the mariner's compass, and his inventions, which he marketed, were seminal to the world navies.

After Kelvin's death, White was chosen to be Kelvin's exclusive agent in the United States by Kelvin's successors and partners, Kelvin, Bottomley & Baird. Kelvin & Wilfrid O. White and Company commenced operations in 1918, but under a business arrangement that put White at a distinct disadvantage. Dissatisfied, and spurred by his own aspirations, White invented the improved "Mariner's Spherical Compass" in 1931, to which he was granted a U.S. patent in 1935. This compass featured a liquid-filled sphere, on gimbals, with a transparent glass top, in which a printed compass card pivoted in all directions to remain horizontal. A separate, sealed chamber, partially filled with a viscous liquid, was attached to the bottom of the compass sphere, providing further stability to the gimbal-action, and further damping out the pitch and roll of the ship.

By minimized internal wall friction, the spherical compass chamber serves to enhance the inertia of the contained fluid, promoting the effective damping by this compass. The spherical shape also provides optical magnification of the compass card and lubber line directly opposite the helmsman, exactly where it is most useful. This compass design and its successors, now almost universally used at sea and in aviation where magnetic compasses are employed, was marketed under the Kelvin-Wilfrid O. White brand, and was sometimes referred to as the Kelvin-White Spherical Compass.

Cooper's *Atlantis* memoirs record: "While at the wheel when swinging ship in July of 1945 in Vineyard Sound, for a compass correction, I heard Mr. White of Kelvin-White, tell Capt. Knight that our spherical compass was the first one that they had ever sold."

Arthur Gaines

Sources:

Eldridge Tide and Pilot Book, 2014. 140th Edition. Robert Eldridge White, Jr. and Linda Foster White, Publishers, Medford, Mass. 272 pp.

Land and Sea Collections, 2014. Kelvin-Wilfrid O. White Binnacle– Provenance. 4125 SW Martin Hwy 10, Palm City, FL 34990

U.S. Patent Office, 1935. Patent 1,987,383. W.O. White Mariner's Spherical Compass, Filed Jan. 6, 1931 2 Sheets, Washington, D.C.

The deck crew awaits orders to let go the anchor (Bill Cooper is partially hidden behind the front man). Photo courtesy WHOI Archives © Woods Hole Oceanographic Institution.

checked for any weed or other debris that might have attached itself to the rotor, thus impeding its rotation and speed.

In areas of much weed, such as the Gulf Stream or the Sargasso, the rotor might have to be cleared every hour, at the change of the wheel watch. If, at any time, we tacked ship, so that the leeward side became the weather side, we had to transfer the log to the new leeward side. Under the bo'-sun we never took any chances at losing the log line and rotor. When changing the log from one side to the other, we hauled the log line in and rotor aboard and then, when attached to the governor, we payed out again on the leeward side. The log would give different readings when fitted to the weather side or the leeward side. There was some theory about how fast water passed the hull, on the different sides.

Captain Knight, being an old-time sailor, paid a great deal of attention to the taffrail log. Before the war or the invention of the Pitot log, the only device to measure distance run and speed was the patent log, or taffrail log. Steamers measured speed by revolutions of the propeller, but this was not always accurate, as the speed of the vessel over the bottom could be different with the same revolutions, when the ship was either bucking the sea or running with it.

It seems to me that I spent a great deal of time, until the installation of the Pitot Meter Log in late 1947, overhauling and clearing the rotor of the taffrail log from weed.

Fresh Water

*A*tlantis carried about 9,000 gallons of fresh or potable water in six separate tanks. In my time on her, we were never at sea much longer than a month, therefore I never experienced any water rationing. Then again, we in the fo'c'sle did not waste fresh water.

The fresh water tanks were steel with a cement lining. When away from Woods Hole, Chief Backus was very fussy where we took on water. He seemed to know the quality of fresh water in every port we entered. The fresh water system was pressurized, which delivered water to all the heads and galley. In 1945, we did not have hot water served to any of the heads.

One of my jobs as an ordinary seaman was to sound the fresh water tanks every day and note the condition of each tank on a blackboard located near the passageway by the sail locker. I reported to Chief Engineer Backus for this job. To sound, I used a length of cod line with a small weight and a piece of blue carpenter's chalk. The line was knotted in four sections: 1/4, 1/2, 3/4, full. I would rub the cod line with the chalk and sound the tank. The fresh water would remove the chalk and thereby show the amount of water in the tank. The sounding and filling pipe plates for the forward tanks were located on the deck in the main saloon. The after tank sounding and filling plates were on the main deck aft, near the poop. These tanks could not be sounded if there were any slop of salt water on the deck.

This was one job that I had as an ordinary seaman, along with filling the fresh water tanks in Woods Hole, that I never saw given to any other ordinary seaman at a later date. I did not mind the daily sounding of the tanks, as it kept me busy, and I had interaction with Chief Backus with whom I got

The bathythermograph winch (BT winch) was the smallest one and the only winch deploying on the port side of the ship. Containing several hundred feet of 1/8 inch wire, it was used to deploy small instruments, such as the bathythermograph, Secchi disks for measuring the clarity of water, and small plankton nets. Since BTs were often deployed every hour or half-hour, he whose bunk lay under this winch (i.e., the Chief Scientist) was awakened frequently by its rattle overhead. Photo courtesy WHOI Archives © Woods Hole Oceanographic Institution.

A crew member operates the hydro winch, used for instrument deployments such as water samplers, deep sea cameras, and small plankton nets. A full spool for this winch contained over 5 miles of wire. With time, sections of the wire had to be cut off, usually from damage at the seafloor. Periodically the spool had to be replaced. Photo by Jan Hahn © Woods Hole Oceanographic Institution.

along very well. He treated me more as an apprentice, as would be in a British ship, than as an ordinary seaman.

Keeping Clean

Atlantis' pressurized water system gave us cool fresh water on the tap in the sinks in the crew's head, but in 1945 there was no shower or tub in the crew's head, or any of the heads for that matter. The crew's head contained two sinks for washing and a large set tub. We used the set tub for scrubbing our clothes. We never knew how they washed themselves or their clothes abaft the mast. The potable water in the tanks was tepid enough to wash with in the tropics, but in the cold winter in the North Atlantic, it was another story. Hot water was obtained from a large kettle kept on the back of the galley stove. One could draw out a quart or two, with the permission of the cook, and then replace it with cold water. Two quarts of hot water was usually enough to do any personal washing in the sink in the head. We always tried to wash some piece of clothing—socks, underwear—in the used water. The clothes were always rinsed in cold water. To take a bath, one would place the hot water from the galley in a 12 quart galvanized bucket. Each member of the crew, fo'c'sle, and messboys, had his own bucket. These buckets were stored stacked and lashed (in heavy weather) on the aft and inboard bulkheads of the crew's head. No one touched anyone else's bucket. With the bucket of hot water, one would stand in the middle of the head and wash with a cloth dipped in the bucket of water. The old sailors called this "a whore's bath in a bucket". When the bath was finished, we washed clothes with whatever hot water was left over. To wash our clothes, we used old-fashioned yellow soap (Fels Naptha). When washing dungarees or khaki pants, they would be placed on the deck in the head and scrubbed with a stiff bristle brush. It was not very difficult to wash our clothes, but we did have to work at it.

In 1945, the deck in the head, which sloped aft, was tiled with small black and white squares. It was watertight with a scupper on the after outboard end. This scupper readily drained all the water out of the head into a sump tank located below, aft of the engine room. Actually, we could wash the head out with a fire hose if it was necessary. With a squarehead crew in the fo'c'sle, this was never necessary, as the head was kept spotlessly clean by the ordinary seamen. AB Willie Gustavesen would check the condition

"Sailor's clothesline" for hanging out laundry without clothespins, one of many skills of seamanship Bill learned from Ernest Siversen. Photo courtesy WHOI Archives © Woods Hole Oceanographic Institution.

of the head each time after I cleaned it. We took pride that the crew's head was the cleanest, by far, on the ship. In the tropic weather of the SOFAR Cruise, we wore very few clothes, so keeping them clean was easy. We normally got a change of sheets and towels about every two weeks from the linen locker. However, the squarehead sailors would not hesitate to wash their sheets, or other linen, if they thought it necessary. They were much fussier about these things than the average American seaman.

Sailor's Clothes Line

Every man forward, including the mess boys, had their own clothes line. This was a very special piece of gear. The bo'sun taught me how to make it up and I, in turn, taught it to the mess boys and the two Yankee ABs—Fay and Remsen. I never saw this simple rig in any book on seamanship or rope work. When we see an old photograph of wash day on the old ships and particularly the "Limey" men-o-war, this was the clothesline they used.

It was made by taking a piece of 9 thread (5/16") manila, probably sisal in 1945, about four fathoms (24 feet long) and un-laying one strand the whole length, removing the strand completely. Now you had a two-stranded piece of rope. To attach the clothes, you would let the clothesline hang slack while each item is inserted into the strands of the rope, just as if using ties or clothespins. When all clothes are in place, haul tight on the line and make fast. I honestly believe the clothes themselves would blow to tatters before they could let go from the two-stranded line—a simple, economical, foolproof and effective old-fashioned idea. We secured our clotheslines any place we could—between shrouds, boat davits, to rungs on the mast to the sea gantline. In any kind of a breeze, the clothes would soon be dry.

Soojee-Moojee

The most distasteful order to be given a sailor was to "mix up a bucket of soojee". The word "soojee" apparently comes from the Japanese "soji", meaning "to clean". "Soojee-moojee", as the old sailors called it, was a bucket of hot (if available) water with a good charge of sal-soda [sodium carbonate] thrown in. Sal-soda was a strong alkaline detergent much in use fifty or more years ago. A strong mix of sal-soda in water seemed potent enough to remove the skin from one's hands. This mix was used for washing paint work. It was a nasty job given mostly to ordinary seamen and ABs of lesser standing. In 1945, I never saw the squarehead seamen "soojeeing".

The rivet heads in *Atlantis*, which were plentiful on all exposed steel work, were a pain to wash around. Worse still was down below where the exposed steel plates were covered with ground cork. The ground cork was worked into a compound and troweled over the steel plate and then painted. The purpose here was to retard condensation in cold weather. This stuff was almost impossible to wash with a soojee rag and do a decent job.

As mentioned earlier, most of the paint washing was done by seamen. The mess boys only washed the galley and their own cabin. If any soojee work was needed in the engine room area, the engineers did that. It seemed to me that "soojee" work on deck was given as a sort of punishment. If the weather was too wet, the mate would give the order to "mix up a bucket of soojee", and wash the bulwarks or house sides wearing seaboots and oilskins, if necessary. This would be mainly to keep the sailors busy as "idle hands will do the work of the devil" (per Chief Mate Mandly).

Wetting the Deck

As ordinary seaman, one of my jobs was to help the bo'sun with the deck hose, first thing in the morning, as we wetted the deck. We would order "water on the hose" from the engine room and wash and wet the decks down. This was a case of just wetting the decks, not necessarily washing under pressure with salt water. *Atlantis* had a 3-inch diameter rubber fire hose that was kept coiled on deck, on the port side of the engine room fiddley. This hose was always hooked up, but a "request" had to be made to the engine room for water before the pump would be turned on and salt water discharged. This hose fulfilled two purposes, fire hose and deck hose. In the event of a fire, there was a bronze nozzle always kept on the end of the hose. Under full force, the water pressure on the deck hose was about 50 lbs. per square inch.

We removed the bronze nozzle from the end of the hose while washing down the decks and replaced it again afterward. The bo'sun was very fussy about keeping the decks with enough moisture on them. This is what kept them from leaking. He did not let them dry out. The bo'sun told me that wooden decks need to be "vet down once a day in summer veather" and morning and night if in the tropics. "If you don't do dis, they dries out and in the first bad veather you get leaks." I never forgot this advice. After 1946, I never saw it practiced in *Atlantis* in my remaining time aboard her, and at times the deck did dry out and leak.

After the deck hose was coiled and put away, I went directly to the main saloon, where the second mate was usually seated having breakfast at the saloon table. He passed me the keys to the chronometer case and I went to the chart room and wound the two chronometers the required number of times. I did this job because the second mate was teaching me celestial navigation after lunch each day, and he believed one of the things I needed to learn was the practice of winding the chronometers.

After I returned the keys to the second mate, I went back to the chartroom and wheelhouse and polished the brass. Then I would sound all the water tanks for the chief engineer and record the soundings on a blackboard mounted near the door to the sail locker. I then checked the whaleboats, if they were in the water, and the catboat launch, and bailed them out if they had taken any water. After all these chores were completed, I reported to the chief mate or the bo'sun.

Bow view of Atlantis *out of the water in a floating dry dock. The frame on the bow was used to deploy the anchor in oceanic water depths using the deep-sea trawl wire. Photo courtesy WHOI Archives © Woods Hole Oceanographic Institution.*

Repairs and Fitting Out

New London

O N J U L Y 8 t h , 1945, following our return from the Bahamas, after a brief stay in Woods Hole we sailed again with a minimum crew for New London to go into shipyard at Electric Boat, then building submarines for the war effort. A sailing vessel, *Atlantis* looked completely out of place and time lying next to the outfitting dock, surrounded by all the submarines in the water and those under construction on the ways. We were hauled on a large marine railway and the hull painted navy gray and the bottom in black antifouling (before this red antifouling copper), exactly the same colors used on the submarines.

The mate, Mr. Christopher, who had been second mate on the Tongue of the Ocean Cruise, was only 23 years old and held an unlimited masters license. He decided to return to the big ships. Before he left, he introduced us to the new second mate, a large, strong-looking man, clean shaven with a crew cut, about 26 years old, who seemed to have a pleasant disposition. His name was Dan Clark [more about Dan Clark later].

After being launched, *Atlantis* returned to the outfitting dock, where damage to the starboard quarter and bulwark and the teak cap rail was repaired. The damage had occurred when the fleet tug *USS Carib* came alongside while we were at anchor in the Tongue of the Ocean to give us fresh water. To do the necessary work to the hull plating, the deck in the wheelhouse was removed. The men who worked on *Atlantis* at Electric Boat were real craftsmen, and in short order all the steel work was straightened out, repaired, and hammered into shape as good as new, teak cap rail and all. Electric Boat Company had plenty of teak, as the submarine decks were teak.

After the new fir decking was laid in the wheelhouse, Captain Knight decided that, since it looked so good, from now on we would scrub it to keep it bright rather than paint it as before. With still a minimum crew, we were using mess boys as seamen to help us with mooring lines. While we were in shipyard here we learned of the first atomic bomb dropped on Japan, August 6th, 1945.

New Crew in Woods Hole

Although Germany had surrendered on May 8th, 1945 and Japan was about to do so, there was still a great deal of war-time shipping, and seamen were in short supply. Captain Knight went to the sailor's boarding-house in Boston and picked up Willie and Ernest Gustavesen, two squarehead ABs who had sailing experience on square riggers and large yachts before the war. Norwegian Nels, who had been on the "Tongue of the Ocean" Cruise with us, had been sent to Canada to come back and make a legal entry into the U.S. in order for him to obtain an American Seamen's passport. Another fellow, who had been sailing as AB on Liberty Ships for the past three and one-half years, was visiting his sister in Falmouth. He came down and signed on. He was Don Fay and was 35 years old at the time. His brother-in-law was working at the Oceanographic.

A short time later, a man in the uniform of a Lieutenant Commander in the Maritime Service came down the dock while we were working, and we were introduced to George Jennings from Belfast, Maine, our new first mate. Charlie Remsen, also of Belfast, soon joined us a new AB. Remsen and Mr. Jennings were friends, both from the same town, and had sailed together on yachts before the war, although at the time we did not know this. Neither Fay nor Remsen had any experience on a sailing vessel the size of *Atlantis* and, looking back now, I don't know why they weren't carried as "ordinaries" for at least one voyage. This would be especially true of Fay, who was really a "steamboat man" and did not know how to sail at the time.

Holy Stones Over the Side

The main and poop decks on *Atlantis* were wood. This wood was riff grain, or vertical grain, Douglas fir of very straight grain, clear stock. It was the practice in the years before the war to keep these decks well scrubbed with a block of pumice attached to a handle, using a liberal amount of water. These tools were known to the sailors as "holy stones".

There were smaller pieces of pumice, about the size of a small brick, used for hand scrubbing in tight areas, called "bibles".

"Holystoning the deck" was usually reserved for rainy days, when no other deck work was possible. The old sailors hated this work. AB Willie G. had spent time holystoning decks in *Atlantis* on the voyage he made in the 1930s, when serving under "that mate Kelly". A few days after Willie and Ernest Gustavesen came on board, they had reason to go to the paint locker in the stern. This locker was in a separate watertight compartment, with its own trunk hatch and watertight cover that could be dogged down at sea. Willie took me with him and sent me down "in that glory hole, because you know what's there." While I was below in the paint locker, I had to move some paints and equipment to get at what was needed. One of the things I moved was the "holystones" with handles. Willie spotted them immediately.

"Does that f—g mate from Maine know these are here?"

"Not that I know of", said I.

Then, looking at his brother, Ernest, he warned him to keep a sharp lookout for the mates. Willie then told me to pass up the "holystones" one at a time. As I did so, I heard the splash of each one going over the side: four "holystones", four splashes. Willie then asked "Are there any bibles?" At first I did not know what he meant. He explained that they would be the size of a brick. I found them and they followed the others over the side.

He said the last time he was on *Atlantis*, he did all the holystoning under the mate Kelly that he ever intended to do. He was not going to take any chances that the mate from Maine would discover the "holystones", and have us at it.

Captain Richard Harding, holder of an unlimited Master's license in steam and in sail, served in *Atlantis* in 1941 as a young boy. When I told him this story, he said: "You did not get them all. There were also smaller "holystones" than the "bibles" that were for use under cleats, and other tight places. These were the "prayer books".

When the "holystones" went over the side, this signaled the end of an era that was not apparent to us at the time. Things changed from pre-war standards to post-war standards after 1945.

For a while we did not have a cook or steward aboard, so we had our meals at the Woods Hole Oceanographic mess which was located in a building next to the present Woods Hole Post Office. One of the woman cooks was Mrs. Soderland, a Swede. The squarehead crew got on very well with her, and, as a result, we were all well fed.

With the large influx of merchant ABs, two things happened that changed the system of *Atlantis*. First the wages that WHOI was paying seamen were still much lower than the going scale. To get these men, with shipping being plentiful, the Institution had to raise the rate, which in 1945 was $175.00 per month, plus room and board. Ernest and I, as well as the engineers, were regular crew and were kept on the old wage system. We received $3.00 per day subsistence money when the mess was closed or if we were in port without food being served aboard.

The second change was to start official WHOI coffee break times of 10 AM and 3 PM. At the afternoon coffee break, the sailors and the bo'sun went out the gate and across the street to the Rendezvous, near the Woods Hole drawbridge, and had their beer. Chief Mate Jennings would send me over to get them if they did not return after a half hour. Whenever I would go in and inform them that they were being summoned by the chief mate, they would order a "Coca Cola for the boy", push me way into the rear, and keep me there. The Rendezvous was not very large so this action was easy to perform. Why Chief Mate Jennings did not send Second Mate Clark over to roust the gang out of the bar, I never knew. The second mate could have brought them back in a hurry.

The Second Mate—"Nulli Secondus" ("Second to None")

AB Willie, the bo'sun and I were in the process of cleaning the muck and debris from the bilge pump rose box (or "strum box", the strainer for bilge pumps) under the heel of the mizzen mast. Rather it was I down in the bilge, with the older men looking on waiting for me to pass the bucket. I heard the second mate's voice talking to Willie, but I could not hear what was being said. After the second mate left, Willie said to the bo'-sun, "Yesus, Ernest, dis ship is yust like a f—g limejuicer; we got a cook who wants to starve us and now the second mate says 'Vil you please come on deck'."

The term "limejuicer" that Willie used refers to the old British sailing ships, famous to the old sailors for the God-awful food and the polite officers – "starvation and ease". Ernest had also sailed on American ships where the food was good, but the officers were buckos with a "belaying pin in each sea boot".

Up the Main Mast

Coming on deck, we found that a discussion had ensued between the captain and his two officers in regard to the height of the main mast. There was doubt about the amount of clearance under the Cape Cod Canal bridges, and it was decided to end all speculation and actually measure the height of the main mast. Somewhere they had found a tape with which to do it. We were to rig the bo'sun's chair on the main gantline (a single part line rigged to a block made fast at the truck or highest part of the mast), and, since junior men were always sent aloft, I was the one to be put in the chair. While going aloft, since the height was so great, the bo'sun gave me a brass whistle to "blow one to heave away, blow one to stop, and blow two to lower". Simple and foolproof. It was the responsibility of the man using the bo'sun's chair to make the gantline fast. Ernest, the bo'sun, and Mr. Mandly, acting chief mate at the time, showed me how it was done the previous year, then untied the knot, a double sheet bend, and let me secure the bo'sun's chair myself (the man using the chair always secured it himself). After all these years, whenever I tie a double sheet bend, I can still hear Mr. Mandly saying, "Don't be so cheap with the length of the end, your life depends on it." No shackle was used.

The main gantline, which rove through a block almost at the truck of the mast, was taken through a snatch block by the main rigging, aft to the electric winch. Willie G. handled the gantline on the winch and, with measuring tape in hand, I was hoisted aloft. I had been aloft quite a few times in the past, so the experience was not new to me and, at that time, I had no fear of height. When I reached the point where the gantline knot in the sling of the chair was almost two-blocked with the main gantline block, I blew one long blast on the whistle as a signal to stop. I could see immediately that I could not reach the truck of the mast with the measuring tape without standing up in the chair! It would have been a little tricky for me to climb out of the chair and still hold on to the tape. Looking back 50 years, I can't imagine sending an 18-year-old boy to do that kind of job. On the other hand, at that time, the government was drafting 18-year-olds to fight and die as infantry, and taking 17-year-olds to serve in the Navy.

The second mate, Mr. Clark, was standing near the bow and must have seen my problem. He started to climb up on the rungs of the mast, and it seemed that in no time he was standing on the upper spreader, about 100 feet up in the air. Now I could talk to him. I told him I was not able to reach

Dan Clark was second mate aboard Atlantis *for only one cruise, but he quickly commanded respect as a gentleman and admiration as a skilled seaman. Dan remained in Woods Hole most of his life as a dock builder and marine engineer. A mentor to many young men in town, he was a legend in his own time. Courtesy Clark family collection.*

the truck of the mast without standing up. He said to wait a bit and he would come up and help me. While I was wondering what he could possibly do, since the mast rungs did not go any higher, he reached out for the rope part of the main halyard and the single part of the starboard lazy jack. Hand over hand on these two lines alone, he hauled himself up the last forty feet to almost the very top of the aft side of the mast. He then placed one foot on each side of the main halyard cheek block shells, which were wide enough for him to stand on, and leaned over the main truck from aft to forward, looking down on me! Dumbfounded at that demonstration of agility, I passed him the end of the tape which he placed at the truck. We learned later the measurement was 138 feet from the deck, and 147 feet from the waterline. [The minimum clearance of the three Canal bridges, railroad bridge up, is about 135 feet.]

"Stay there a minute", he then said, and immediately swung about the mast to the forward side and lowered himself down by whatever ropes he could grasp to the level of my bo'sun chair. He then placed one foot on the chair on either side of me and held on to the gantline. I blew two long blasts on the whistle to lower and down we went to the deck. I doubt the second mate spoke more than a dozen words the whole time.

While disconnecting the bo'sun's chair from the gantline, I asked the bo'sun, "Ernest, did you see the second mate climb from the second spreader to the main truck?" "Ya," answered the bo'sun, and then added, "I knew he vas a yentleman, but now it looks like he's a sailor too."

Many years were to pass before I realized the real depth of that compliment given by that old "shellback" to the much younger Dan Clark. Squarehead sailors rarely if ever complimented anyone. They expected that everything would be done well at all times. That was what you are getting paid for, was it not? "You call yourself a seaman, don't you?"

With the crew in the fo'c'sle all in place, we had a bo'sun, five able bodied seamen, and one ordinary seaman (that was me). This was the only voyage I ever made on *Atlantis* with five ABs in the fo'c'sle. The usual ratio was half and half, or usually more ordinary seamen than ABs. One year later in September of 1946, I would be, at 19 years of age, the only AB and all the rest ordinaries.

Photo courtesy WHOI Archives © Woods Hole Oceanographic Institution.

The SOFAR Cruises

WE LEFT Woods Hole, bound for the Underwater Sound Laboratory in New London, late in the afternoon on August 14th, 1945, with the intention of having a fair tide through the Race, the entrance to Long Island Sound. As we proceeded down Vineyard Sound, in a pleasant SW wind on a real summer day, Captain Knight told the bo'sun that he wanted to set all sail once clear of Gay Head. Looking back, I am sure the "old man" believed that his squarehead ABs and the bo'sun could handle *Atlantis* under sail, but the two mates and the two ABs were not familiar with the ship or her gear. She might have been rigged as a yacht, but her gear was heavy and it required some training and experience to handle it. Setting all sail in these conditions (a 15 knot SW wind—easy sailing conditions for *Atlantis*) was probably just what the green officers and crew needed.

The ship was operated in what was called "deep water style" and not in the style of a fishing schooner. This required an exact procedure in issuing orders, acknowledgement of these orders, and the various customs such as "heave way on the jib halyard gig", "vast heaving", "make fast up behind", and "all fast". It was a seaman's vocabulary that all seamen understood. We always addressed the officers as "Mr." and we always said "Sir". We did not associate or fraternize with the officers in any way. Most of the time, we only spoke when spoken to.

One problem that the new men had (excluding the squareheads) was understanding the bo'sun when he was excited. Then his orders were almost untranslatable. The squarehead ABs, being seamen in the classic sense of the word, seemed to know intuitively what the order was. One day Captain Knight said to me, after watching the bo'sun give me a hard time, "I put you in Ernest's watch because you are the only one who can understand him and can translate the order when he gets excited" (I had been with Ernest for a year and was able to understand him most of the time). Ernest, the bo'sun, always demanded orders to be obeyed with "a jump" as the saying went, and not questioned in the slightest. The squarehead sailors did this and they were always a pleasure to be with on deck, handling sail or any type of gear. They seemed to know what to do at all times and did it smartly. The Yankee sailor wants to question everything—to see if it is the way he would do it.

It was a pleasant sail beating down Block Island Sound into the August night and we tacked ship a few times, even in the dark. This was easy to do because at that time, the watches had not been set and there were enough bodies to do the work of handling the multitude of lines. Later, when the watches were set, the bo'sun's watch, which included Don Fay and myself, took care of the forestaysail (jumbo) and jib. The term "jumbo" was of fishermen origin, but seemed to stick as it was easier for the bo'sun and the other squareheads to say "Yumbo" than "forestaysail".

Tacking Ship

Captain Knight must have felt confident with the crew to handle *Atlantis* as we carried on under full sail well into the night. About midnight, we were off the Race, the entrance into Long Island Sound. The order came for "all hands stand by to come about." Don Fay and I went to our stations near the jumbo and jib. When tacking a vessel the size and type of *Atlantis*, a procedure had to be followed, especially in any kind of a sea. The jib and jumbo must be kept aback to help the vessel's head come around. It was also necessary to keep the jib and jumbo from unnecessary slatting or shaking which could damage the sails, particularly the stitching.

In the process of tacking at night with the generator running, it was difficult to hear the order of "hard alee". We were very attentive however, and could see and feel the vessel swinging through the eye of the wind. I vaguely remember seeing the Race Light and thinking at the time, "This is fun—we are going to sail through the Race."

The jumbo boom had a large line about 1 1/2 inches in diameter, attached to the inboard end which the bo'sun called the "bowline". This line normally kept the boom, which was 18-feet long, from jumping up and down or working in a seaway. It was also used to hold the "jumbo" to weather when hove-to or when tacking ship (as in this case). Other than that, the jumbo boom sheet was on a traveler and was self-tacking. After the order to "stand by to come about" was given, there were a number of things to get ready. First the preventer or running backstays on the leeward side had to be readied and cleared, the runner hook released from holding position near the lower shrouds and hauled aft and hooked in place. The runner was attached to a jig or jig affair. Then the main boom topping lifts (there were two on each side of the main boom) had to be sweated up so that the boom sheets could clear the boom crotch on the upper lab and the life raft that was stored there. Boom tackles had to be slacked away ready for easy running. The main boom "bowline" had to be let go. The funnel had to be lowered. The jumbo boom topping lift had to be taken up so that the jumbo boom could clear the "Charlie Noble" (the smoke pipe for the galley stove).

We did all this in the dark at midnight without any deck lights to help us. There must have been some moon, however, as I don't remember it being all that dark. Don Fay and I were on the leeward side near the main rigging at this time. We had sweated up the jumbo boom topping lift, took a strain on the leeward lazy jacks and helped the ABs who were handling the mainsail gear attach the leeward backstay runner hook (it would become the weather backstay as soon as we changed tacks) and then straightened out some of the lines, as the vessel began to change tacks. Don Fay told me later he had no idea what we were doing at that time.

The bo'sun was standing by watching everything. As the bow passed through the eye of the wind, the jib and jumbo came aback. It was exciting—we were tacking right near the Race. I was coiling one of the lines, probably the jumbo boom topping lift, when the bo'sun gave the order: "Let go yib sheets, let go the bowline." Fay let the jib sheet go; my job was the jumbo boom line. I was just about to get the coil of rope on the belaying pin, when the order to "Let go the bowline" was given. "Just a minute", I said as I was finishing my coil. I was looking out of the corner of my eye. I thought I had time. The bo'sun came over very quickly and belted me with his fist and knocked me down on the deck. Without a word, I cast off the jumbo boom bowline.

Now that *Atlantis* was tacked over, we had enough to keep us busy, trimming jib sheets and coiling lines. I forgot all about the blow I had received. I'd heard enough about sailing ships to know that this could happen. Don Fay was appalled by the bo'sun's action. The next day, Willie Gustavesen, after Don Fay had told him what happened, laughing, said to me "Now you know to 'yump' when an order is given." I never spoke back to the bo'sun again.

We lowered all sail off the mouth of New London harbor and proceeded under power to the Underwater Sound Lab pier, where we arrived in the wee hours of the morning to load sonic recording equipment for the upcoming cruise. The pier where *Atlantis* lay at the underwater Sound Lab, right next door to Fort Trumbull, seemed deserted. The war was winding down. I remember a large steam yacht laying next to us and the Navy crew stripping the wartime gray paint off the bright work prior to returning the yacht to her owner.

We loaded wire, which I assumed was for the hydrophone, and also received on board two Navy radio operators. The Navy radio operators were really nice fellows and we got along with them very well. They berthed aft and messed with the officers and scientists in the main saloon, and they never ventured into the crew's quarters. Also on board at this time were three scientists or technicians, Stanley Bergstrom, Alfred Woodcock, and Joe Worzell.

Felix Comes Aboard

The Underwater Sound Lab and Fort Trumbull were on the New London side of the Thames River, so in the evening practically all hands went ashore to visit the city. I went with the mess boys, Bob Metell and Bill Shannon, they being my own age, and therefore we could not visit bars with the rest of the crew.

When the mess boys and I returned to *Atlantis*, the guard at the gate asked us if we wanted a kitten. The little black kitten had been hanging around the gate house and he wanted someone to take it. There was coal dust on the ground and the kitten looked as though the dust was ground into his coat. We took it back to the vessel, fed it some canned milk and placed it on a folded towel in a corner in the mess boys' small cabin. After finishing his milk, the kitten went to sleep and slept through the night, well into the next morning. We did not tell anyone we had the black kitten on board.

While we were preparing to get underway for sea the following morning, with all hands on deck, the kitten suddenly appeared in the fo'c'sle companionway. How he ever climbed the ladder, I never knew. When the bo'sun saw him he said, "You cannot keep him", and proceeded to place the kitten

Felix was one of several in a line of cats to serve as mascot aboard Atlantis. *Given that only one cat was aboard at a time, their repeating behavior patterns suggest a surprising intelligence and adaptability of cats to shipboard life. Photo by Don Fay © Woods Hole Oceanographic Institution.*

on the pier. One of the mess boys placed a small dish of milk on the pier, which kept the kitten occupied for a few minutes.

The tide was low, and, as I remember, the top of the pier was a few feet below the bulwark cap rail of *Atlantis*. We were laying port side-to, with the bow toward shore. About the time when all lines were let go and hauled aboard, I heard the engine room telegraph ring the order for "slow astern". I ran over to the side of the ship, outboard between the bulwark rail and the bow of the whaleboats—no one saw me—for a last look at the kitten.

Atlantis started to move slowly away from the pier. For some reason I leaned down and scooped up the kitten. Most of the crew and the bo'sun were working near the open sail locker hatch, stowing away the mooring lines. One of the mess boys, Bob Metell, was standing nearby. I quickly passed the kitten to him, and he in turn took the critter below, apparently without anyone seeing us.

Atlantis moved slowly out of New London harbor under power while everything was being secured for sea. The crew was completely sober, as were the officers, so there were enough hands to make the work easy. When we reached the mouth of the harbor we had a breather when we could look around or "sightsee", as the bo'sun would say, before we would do the last task, unship and secure the port anchor for sea. About this time the kitten again came up the ladder of the fo'c'sle companionway and sat down right alongside the bo'sun, who was standing and looking aft. When the bo'sun saw him, I thought "Oh God, what now?" I was sure he would pick up the kitten and throw him over the side. I was ready to dive in after him. It went through my mind, "They would have to pick me up."

The worst expected did not happen.

"Vell," said the bo'sun, looking at the kitten, "I thought I put dot cat ashore, but he must have come back on board." Looking directly at me he said, "You can keep him, but he has to sleep vid the mess boys." The mess boys were the lowest in rank on board, but had their own little cabin aft of the galley on the port side.

In a few days time, the kitten took to the sea like an old salt. He cleaned himself up, got in a lot of sleep, and after he had gotten the "wrinkles out of his belly", he decided to look around and explore this new home. On the kitten's first visit to the fo'c'sle, it was decided by the senior AB, Willie Gustavesen, that he had to have a name. Charlie Remsen wanted to call him "Blackie". I suggested "Felix". After a moment's reflection, Willie announced in a voice packed with authority, "His name is Felix." That settled it, although Charlie continued to call him "Blackie".

The little kitten proved to be a very intelligent and beautiful angora cat. We never had to housebreak him. He used the waterways near the scuppers, at the break of the poop deck. Fifty years later, former Second Mate Dan Clark was still amazed that the kitten learned this on his own. He told me, "I can still see him now, sitting over the scupper and jumping out of the way when the ship rolled down until the water forced air up the scupper; he would move back into position as soon as the ship started rolling back the other way." Felix's cleanliness endeared him to the squarehead crew also.

For now, Felix seemed content to sleep with the mess boys. He soon found the officer's companionway ladder closer to the scuppers (his latrine), and no longer climbed the fo'c'sle ladder. Eight months later, in April 1946, when we were underway from Guantanamo Bay, Cuba, I was at the wheel at 6 AM. I heard the captain tell the mess boy who brought him morning coffee, "Don't make up my berth too early. Felix is sleeping in it and I don't want him disturbed." In eight months time, Felix went through all the berths in the fo'c'sle, slept with the first and second mates and finally ended up with the captain. He never slept with the scientists, the cooks, or the engineers.

Bermuda

Once we cleared New London Harbor, we set mizzen and jibs and proceeded down the Long Island Sound, through the Race. When off Montauk Point, in the freshening SW breeze, we set the mainsail. All hands were on deck at this time, as I remember being able to watch the whole procedure. Captain Knight was forward observing the mainsail slatting and snapping in the breeze as it was slowly hoisted. He told me to go over and look aloft over the mainsail. The sight astounded me. The mainmast was twisting, bending and shaking like a piece of spaghetti. This was the first time I had ever been able to look aloft when the main was being set.

Carrying all sail, we set course for Bermuda, on that lovely summer day. The watches were set and the ship's routine begun. A day or two after we departed New London, we learned of V-J day, August 14th, 1945. At sea, just an ordinary day for us.

The weather for the leg to Bermuda continued warm and sunny. Nothing like the usual heavy overcast that is normally found in crossing the Gulf Stream. Through some fault in navigation, we missed the island and as a result, had to spend a day or so steaming back. Captain Knight was furious that we had missed Bermuda. He blamed the chief mate, who was doing the navigating. "The only sight he could take was 'Polaris'" and he could not see 'Polaris'." The old men did not seem much concerned about this; they considered the two young officers as "yust kids". They had as much time at sea as the officers had been alive.

Breaking Out the Flags

When we arrived off St. George, Bermuda, we hove-to to await the pilot. At this time we hoisted the code flag "G", ("George" in those days, which meant, "I require a pilot") to the lower spreader. We were about to begin hoisting the British Merchant flag (the "Red Duster") to the second spreader (about 100 feet above the deck), when the bo'sun decided to give me a lesson in how to hoist a signal flag "made up" and when peaked, "break it out". At that time, with war rules in effect, we also hoisted the *Atlantis'* international call letters, the code flags WCFB.

To do this, one carefully folded the flag and then rolled it up into a tight cylinder. The made-up cylinder was then wrapped tightly with the flag halyard. The bight of the standing or lower part of the halyard was placed under the turns, after it was ascertained that the whole thing was right side up. This made-up flag (cloth cylinder) was then hoisted aloft and when "two blocked", the hauling part of the halyard was made fast. A sharp pull on the lower or standing part of the halyard would break it out into an instant bloom.

Continuing with this lesson: after the pilot boat hove in view, we lowered "G" and made up flag "H" (pilot on board), and hoisted it in place on the lower spreader, ready to break out when the pilot came up the ladder and stepped on deck. The bo'sun, at this time, seemed quite relaxed, and speaking slowly and quietly, explained the breaking out of the flags to me. He said, on a large yacht, lying in a harbor where the yacht club fired the morning gun, the flags were always broken out. When the morning gun (8 AM) was fired, the national ensign was slowly hoisted to the peak. When the ensign was peaked, all other flags—owner's, yacht club, jack—were broken out. The national ensign was never broken out, but was always hoisted flying, as a point of honor.

St. George

In Bermuda of 1945, there were no automobiles allowed. The only motorized vehicles I remember were some jeeps and trucks belonging to the British Army and Navy. St. George's Harbor was full of large wooden seagoing tugs, laying to the mooring buoys. None of these tugs seemed to be manned. The rumor was that they were completed too late for the "D-Day" invasion. The bo'sun insisted the tugs were West Coast built— "too much vood for East Coast."

Almost as soon as *Atlantis* was secured to the wharf, AB Willie G., speaking for the crew, went to see the cook, whom they called "Portagee Yoe". Cooks were hard to come by in 1945, and I believe this fellow came from a New Bedford fishing boat. The squareheads did not like his cooking, nor the cleanliness of the galley, therefore Willie G. told him to pack his bag and go ashore, and if he refused, they would throw him ashore and his gear after him. Willie and Ernest G. were two tough "hombres" and the cook had no choice. He appealed to Captain Knight, but found the captain sympathetic to the squareheads. "Portagee Yoe" left us in St. George. We acquired a Bermudian in place of "Yoe" but nothing improved.

After he paid off the cook, Captain Knight came to the fo'c'sle with a bottle of whiskey to give all hands a drink. No other captain I ever served under had the relationship with the crew that Captain Knight had with the squareheads in the SOFAR Cruise. He seemed very fond of them and enjoyed their company. They were all seamen of the "old school". I remember that they would tease the captain at times, saying that he was not really an AB on squareriggers, but "yust super cargo" (along for the ride). Captain Knight was not vain as a seaman, and he took it all in good spirit.

That evening all hands went ashore to the White Horse Tavern, except for me and the two mess boys, as we were too young. That did not bother us. We went swimming over the side and practiced jumping off the bow wearing old-fashioned cork life preservers, which we had to hold down when we hit the water. Afterward we went ashore to get some Bermuda ice cream. I remember it was rather bland compared with what we were used to. We did not mind this; after all it was "yust like Limeyland".

One afternoon, the mess boys and I rented bicycles from a shop across from the wharf where *Atlantis* was lying. The owner of the shop remembered *Atlantis* favorably from before the war, and did not require any deposit from us. The bicycles were Raleigh three-speeds. This was the first time we had ever seen anything like them. We rode the bikes all over St. George town and since there were no cars it was lots of fun. We were moving pretty fast down one of the hills, when we were stopped by a constable for speeding. We were exceeding the speed limit in a 15 mph zone. He said he would "let us off this time, but see that it does not happen again." Remembering what Chief Nordquist had told us two months before, about "Limeyland and yail", we were very careful after that. We rode at the slow pace of the Bermudans and even walked the bikes up hill the way they did, instead of riding as we normally would. The Bermudans told us "only Yanks ride bicycles up hill."

The Bicycle Chase

I was discussing the slow pace of 1945 Bermuda with former Second Mate Dan Clark, about 50 years later. He told me a story I had forgotten over the years. It seems that the two young officers ("yust kids" as the older squareheads called them), decided to visit Hamilton for the evening night life, there being none in St. George. They rented two bicycles in St. George, so they would be able to get back from Hamilton later that night. There was a train (one or two cars) that ran between St. George and Hamilton. The old-timers called it the "Tooterville Trolley". If one were going to Hamilton, one could load his bike on the outside platform and ride the train.

The train ride was a scenic run through the back areas of Bermuda, and, as I remember, went past many interesting small farms. Second Mate Clark and Chief Mate Jennings had a wonderful evening in the night clubs of Hamilton. At this time in 1945, there were no tourists to speak of, the war being over for only a short time. At one night club there was sort of a victory celebration in progress and Dan Clark told me they were displaying all the Allied flags. These consisted of British, American, French and the flag of the Soviet Union. The Americans who knew anything about the Soviets at that time had no great love for them, especially if they had served on convoy duty to Murmansk. Mr. Clark and Mr. Jennings decided they did not like the Soviet flag hanging there, so they stole it from the bar. The chase began.

They ran out of the night club with the Red flag, jumped on their bicycles, which they had left outside, and rode away. The people in the night club were all yelling and were heard by a constable with a bicycle nearby. Dan Clark, remembering back 50 years, laughed as he recounted that scene in 1945. He and George Jennings were husky and strong, and were peddling furiously, riding away, being chased by the Bermudan constable on a bicycle, blowing his whistle and, in time, joined by other constables. He said, "I have to laugh every time I think of it. Here we were escaping on bicycles and the 'fuzz' chasing us on bicycles."

They were madly riding through the empty streets of Hamilton, trying to get their bearings for St. George (there were no street lights once clear of the main drag) , and being chased by a posse of police on bicycles. It was a good thing that the younger, stronger and, above all, Yankee legs outpaced the slower-moving Bermudans, or *Atlantis* would have sailed minus two officers. Neither Mr. Clark nor Mr. Jennings had heard Chief Mate Nordquist's warning "Dis place iss yust like Limeyland, boys. If you goes to yail here, you stay there no matter who you are."

Queen Anne Scotch

I don't remember when ABs Willie, Ernest Gustavesen, Don Fay and Norwegian Nels got the idea to secure a case of bonded liquor while we were in Bermuda. This could not be done without the captain's permission; only the captain could order from the bonded warehouse, and only he could receive the bonded, tax free liquor on board, one-half hour or so before sailing time.

Willie G. went aft to see Captain Knight, with whom he got on very well, both being square-rigger men, and I believe they were probably shipmates sometime in the past. Captain Knight gave permission for one case of bonded liquor for the gang in the fo'c'sle, and agreed to make an advance on the sailors' wages to pay for it. Sailors always try to get an advance on their wages when in port. We came home from one three month voyage (to Cuba) when one of the men had no pay coming, but actually owed the ship money!

Now the decision was to be made as just what kind of liquor they would buy. Ernest, the bo'sun, only said that he did not want them to buy any "cheap rot gut". I was only 18 and knew nothing about the subject. The discussions, however, on the different types and brand names, were one part of my "intellectual" education in the fo'c'sle. The older, senior men made the decision, although they accepted input from the younger ABs. Scotch was the liquor of choice, supposedly as it did not cause hangovers and Queen Anne Scotch was the brand settled on. The next day before the case of Scotch arrived on board, Willie informed me that the crew were in complete agreement with the captain's request that I was chosen to store the 12 bottles of Queen Anne in my foot locker and issue them to the crew when requested.

After we sailed from St. George, I went aft to take possession of the case of Scotch. At that time the captain told me I was to issue one fifth every two days, and maybe one extra on special occasions. I packed the 12 bottles in my foot locker or chest, padding them from each other with my spare clothing. Our foot lockers were basically settees by each double set of pipe berths, each locker about one and one-half feet wide and two feet long. The tops hinged up for access and there was no way to lock them. Actually, anyone could have opened the top at anytime. Of course, no one ever did. The system of honor and respect for other's gear in the fo'c'sle was in force and observed by all, even, when in one instance, I refused to issue an extra bottle when it was requested, the code was not violated.

When I think about this today, 50 years later, I find it amazing no one ever touched the liquor without my permission. Four of these men were old enough to be my father and the bo'sun old enough to be my grandfather. The remaining ABs, Don Fay and Charlie Remsen, were my seniors by 17 years and eight years, respectively. The squareheads and the other ABs handled their liquor very well, with a fifth every two days. I gave them the bottle at 7 bells in the afternoon watch (3:30 PM) just before the change of the second mate's watch to the first mate's watch. This time was also the start of the daily cribbage game.

Discipline Aboard Ship

Discipline was maintained usually by the physical force of the officers. At no time in my years on *Atlantis* was there ever an instance when one or both officers would not have been able to overcome any breach of discipline by the threat or use of physical force. A case in point: when we were about to sail from St. George, Norwegian Nels, who was in the second mate's watch, had had quite a lot to drink and was acting up. He was on the dock letting go most of the lines when he suddenly decided he was going to stay ashore. Second Mate Dan Clark got a line around him quickly and then asked Captain Knight, as the ship was about to move away from the wharf, "Do you want him to come?" "Yes", replied the captain. The second mate took a firm hold of the line and let Nels know "You come on board or I'll pull you off the dock and drag you out in the harbor." Nels got the message and, booze or no booze, he meekly jumped on board. Nothing more was said. Nels could not swim and really had great respect for the second mate.

Clearing Bermuda

WE LEFT St. George, Bermuda, without any other incident and with all hands on board—no one left in jail. As soon as we dropped off the pilot we were able to set all sail and proceed on course SSE. It was beautiful summer weather, as it can be in that part of the world. We were really in the middle of the hurricane season, but we, in the fo'c'sle, did not give any thought to that. Hurricanes were not forecast then as they are now. It was only through wireless reports of storms from other ships that one would know of an approaching storm.

We fell immediately into our sea routine, watch following watch. I was in the 8-12 watch: 8 AM to 12 noon, and 8 PM to midnight. The 8-12 was really the captain's watch, but was stood for him by the bo'sun. For me this meant that I was under the bo'sun's critical eye for eight hours each day. What was worse, I was the only ordinary seaman on board, the only one for him to harass.

After a day or so the wind died down completely. We had a destination, so we proceeded under power, through a flat calm sea of the most beautiful blue that seemed to grow thicker with weed with each mile travelled. Soon there seemed to be acres of weed as far as the eye could see—to the horizon all around. Occasionally a flying fish would break the surface, fly along, and drop back in to the ocean again, hopefully escaping its pursuer. These scenes gave reality to the description of this cruise, as termed by the old seamen "flying fish weather". It seemed that we had to clear the taffrail log of weed after every wheel watch.

One night, I believe, during the second mate's watch, a flying fish came crashing aboard near the break of the poop deck. Felix, the ship kitten, happened to be near by and was pretty excited by it. He was too small to tack-

For seamen, flying fish are emblematic of tropical seas and fair weather. To the shipboard cat's delight, they sometimes landed aboard ship. Photo by David Levin © Woods Hole Oceanographic Institution.

le the lively fish, but with the help of the second mate, who subdued it, and AB Willie G., who cut it into small pieces for him, he enjoyed his first feast of flying fish. After this incident, he took station aft many nights in hope of another late meal landing on the deck.

The Wheelhouse Deck

When the new deck was installed in the wheelhouse, Captain Knight decided he wanted it kept bright or scrubbed. To comply with this order, the bo'sun gave me the job, to be done every day, if possible. On this cruise my watch mate, Don Fay, usually took the first watch at the wheel. This allowed me to wash the deck with the bo'sun and scrub the wheelhouse deck after that. With a bucket of salt water from over the side, I would wet the deck and scrub it with a bristle brush. No one ever asked why I did not use a holystone. Of course we had none since Willie G. had thrown them all over the side in Woods Hole. After scrubbing I swabbed the deck as dry as I could.

All the time the scrubbing was taking place, Fay would be performing a balancing act, standing to one side with as little of his feet on the deck as possible and steering the ship at the same time. All this was done under the watchful eye of the bo'sun.

Trim Ship

Don Fay had a lot of gear—shoes, shirts, pants, sweaters—that were GI issue which he had acquired from a Liberty Ship he had served in. The ship had been bombed and some of the cargo damaged and condemned. Don Fay told me the crew picked through whatever the army did not take, and found many pieces of clothing and shoes in good condition. He gave me a number of pieces of this clothing and a pair of GI shoes with the smooth leather on the inside, and the rough or suede outside. I loved those shoes, with the smooth leather inside, I could wear them with my bare feet and get them on and off very easily.

The decks were getting very hot now and the pitch (tar) in the seams began to boil in the midday sun. This precluded walking in bare feet. I wore the GI shoes on watch and when at the wheel, I would take them off and place them outside the wheelhouse door. I did everything I could to keep the wheelhouse deck clean.

The bo'sun did not take kindly to the sight of my two "gun boats" (as he called them) outside the wheelhouse door. He ordered me to place one shoe on either side of the wheelhouse (one port and the other starboard) to "trim ship" he explained in a rather serious tone. Thereafter, whenever I had the wheel watch, I placed one shoe either side of the wheelhouse, before I relieved the wheel. One time Captain Knight, sitting on the settee, watched as I placed one shoe on each side of the wheelhouse before relieving the wheel. After everyone else was out of the wheelhouse, he asked me "Why the hell did you do that?" "Ernest ordered me to stow them that way, to trim ship", I answered. The captain said nothing, but smiled and shook his head.

Diesel Oil Shoes

Chief Engineer Backus would usually pay a visit to the wheelhouse about mid-watch in the mornings and again in the evenings. He wore an old pair of shoes with leather soles and heels that looked to me as if they had been soaked in a bucket of diesel oil for six months. The leather soles and heels resisted the rot of diesel oil, which easily destroyed rubber. They looked far worse than they were. I was upset every time I saw those shoes make contact with the scrubbed wheelhouse decks. This would be at the time when the deck had just dried and looked its best. It was a wonder the shoes never soiled the deck.

Regardless of how I felt, I could say nothing. Chief Engineer Backus was a senior officer, and I was only an ordinary seaman. I reasoned if I said anything sassy to the chief about his shoes, the bo'sun might get after me so I kept my mouth shut. Besides, I liked Chief Backus; he was a real professional and I loved to hear the stories he would tell the captain and the bo'sun during his daily visits to the wheelhouse.

One morning just after 6 bells (11 AM), Chief Engineer Backus, as was his custom, came to the wheelhouse. It was my watch at the wheel. This gave me the opportunity to listen to the conversation between Chief Backus and Captain Knight. This was one time I did not want the wheel watch to pass too quickly.

The question of the proper tack (port or starboard) to heave-to on, in case we encountered a hurricane, came up. Captain Knight said that from what he had read in "Bowditch", we should heave-to on the starboard tack, if the necessity arose. Chief Backus said, that during the hurricanes he experienced in *Atlantis* at sea, they had hove-to on the port tack. The reason for this was, that in the full strength of wind and under "bare poles", *Atlantis* would lay down with her deck half under water. If hove-to on the starboard tack, this condition could swamp the whaleboats, which were nested on the port side.

Laying with the deck this far under water, required that everything be buttoned up tight. This meant the ventilators and the companionways had to be covered and lashed up tight to keep the water out. Access to the interior of the vessel would be through the companionway inside the wheelhouse or the trunk hatch by the mainmast. With everything thus "buttoned up", Chief Backus believed "she would ride out any hurricane safely."

Captain Knight wondered if, under severe conditions, whether the wheelhouse would stay on. Chief Backus had watched the teak wheelhouse being built, and told the skipper the house had a steel frame. There was no question in his mind that the wheelhouse could withstand most anything. Captain Knight's reply was, "Yes, chief, but anything can happen at sea."

A Snake Would Break his Back

Standing wheel watches at night seemed hard for me at that young age. We stood two one-hour watches on the wheel between 8 PM and midnight, alternating between one hour wheel, one hour lookout, one hour wheel, and one hour lookout.

Atlantis, when under power in a fairly calm sea, steered very easily. "One-half spoke of the wheel", the bo'sun would say, meaning one needed to move the top spoke (king spoke) only the distance between one spoke either side of center. In the nighttime hours, the bo'sun would take the reading of the taffrail log immediately the wheelhouse clock started striking hour bells (2 bells, 4 bells, 6 bells, 8 bells meant 9, 10, 11 and 12 o'clock, respectively). In that way, he could get an accurate reading of the distance travelled in one hour. He would have an idea of how far off course we had wandered, or if the helmsman was steering a straight course. He would also tell us, Don Fay and me, which one of us steered the straightest or best, according to the distance run. We steered using points, not degrees, and the compass was a Kelvin-White spherical model, about 8 inches in diameter. It was lit by a small light—the only light in the wheelhouse at night. While at the wheel when swinging ship in July of 1945 in Vineyard Sound, for a compass correction, I heard Mr. White, of Kelvin-White, tell Captain Knight that our spherical compass was the first one that they had ever sold.

The wheelhouse was located right over the propeller, which caused a slight vibration in the steering compass. I found this very mesmerizing at times and sometimes lost positive control of *Atlantis* and might wander off course 1/2 a point or so. The anxious effort to get the ship back on course always seemed to result in over-correction, and although these actions would be small, the bo'sun never failed to notice them. He kept a sharp lookout and always seemed to have a star sighted to the forward part of the main rigging as a point of reference. If he noticed any deviation in course, he then studied the wake. If there were any bioluminescence, he could see the wake of the propeller clearly. Just about the time I would have her quieted down and back on course, he would come in the wheelhouse and comment on my performance, "A snake would break his back to follow you."

Hurricane Yoe

When we left Bermuda, Captain Knight knew, of course, that we were heading into "hurricane country" at the height of the season. I don't know how much he discussed with his two officers about this matter, but I heard him talk about hurricanes and heavy weather with Chief Backus. I had also noticed, while polishing brass in the chart room, a copy of *Bowditch* opened to the part titled "Cyclones in the Northern Hemisphere".

Just after breakfast on or about the third day out of Bermuda, we were informed by the bo'sun that all hands would turn out to remove, examine and repack storm sails in the sail locker (there was no such thing as overtime in *Atlantis* in 1945). The sea was still flat calm, beautiful "flying fish weather". The main hatch on deck over the sail locker was opened and the made up sails were hauled on deck. This was a job for all hands. Looking back 50 years, I think this was a proper procedure for the Captain to have ordered done. Maybe it was because of the story he told Chief Backus about the *Parma*, nearly lost in a hurricane, that made him decide that preparation should be made now while there was a chance. Anyway we began to prepare to meet a hurricane.

Atlantis' sails were all very heavy #00 duck and made up deep-water style, which meant they were not folded in any way. Instead they were made up loosely, in sort of a long roll, tied at regular intervals with rope yarns, with the head, tack and clew cringles readily exposed. The sail locker was full of sail—jibs, jumbo and a number of trysails for both main and mizzen. Neither of our officers had any idea what was in there. The sails were passed up one at a time through the open hatch and laid out on deck running forward on the starboard side. The squareheads who had done this kind of work many times in the past called it "sail drill". We hauled out one flax canvas main trysail with hand-sewn seams and the most beautiful leather and grommet work for the various cringles. The bo'sun said he believed this trysail came from the J-boat *Yankee*. There were also a couple of mizzen trysails.

It was hard, heavy work, in the hot sun, shifting the sails out of the locker, cutting all the rope yarn lashings, pulling everything apart and examining it. Then the process was reversed and all had to be tied up again and the sail, with all hands hauling, dragged forward out of the way, for now. Because of this constant "sail drill" the squarehead crew began to rebel. They spoke of Captain Knight as "Hurricane Yoe", with AB Willie G. saying, "You would tink, vid all dis sail drill, dis vas a f—g Yay boat." But, as the old rule of a sailing ship was "Grumble you may, but go you must", the work continued on.

We knocked off for dinner (noon) and took up the work afterwards. At the time, I was not privy to know what they were examining or why, but did have the feeling they wanted to know what was there and what condition it was in. As the afternoon wore on, we began to re-stow the sails in the locker, keeping the ones that might be needed on the top. I was in the sail locker during the stow which was being directed by Chief Mate Jennings. After the last sails had been passed down and the hatch covers replaced, Mr. Jennings asked me if this was a "Queen Anne Day". I said no, that yesterday had been. He told me to issue an extra bottle at eight bells (4 PM) which accordingly I did. I enjoyed telling AB Willie G., as he came off watch, that the order for the extra bottle was given by the "f—g mate from Maine".

The next day we got out all the covers that were available: the whaleboat covers, all ventilator covers and the companionway covers. All these were hand sewn canvas, made up before the war, and were painted a brown color. I assume this was the style then. Captain Knight, in his discussion with the bo'sun, was much concerned with the ventilator covers. They only covered the mouth of the vents and would not be strong enough to keep a sea out if necessary. We did have wooden plugs for the vent pipes after the cowls were removed, but no canvas covers to go over these (the canvas covers for these plugs would not be made until September 1946, a full year later).

I realized much later the depth of the captain's concern that it was necessary to secure and make as watertight as possible every deck opening. A prudent seaman would have this all completed long before it became necessary. Captain Knight was, if anything, a prudent seaman. The schooner *Vema* had almost foundered in a hurricane in the North Atlantic in 1933, because she took in a great deal of water through deck openings. The *Vema* was 202-feet OA, a three-masted schooner (in later years it was acquired by Dr. Maurice Ewing for Columbia's Lamont Geophysical Laboratory).

These openings were below the water when she was hove down because of the force of the wind. Her captain, James Barker, had been master of many British Cape Horners and had a great many years (50) of experience at sea. It apparently did not occur to him or the officers that when *Vema's* deck went under, as wind in spars and rigging laid her over to 35° to 40°, there were a lot of vent pipes that were open to the sea. The bilge pumps could not handle the amount of water pouring in. The vents were under water and could not be reached. The crew had to tear open much fine joiner work down below to get at the leaking pipes and vents and try to plug them. Captain Barker told *Vema's* owner after the storm that he believed, if the hurricane had lasted another hour or two, the ship would have foundered.

After about four days steaming (running under power), we reached the position where *Atlantis* was to anchor for her Woodcock station. The ocean was still flat calm and the water was a beautiful cobalt blue, which the mess boys and I never got tired of looking at. On the way out from Bermuda, I do not remember making any hydrographic stations, although they made BT casts every half hour or so. Also, one of the technicians would place a weighted white disc on the BT wire and lower it down until it could not be seen any longer. I think we could still see the white disc at over 100 feet deep in the water, demonstrating plainly how clear the water was.

Anchoring in Mid-Ocean

The anchor was a Danforth type, weighing about 200 pounds, with a short length of chain, an iron ball of about 500 pounds attached, followed by another 100 feet of chain. The 5/8-inch wire cable from the main trawl winch was attached to the end of the chain. This was basically the same rig we had used a few months before when we anchored in about 1200 feet of water in the Tongue of the Ocean in the Bahamas. The difficulty of getting this anchor rig over the side lay in the fact that the lead block attached to the bow gallows, although very large in diameter, was made for the 5/8-inch trawl wire only. Getting all this gear ready took three or four hours.

The Danforth anchor with its accompanying iron ball and chain had to be lowered first. To do this, Second Mate Dan Clark led the bitter end of the chain to the forward starboard mooring bitts. The anchor chain and ball were hoisted over the bow with anchor davit, with a rope strap made fast around the chain and, when all was clear, the strap was cut. The fall into the sea of the anchor, ball and length of chain were snubbed up by the second mate on the aforementioned bitts.

Valentine Worthington, a physical oceanographer, launches the BT. This instrument, which recorded the temperature profile of the upper ocean, was often deployed throughout a cruise and over the years hundreds of thousands of BT records were collected. Photo by Don Fay © Woods Hole Oceanographic Institution.

I was standing by in the fo'c'sle companionway, well out of the way, when I observed the second mate snub the fall of the anchor, ball and chain. The bitts seemed to me to raise about two inches into the air when the shock of the falling anchor gear reached them. A messenger line was rigged from the bollard on the main winch to the chain still on deck and thereby lowered until the strain was taken by the 5/8-inch trawl wire. Then the rope messenger was cut free.

The trawl wire from the trawling winch below, aft of the engine room, was payed out. The depth of the ocean at this spot was 3,060 fathoms (or

Bathythermograph (BT)

The bathythermograph (or "BT") is an instrument used to quickly and easily record a temperature profile in the upper ocean to a depth of several hundred feet. Over the years, several designs have been produced although typically, in Bill's time, the BT was a streamlined pipe about three feet long that could be deployed from a moving ship. Major advances in oceanography often follow development of a new instrument that allows scientists to "see" some feature of the ocean better. The BT was such an instrument and its development led to major advances in understanding the oceans. Many of those responsible for its development were to become leaders in the field of oceanography.

The predecessor of the BT was called the "meteograph". It was used to record temperature and pressure in the atmosphere. The first meteographs were deployed from kites and achieved elevations of up to about two miles. The instrument could be retrieved using a steam-powered winch, which spooled in the wire tether holding the kite and instruments. In 1899 French atmospheric scientists substituted balloons to carry the instruments and were able to take measurements up to about 8 miles.

Carl-Gustaf Rossby was a Swedish-born meteorologist/oceanographer who, in 1921 while working at the Lindenberg Observatory in Germany, used meteographs to make upper air measurements by kite and balloon. From this early work he helped develop the concept of the Polar Front, a polar atmospheric feature whose dynamics continue to be seminal to weather prediction in the mid-latitudes. Rossby continued in a distinguished career to push the frontiers of meteorology and oceanography.

In 1928 Rossby came to the Massachusetts Institute of Technology and, in 1931, was also appointed a Research Associate at the new Oceanographic Institution. Working at Woods Hole in 1934, Carl Rossby, Raymond Montgomery, and K.O. Lange designed and tested an "oceanograph", based on the meteograph, to obtain a continuous record of water temperature beneath the surface of the ocean, now deploying the instrument downward from a ship, rather than upward. Pressure was measured using an aneroid bellows and temperature using a bimetallic stylus. The two sensors were linked in such fashion as to scratch a line recording temperature versus pressure on a smoked brass foil. The oceanograph was said to be of limited utility.

A bathythermograph ("BT") is prepared on deck for deployment. A smoked slide is inserted into the rectangular slot to record the action of the stylus which responds to temperature and depth. The BT winch (left) spools out wire to let the BT descend and then rewinds it to retrieve the instrument and its data. A short boom holds the wire away from the ship's hull. Photo by Jan Hahn © Woods Hole Oceanographic Institution.

At Rossby's request, his student at Woods Hole, Athelstan Spilhaus (himself at the beginning of a distinguished career) redesigned the instrument and named it the "bathythermograph", or "BT". By 1939 Spilhaus had an instrument that, as it was lowered from a ship, would scratch a record of temperature versus pressure on a smoked glass slide, forming a waterproof record. A later model substituted a bourdon tube for the aneroid bellows to sense pressure. When calibrated, the resulting signature represented temperature versus depth.

Later Maurice Ewing and Allyn Vine (both to become icons in oceanography), also working at WHOI, improved the instrument's sensitivity, robustness, and streamlining so that it could be deployed and recovered on a wire from a moving ship. When the importance of temperature stratification to submarine warfare became clear, a modified design of the BT was developed that could be attached to the outside of a submarine producing a record that could be read inside the hull. By knowing the temperature stratification it was often possible to position a submarine within an acoustic

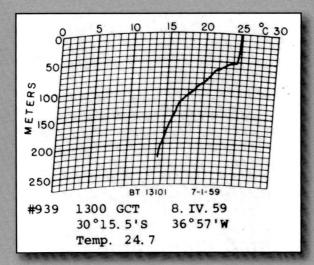

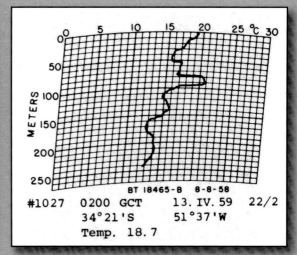

**Corrected BT Traces
(250 meters = 825 feet;
30 degrees centigrade =
86 degrees Fahrenheit).**

Above left: *BT record
from 700 miles off the coast
of Brazil, showing a common
temperature-depth profile: a
uniform surface mixed layer,
a sharp decline within the
thermocline layer, and a more
gradual decline in temperature to the ocean depths.*

Above right: *BT record
from 85 miles off the coast of
Argentina near the shelf edge,
showing the complex temperature pattern of interleaving
coastal and oceanic waters.*

"shadow zone", such that sonar signals from a surface vessel would be deflected away from the submarine, making it "invisible". This acoustic property of the upper ocean made the BT of vital interest to the Navy, as both the pursuer and the pursued.

During the war the BT continued to be modified to make deeper and deeper temperature records. The instrument continued to be used by oceanographers, and over the years hundreds of thousands of BT records have been filed in temperature atlases of the world oceans. The BT has been paramount to understanding the physical oceanography of the sea.

In more recent decades, the "expendable BT" has been developed, which can be deployed from ships or planes. As it sinks, a probe transmits a temperature-dependent signal up a fine wire directly to a ship, or up a wire to a small buoy that transmits the signal by radio to a ship or plane.

Arthur Gaines

Sources:

Lewis, J. M., 1992. Carl-Gustaf Rossby: A *Study in Mentorship.* Bull. Amer. Meteor. Soc., 73, 1425–1438.

Revelle, R. 1980. *The Oceanographic and How it Grew.* P. 10-24 [In] M. Sears and D. Merriman [Eds.] Oceanography: The Past. Springer-Verlag, New York. 812 pp.

BT slides: Fuglister, F.C., 1960. *Atlantic Ocean Atlas: Temperature and Salinity Profiles and Data from the International Geophysical Year of 1957-1958.* Woods Hole Oceanographic Institution, Woods hole, Mass. 209 pp.

Woods Hole Oceanographic Institution Archives. Instrument files: Bathythermograph.

nearly 3.5 land miles), a number branded in my memory. We had a large 1933 fathometer which pinged like sonar in shallow water. I don't know how they knew when the anchor was on the bottom, maybe by the amount of wire payed out by the winch. It was said the winch contained five miles of wire. The trawl winch was a very large affair, with controls on deck, which required the main engine to generate the power necessary to operate its DC electric motor. It did not free wheel, but was run under power in reverse.

After a few thousand feet were payed out, the wire was as taut as an iron rod and hung from the lead block in the gallows completely vertical. There was very little swell running at this time. Weight of wire at the bow block was about 5.4 tons.

The bo'sun sent me to the fore peak to get the black cloth anchor ball. When it was ascertained that the anchor was on the bottom, or "vessel anchored in 3,060 fathoms", we hoisted this ball to the second spreader (the daytime signal for a vessel at anchor). For the crew of another ship to come upon this scene, at this time in 1945, and find a sailing vessel—the largest ketch in the world—anchored 660 miles SSE of Bermuda, in mid-ocean in over 3000 fathoms, would have been unbelievable. To our knowledge, this was the deepest any ship had been anchored to the bottom.

To the men in the fo'c'sle, it was reason enough to "splice the main brace" and accordingly, I issued an extra bottle of Queen Anne Scotch when requested to do so. In the morning, the day after we anchored, we saw a steamer hull down on the horizon in the SW quadrant. She seemed to be heading in our direction. In due time, she passed close by us and we could see that she was flying the "Red Duster". She was a British ship with passengers lining the rails on her starboard side. *Atlantis* had the black anchor ball hoisted to the second spreader and we wondered if they believed we were really anchored.

The British ship inquired through a megaphone, "Are you all right?" Captain Knight called me aft and made a quick check in the International Book of Signals, then told me to get the signal flags "How" and "Dog", and break them out on the lower spreader of the main mast. These two signals meant "engaged in submarine survey work, keep clear". She was the only ship we saw from the time we left Bermuda to the time we returned.

AB Don Fay pays out wire from the deep sea winch using the topside control box, a process that could require 30 minutes or more. Second Engineer Hans Cook looks on. Photo by David Owen © Woods Hole Oceanographic Institution.

Because of its size and massive weight (23,000 pounds), the main trawl winch (deep sea winch) was located in the bowels of the ship. When containing a full spool, this winch carried over 5 miles of heavy wire. In addition to its more common scientific applications, such as for coring, large net deployment, and dredging, its heavy wire was occasionally used to anchor Atlantis in oceanic water depths. Second Engineer Hans Cook is seen here monitoring the winch. Photo courtesy WHOI Archives© Woods Hole Oceanographic Institution.

Swimming Over the Side—Mid-Ocean

After we were anchored, AB Charlie Remsen made a request to the chief mate, George Jennings, who in turn received permission from the captain that we would be allowed to go swimming over the side of the ship. We secured the pilot boarding ladder (a rope ladder, also called a Jacob's ladder) to the bulwark rail amidship; this ladder reached all the way down the side to the waterline.

I, with the two mess boys, Charlie Remsen, and some of the scientific party, went swimming in the beautiful, clear blue water of the mid-ocean. I can remember swimming a distance from *Atlantis*, diving under water and getting the sight of the whole underwater shape of the ship, as if I were looking at a model in a case. I could see every detail of the hull perfectly. Also since it was the first time I had ever been swimming in mid-ocean, it gave me a strange feeling to realize the bottom was three and a half miles below. Only the younger members of the crew went swimming. When we dived in we never gave it a thought that there might be sharks around. I always felt that, in 1945, it was the general belief that mid-ocean was devoid of fish. How wrong that was, as we were soon to find out.

The squarehead sailors thought we were crazy. No one ever swam off a square-rigged ship at sea. Chief Engineer Backus told me in no uncertain terms that if it had been up to him, he would not have allowed it. I knew at the time that none of the old-time seamen could swim a stroke, not even the bo'sun who had been going to sea for over 50 years. Chief Mate Mandly once told me that if he and I were both forced into the water because of a foundering vessel, he would die much easier than me because he never learned to swim. I, he claimed, would struggle and suffer much longer because I could swim.

I realized in later years that the philosophy expounded by Captain Mandly was held by many old-time sailors. "If you can't swim, you will die easily." The men who went to sea in the sailing ships accepted the fact that they could drown at any time. If one fell over the side, the chances of being recovered were very slim, at best. The bo'sun told me, that in his experiences at sea, they very rarely recovered anyone who had the misfortune to fall over the side.

Anchor Cable Parts

At the time we dropped the anchor, there was not much of a swell running. The strain on the tension gauge was almost at the limit. During the 8-12 watch the first night we were anchored, Captain Knight checked the wire cable and the strain gauge constantly. The wire ran out from below to a lead block on deck to the block in the gallows frame, as if it were a stiff rod. *Atlantis* pitched up and down on this wire. The wire in the water never moved at all. Captain Knight would pay out wire to keep too much wear from occurring on the area at the fair lead block on the bow gallows. I doubt he slept very much the first night, constantly checking the gallows block and the condition of the anchor wire with a flashlight (he had a large five cell flashlight at the time).

The next day a bit of the trade wind came up with the sun, and after that more ocean swells. *Atlantis* began to jump more and more around her anchor cable. Captain Knight, at this stage, began to worry the wire cable might part. He continued to order more wire payed out to reduce chafe. The measuring device for the strain gauge was bottoming out. I don't remember any discussion of what would happen if the wire parted on deck. We probably believed that the wire would part down near the ocean bottom. We, in the fo'c'sle, did not give any of this much attention.

That evening between 5 PM and 6 PM, all hands were below having supper. As we were anchored in mid-ocean, there was no necessity for a wheel-watch and lookout was not necessary every minute. Therefore, in the fo'c'sle, we were all below. The swell had increased a good deal during the day, but still one could not call it rough.

Suddenly, while in the midst of our evening meal, we heard a big bang, like a small explosion, and then a whirling sound as if many wires were spinning around rapidly, hitting the deck and the house sides. The anchor wire had parted, and as luck would have it, no one was on deck at the time. Most wire rope used on yachts today is pre-formed, meaning as the wire rope is made up, the strands are twisted and formed before the rope is laid up. Therefore, when this modern wire is cut, it does not unlay. The 5/8-inch trawl wire *Atlantis* used was not pre-formed, so if one were to cut it for any reason, it would be necessary to first put a good seizing on each side of the proposed cut. When the trawl wire would part under great strain, one strand would let go first and then followed in rapid order by the other five. The strands would spin around madly for about 10 or 15 feet. If anyone happened to be near, he could be cut up seriously, if not cut in half. As much as he did not want to see the anchor cable fail, Captain Knight was extremely happy it parted when it did with all hands safe below.

We immediately set the mizzen and jumbo and hove-to on the starboard tack. It was not until many years later that I realized the reason we always hove-to on the starboard tack. This tack gave us right-of-way over all vessels. Years later when reading cases and rulings of Admiralty Law, I read of a case where two vessels hove-to had a collision at sea. One vessel was on the port tack and the other on starboard. I believe they drifted into each other in a snowstorm at night. The court found the port tack vessel at fault, because under the rules of the road, a close-hauled starboard tack vessel has right-of-way over every other vessel. The only exception to this rule would be in the rare instance of another starboard tack vessel hove-to to the weather of us.

Mid-Ocean and the Bahamas Dinghy

*A*tlantis carried a 12-foot dinghy of the Bahamian model, stored on top of the house over the main saloon. The day after we anchored, one of the scientists, Al Woodcock, asked to have the dinghy launched for an experiment he planned to conduct. He was to row the dinghy about a mile or so away from *Atlantis*, beam to the sea or the swells we had at the time, to set out at intervals, red colored bottles. His idea was to attempt to locate the areas of the recirculation of the cooler subsurface water and the warm surface water. At least that was the way I understood it.

We launched the dinghy, many hands making an easy job of it, and I was ordered to accompany Al Woodcock. As I look at the photo of us in the dinghy 50 years later, I am amazed at our foolishness. We had nothing but one pair of oars and a small wood bailing dish. We did not have life jackets, no flares, no flag, no reserve fresh water and no clothing except what we had on. I wore only a pair of shorts and nothing to protect my head. We were in mid-ocean, well south of Bermuda, in mid-August. I don't know why we did not suffer more from exposure to the sun. I believe now, for us to be in this small boat, considering the sea that was running, was a very dangerous operation. I was too young and inexperienced to know any better. Al Woodcock and the officers should have.

Al Woodcock was at the oars as we rowed away from *Atlantis* for a mile or so, while I dropped the red colored bottles whenever he said "drop". In the swell running, we would be one minute in the valley of the sea, with walls of water all around us, and in the next, as we rose to the crest, we could get a glimpse of *Atlantis* in the distance. He explained to me what he was trying to find out. If the circulation theory worked as expected, the bottles would line-up perpendicular to the send of the sea. Apparently this would be where the surface water was going down. As I looked astern at all the bottles we dropped, there did not appear to me to be any line-up. The bottles seemed to be spread all over the place.

The lookout aboard the *Atlantis* had a difficult time keeping track of us in the swells. Apparently Captain Knight did not like us out there in the dinghy. He decided that Number 1 whaleboat should be launched under the command of the second mate, with two men, to sail back and forth on patrol, near our dinghy. The crew in the whaleboat with Second Mate Clark was Don Fay and Charlie Remsen. *Atlantis'* Number 1 whaleboat was about 23 feet overall, lapstrake (or clinker built), a beautiful Beetle model. She was painted French gray on the topsides and light green antifouling on the bottom. She was sloop-rigged with a standing lug main sail and the jib was set flying. How I envied the men in the whaleboat, and how beautiful she looked to my young eyes, dancing over the sea.

After the second day of being in the dinghy with Al Woodcock, I was bored with the inactivity of just dropping a bottle whenever I was told to. He would not let me row. He insisted on doing all the rowing, saying that we had to keep a certain course in the troughs across the sea. It was easier for him to do this himself, rather than to constantly try to tell me what direction to go, if I were rowing.

Handling the Whaleboat

At the end of the day, after we hauled the dinghy aboard, all hands would haul the whaleboat back on board *Atlantis*. This gave us great practice handling the boat in the davits with a good size swell running.

Above left: *Scientist Alfred Woodcock conducted physical oceanography research on several of Bill's cruises. Woodcock was among the physical oceanographers at WHOI (including Worthington) who did not hold the Ph.D., yet were considered among the best in the world. Photo courtesy WHOI Archives © Woods Hole Oceanographic Institution.*

Above: *Whaleboats were designed for use on the high seas. Uneasy with Woodcock and Cooper rowing the small Bahamas dinghy far off from the ship, Captain Knight sent out the Number 1 whaleboat to patrol back and forth for added safety. Photo courtesy WHOI Archives © Woods Hole Oceanographic Institution.*

At cocktail time, on the first day, after we had hauled the whaleboat back aboard with a good swell running, Norwegian Nels asked me a question: "Vat iss dot line called that we rigged to hold the lifeboat falls close to the ship's side, so she don't sving vay out and smack back into us?"

Of course, I didn't know the answer. I realized, even then, that he was asking this to "put me in my place." Nels proceeded to tell me in his Norwegian accent while sipping his Queen Anne, that "it vas a 'frapping line.'" He then explained that in the big schooners with dead eyes and lanyards securing the standing rigging, it was necessary to tie the shrouds together near the hounds to tighten them in calm weather, and, when there was a sea running, to keep the spars from "yumping out". Under these conditions, the schooners would roll so badly with the shrouds slack, they could roll their spars right out. The term for this was "frapping the rigging". I never forgot what a frapping line was, or how to use it.

On deck I learned about the real purpose of the "sea painter" and the "frapping line". The long sea painter (about 50 to 60 feet) gave enough slack so the whaleboat could lay away somewhat from the side of *Atlantis*, while the falls were being readied. The "frapping lines" were around the boat falls

Langmuir Circulation

Irving Langmuir had a distinguished career in basic physics and chemistry, but he is known to oceanographers for his work on surface circulation of the ocean. His curiosity was aroused during a transatlantic ship voyage on which he observed long lines of floating seaweed aligned with the wind direction. Photo courtesy of Roger R. Summerhayes.

Born in Brooklyn, N.Y., in 1881, Irving Langmuir was a distinguished American physical chemist and engineer who, among many honorary degrees and awards, received the 1932 Nobel Prize "...for his outstanding discoveries and investigations within the field of surface chemistry". While working at General Electric in Schenectady (1909-1950), Langmuir perfected the incandescent light bulb by introducing an inert gas to reduce deterioration of the tungsten filament, and improve its brightness and longevity.

Although accomplished in pure research on physical and atomic chemistry, in which he made many major contributions, he also pressed forward for useful applications and held some 60 patents. In his lifetime among those with whom he was conversant included such legends as Walther Nernst, Max Planck, Thomas Edison, Niels Bohr, Albert Einstein, and Werner Heisenberg. He was taught to fly a plane by Charles Lindbergh.

To oceanographers, however, Langmuir is known for his study of surface circulation in the ocean and in lakes. During a 1927 transatlantic voyage aboard S. S. *Rotterdam* Langmuir observed Sargassum seaweed forming long floating windrows, oriented parallel to the wind direction. Later he conducted field studies on Lake George in NY, near where he maintained a vacation house. In these studies he measured the speed and direction of currents by observing the movement and alignment of drifting leaves and neutrally buoyant artificial drifters, such as carefully weighted umbrellas.

The circulation pattern he described, now called "Langmuir Circulation", was published in 1938 in the journal *Science*. This pattern consists of horizontal rows of adjacent, slowly twisting helixes, parallel to the wind direction, that converge at the surface along one side and diverge at opposite sides. The result is that floating objects are brought together where the cells converge and drift apart where divergence occurs, to form a pattern of floating bands.

It was this mid-ocean circulation pattern oceanographer Alfred Woodcock was attempting to study when he rowed Bill Cooper around in a small boat on the high seas, instructing Bill to throw bottles overboard at intervals. Since the Langmuir cells involve low velocities it is imperative to get away from the disruptive effect of the wake or surge of a large ship.

Woodcock prepared scores of small, brightly colored bottles, each care-

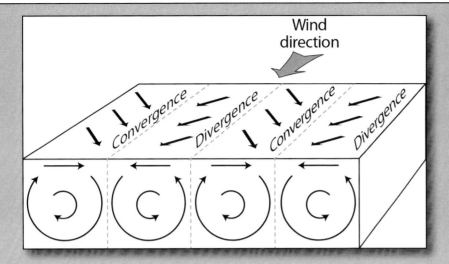

Wind direction

Convergence Divergence Convergence Divergence

fully flooded so that it would barely float at the surface, each bottle bearing a consecutive number. In this way the bottles were coupled more strongly with the water than with the wind, and their trajectory could be determined at recovery. The plan was to deploy them along a transect perpendicular to the wind direction, and to observe this array as the bottles rearranged their distribution to reflect the expected Langmuir pattern—rows now parallel to the wind. According to what Woodcock wrote, "Within three to five minutes all of these bottles were always rearranged into new lines parallel to the wind direction. . . and at right angles to the original line of distribution…"

Over the years, Langmuir Circulation has come to be recognized as an important process in ocean surface mixing, and is attributed with affecting the distribution of plankton and the behavior of their predators.

Irving Langmuir died of a heart attack on August 16, 1957 at age 76, while visiting his nephew in Falmouth Heights, a few miles from Woods Hole. The Certificate of Death lists his "usual occupation" as "physicist" at "General Electric Co.", a remarkable and sad understatement!

Arthur Gaines

The circulation pattern he described, later called "Langmuir Circulation", involves horizontal, parallel, twisting helixes near the ocean surface, responding to wind stress. Along zones of convergence the water descends and floating objects concentrate; along zones of divergence water comes to the surface and floating objects move apart. Graphic by Jack Cook.

Sources:
Langmuir, I., 1938. *Surface Motion of Water Induced by Wind*. Science, New Series, Vol. 87, No. 2250 (Feb. 11, 1938), p. 119-123.
Pregl, F.W., F. Zsigmondy, R. Adolf et. al. and N. Aston, 1966. *Nobel Lectures Including Presentation Speeches and Laureates' Biographies*. Chemistry, 1922-1941. Elsevier Publishing Company, Amsterdam.
Summerhayes, R.R., 1998. *Langmuir's World: The award-winning biography of America's first industrial scientist to win the Nobel Prize*. DVD. Running time 57 minutes.
Town of Falmouth, 1957. Standard Certificate of Death [certified copy]. Irving Langmuir. August 17, 1957. 59 Town Hall Square, Falmouth, MA.

Atlantis' *whaleboats were hung from the davits on rope falls. Launching and hauling the boats used human power, also known as "Norwegian steam", on the block-and-tackles. Photo by David Owen © Woods Hole Oceanographic Institution.*

(or tackle) to hold these in snug so that the boat did not swing out and then crash back into the side of the vessel (boat falls or tackle were made of the finest 4-strand manila; this made them less liable to kink).

If one were in the whale boat alongside, with a sea running, one would be looking at the deck of the ship and then in the next instant, looking up at the turn of the bilge. The automatic releasing hooks attached to the boat falls had lanyards attached which were fed through the lifting eye in the boat. The trick was to get both falls hooked in with the boat on the top of the swell, and then all hands heave away quickly. While hoisting, the two men in the boat had to heave down on that part of the fall that would help compensate for their weight in the boat.

The bo'sun and the squarehead ABs seemed quite proficient at launching and hauling the whaleboat on the davits. Since at this time, we had had a good deal of practice, we never had any trouble and did not damage the boat in the least. Even though it was "Norwegian steam", Second Mate Clark added quite a bit of "beef to the boat-falls" and with all hands on the falls of both davits we got the boat up very easily.

That evening I talked my watch partner, Don Fay, into trading places with me in the Bahamas dinghy. Since Don had been in the whaleboat,

WHOI Scientist Stanley Bergstrom at work in the electronics lab. Photo courtesy WHOI Archives © Woods Hole Oceanographic Institution.

that's where I would be the next day, so I thought. In the morning, I told the bo'sun and Al Woodcock I did not want to go again in the dinghy. The bo'-sun was somewhat taken aback at my impudence and wanted to report the matter to the mate. Al Woodcock said "no"; he wanted a volunteer and gladly accepted Don Fay in my place. Right after the whaleboat was launched, the bo'sun told Norwegian Nels to go with the second mate and to me he said sternly, "Mix up a bucket of 'soogee.'" He gave me punishment duty— "soogee the bulwarks!" That was the end of my small boat duty.

SOFAR—Sound Fixing and Ranging

The Navy radio operators aboard *Atlantis* had made contact with the Destroyer Escort (DE) off Dakar, Africa, on the wireless the previous night to let her know we were on station and the tests were to begin. To get the required distance on the wireless, transmissions could only be made at night. During the war, there were many new words added to the seaman's vocabulary —words such as LORAN, Radar, sonar, and SOFAR. The apparatus these words described all worked on radio waves or sound waves.

The Sound Channel and SOFAR

The sound channel is a feature of the deep ocean through which sound spreads for long distances. Given that the ocean quickly absorbs light or radio transmission, the sound channel has been useful where the ocean's sound transparency and focusing can support acoustic signaling or detection applications.

The deep sound channel is caused by the variation with depth of sound speed, which depends on temperature, pressure and salinity. A minimum of sound speed is located at a depth of around 4,000 feet near Bermuda (shallower toward the poles). Above this depth, sound speed increases, primarily due to warmer near-surface water, which causes sound rays to refract downward. Below this depth, sound speed increases, primarily due to an increase of pressure, which causes sound rays to refract upwards. The result is a middle layer where sound is focused and spreads horizontally over long ranges of hundreds and even thousands of miles. An extreme example of long-range acoustic transmission is a depth charge exploded in the ocean near Australia that was heard by a hydrophone near Bermuda.

Soon after the sound channel was discovered an early application of this knowledge was long-range SOund Fixing And Ranging (SOFAR), studied on some of Cooper's cruises. SOFAR was originally conceived as a means to locate aircraft downed at sea. The pilot could release a small bomb set to detonate at depth, which signal, detected by hydrophones, could be used to triangulate the plane's position. Later, the Navy considered applying a modification of the method to locating the position of military rocket splashdown in tests from the U.S. east coast.

During World War II, and much more in recent decades, sounds recorded in the deep sound channel have been used to identify and track submarines. A network of deep listening stations monitors the oceans for submarines, especially near the coast of the United States. In a cat-and-mouse game with our adversaries, the Navy employs ever-quieter submarines and ever more sensitive acoustic hydrophones. This was no doubt the motivation of the Navy in sponsoring research for some of the groundwork for these methodologies conducted while Bill Cooper was aboard *Atlantis*.

Today the deep sound channel is often used by scientists to obtain the tracks of freely-drifting acoustic floats over long ranges, and also the tracks of whales. The trajectory of neutrally buoyant floats, tracking deep ocean currents, ocean eddies, and dispersion, can be monitored from shore stations or ships that locate the moving source of the emitted acoustic pings. Another use is acoustic tomography, which repeatedly measures ocean temperature and its variations by sending sound rays long distances through the ocean depths. The different arrival times of sound rays recorded by a network of hydrophones in the sound channel reveals ocean temperatures at various depths above and below the deep sound channel.

Phillip Richardson

Sources:

Schlee, S., 1978. *On Almost Any Wind: The Saga of the Oceanographic Research Vessel Atlantis*. Cornell University Press, Ithaca and London. 301 pp.

Drake, C.L., J. Imbrie, J.A. Knauss and K.K. Turekian, 1978. Oceanography. Holt, Rinehart and Winston, New York. 447 pp.

It was Stan Bergstrom who first explained the operation SOFAR to the mess boys and me. As I remember; this is how he explained it: if an aircraft were to crash in the ocean, there would be a small bomb on board that could be dropped or set off with a hydrostatic charge if the plane sunk. The sound waves produced by the explosion could be picked up by hydrophones located in deep water along the coast. If there were two or more hydrophone locations, one could get a triangular reading. These bearings would thereby help locate the downed aircraft.

Stan said we were to proceed to a point in mid-ocean, anchor to remain stationary, and lower a hydrophone to the proper depth. A destroyer escort (DE) would be cruising near Dakar, off the coast of Africa, (about 3,000 miles away) and would drop bombs at specified times. Sound waves travel slowly in water as compared to radio waves in the air. After the DE dropped the bomb, it would take approximately one half hour for the sound to reach us. The Navy operators were aboard to maintain radio contact with the DE to set up the schedule of bomb dropping times.

In the daytime, *Atlantis'* wireless did not have range enough to reach Africa but could do so at night, bouncing the wireless waves off the atmosphere. In other words, we could only communicate with the DE at night. In 1945, there was an invisible barrier between the men before the mast and those aft, especially in the scientific party. The older seamen had nothing to do with the scientists. The bo'sun called all technicians "rah-rah boys". However, he got on well with Al Woodcock and was always respectful to any chief scientist, if we had one on board, such as Dr. Fye, Dr. Ewing, and Dr. Stetson. He may have had a vague idea of what they were doing, but that was all.

The young ABs on this cruise, Don Fay and Charlie Remsen, certainly had more interest and curiosity than the older men. Because of our young age, and the fact that the mess boys had social contact with the scientists and technicians, the mess boys, Bob Metell, Bill Shannon and I, were not as keenly aware of this invisible barrier. We visited the deck laboratory and, if it were interesting to us, we would stay and watch and ask questions, although we might not have understood the answers. One time, Stan Bergstrom told us that a bomb would be dropped about 2 PM, and if we came to the deck lab he would let us listen to the sound. If I remember correctly, he had an amplifier rigged up with a speaker, which enabled us to hear the sound coming from the bomb dropped by the DE off Dakar. It sounded to me like a marble rolling down the stairs and it seemed that we could hear the sound coming and then going away.

Mid-Ocean Fishing

One loses all track of time at sea, usually after about two weeks or so. Watch runs into watch and the time flows together, especially true if it is not punctuated by bad weather. For us, the beautiful trade wind weather continued, the sun shining every day, and very warm. The destroyer escort must have been steaming various courses dropping bombs, and the men aft listening on the hydrophone.

A short time after we layed hove-to, we began to notice a small species of fish swimming around the hull, just below the water line. The crew called them "rudder fish". Whether this is the correct name or not, I do not know. From somewhere, some small fish hooks and lines appeared and with the hooks baited, we commenced hand-lining over the side.

We caught enough fish the first day for all hands to enjoy them for

Second Engineer Hans Cook displays his catch, a dolphin fish (right hand) and a pomphret (left hand). Photo courtesy WHOI Archives © Woods Hole Oceanographic Institution.

supper. Everyone seemed surprised that there were any fish here in the middle of the ocean. A day or two later, sharks with their pilot fish appeared. This was certainly unexpected by the older sailors, at this time. No one in the crew had ever been hove-to in one spot in the ocean before for so long a period of time. They had not the chance to observe the marine life in mid-ocean, which certainly did exist, contrary to accepted beliefs of the day.

The older men in the crew decided they wanted to catch a shark. We had shark hooks with chain leaders in the fore peak; after obtaining a piece of bad meat from the galley, they lowered a couple of baited hooks over the side. Eventually they caught their shark. I remember it was a pretty large one and the men were not able to haul it aboard. Somehow or other they managed to get a line hitched around the shark's tail. Since they were on the starboard side amidships, they were able to use the cargo boom attached to the mizzen mast and, using power from the electric winch, were able to get him aboard. The shark was still alive when landed on deck. The square-heads attacked the shark with boat hatchets, the big fire axes and their sheath knives. Fifty years later, former Second Mate Clark said to me, "I cannot forget, after all these years, the unbelievable frenzy with which those squareheads attacked that shark." Sharks are not easy to kill, so the process took some time. Deep-water sailors had an absolute hatred of sharks. The squareheads then cut out some steaks and had the cook serve them up for supper that evening. I declined the shark steak.

Homeward Bound

We finally left our ocean station, and got underway for home. We stopped at St. George, Bermuda, again and probably took on fresh water and fuel.

The only good sailing breeze we encountered was after we left Bermuda and picked up a fair, fresh SW wind. We carried full sail and *Atlantis* was probably making an easy 10 or 11 knots. I only know this now from observations made after the Pitot meter log was installed in 1947, which gave accurate speed measurements. I don't believe we ever really got an accurate reading of speed with the taffrail log in the area of the Gulf Stream, because of all the fouling with gulf weed. At over 11 knots, the bow wave of *Atlantis* began to be quite noticeable, and if anywhere near 13 knots or so it became a constant roar. The bo'sun always said, "Dis ship's bow iss too full for any speed", and "Dis ship vas built vid a lightship bow and not built to sail fast." Even if this were true, she could sail up to 11 knots easily.

Atlantis was romping along at a good clip for home. So good that a happy Chief Backus, when on deck, said to messboy Bob Metell and myself, "the Woods Hole girls have hold of the towline, boys." All well and good, thought Bob and I, but we hoped that the Quissett girls had hold of the towline, too.

Chief Backus also gave us an old sailing ship saying:

"When Bermuda you do pass,
watch out for Cape Hatteras.
If at Hatteras, all is well,
watch that Cape Cod doesn't give you hell."

The bo'sun always seemed to be in a happy mood the last few days before we reached Woods Hole. Just before going below, at the end of the watch at midnight, he sang a ditty that he sang quite often. Looking out at the sea, he sang as the ship rolled along steadily for home:

"Everyone marries but me,
the dogs and the cats,
the mice and the rats
and the fishes that live in the sea."

We arrived in Woods Hole about the second week of September 1945, and tied up at the Fisheries wharf, which was still a shambles from the 1944 hurricane. The wartime atmosphere was still prevalent, with Navy crash boats moored to the old town wharf, joined occasionally by a "Fairmile"-type sub-chaser [The Fairmile boat was a versatile British design mainly equipped for anti-submarine use. It was about 112-feet overall, capable of about 15 knots, and designed to be built as components of a kit by small, dispersed shops, later to be assembled at ship yards. About 650 were built between 1940-1945, largely in Commonwealth countries.] The Army also had 63-foot crash boats in the area. These boats were to serve the planes that came from Otis Flying Field (the name used in 1945 for Camp Edwards). Whenever these boats lay in Woods Hole over night, they tied up alongside *Atlantis*.

Atlantis *in heavy weather suggests something of the hardship of serving "before the mast". Accommodations before the mast included 8 pipe berths, 8 steel lockers, a crew's head, and mess area. Photo courtesy WHOI Archives © Woods Hole Oceanographic Institution.*

Heavy Weather off New England

12

THAT FALL, starting the 11th of October 1945, we began a series of short cruises out to the Continental Shelf or the 100 fathom curve. These cruises had something to do with the transmission of sound through the Gulf Stream. The warm water apparently diminished sound waves passing through. We worked with a large Navy converted diesel yacht, named *Mentor*. This vessel supposedly had been built for Major Fleischman, of Fleischman's Yeast, just before the war. She was quite a handsome vessel, but the weather conditions offshore in the fall were a bit rough on her, and her crew had a hard time. She was equipped with LORAN and Radar, however.

Second Mate Clark left *Atlantis* sometime about mid-October, 1945, I am sure to the regret of the men forward, and his replacement arrived shortly after. I was working on deck early one afternoon, when I happened to look out into the street, between the Fisheries buildings, and caught sight of a large rugged man walking toward *Atlantis* and the dock where she lay. He had the same gait as Ernest, the bo'sun, so I supposed he was a seaman, "by the cut of his jib", as the old sailors would say. I could see that he was a squarehead, a Swede in fact.

When he came near to where I was working, he asked me if the captain was aboard. I met him at the gangway and escorted him through the wheelhouse to the captain's cabin, just off the chartroom. As I left the chartroom and climbed the steps to the wheelhouse, I heard the newcomer say to Captain Knight, "I vas the new second mate, my name iss Arvid Karlson." He was Dan Clark's replacement.

Arvid Karlson was born in 1891 and was 54 years old when he joined *Atlantis* as second mate. From the stories he later told, we learned that he was orphaned at a very young age, went to sea about age 14, serving first in

Baltic schooners. Later he served in German square rig ships of the famous Laeisz-owned "flying P-line" (all ships names began with the letter "p". The *Peking* in South Street Seaport in New York City is a former Laeisz ship). These ships were big Cape Horners, sailing between Hamburg and the west coast of Chile, returning home loaded with nitrates. This was before the First World War. Arvid Karlson, in the spring of 1946, became the chief mate of *Atlantis*, and served in this position for about eight years, then being promoted to master of the ketch *Caryn*.

At the end of October we lost our two mess boys, who had been with us since the previous April. Bill Shannon suffered from chronic seasickness, so bad that Captain Knight told him he could not sail in *Atlantis* any more. Bob Metell did not like the idea of winter in *Atlantis,* and did not want to go on deck as a seaman. Chief Backus had wanted him to go into the engine room and train as a third assistant engineer. Chief Backus told me later that Bob could not throw the clutch of the Burmeister-Wain diesel into gear; therefore they could not take him in the engine room. I am sure he could have done it with a little practice.

The Ethyl Alcohol

Atlantis' decks below were plated with steel and, as was the custom at the time of her building, the steel decks were covered with canvas. The canvas was then painted with red shellac—actually maroon in color. After many coats of red shellac, the canvas took on the appearance of maroon battleship linoleum. In wet weather with boots tramping the decks below, the top layers of the red shellac wore off quickly. Therefore, it was general practice, if possible, to re-shellac the worn decks the last day before we arrived in port. Then, when we arrived, everything below would be in good condition. Many times the weather was adverse right up to the time of our arrival. In such a case, shellacking below in the lower alleyways and saloon would be done a day or two later. The fast drying of the shellac made this possible.

We used alcohol to clean the brushes and, at times, to thin the shellac. Right after we came back from Bermuda in the fall of 1945, we had run out of alcohol. Our alcohol came from the WHOI stockroom, then in the

Above: *The 127-foot yacht Haida was built in 1941 for Max C. Fleischman. In 1942 she was acquired by the Navy, renamed Mentor (PYc 37), and loaned to WHOI from 1946 to 1950. She is seen here off the WHOI dock. Photo courtesy WHOI Archives © Woods Hole Oceanographic Institution.*

Left: *Arvid Karlson came on board as second mate in October 1945. An old-school Cape Horner, he was promoted to chief mate a few months later and held that position for eight years. Photo by Jan Hahn © Woods Hole Oceanographic Institution.*

Penzance Garage on the main street of Woods Hole. I believe it was a Saturday afternoon in October, and we were preparing to sail on a short cruise. No one was in the stockroom. John Churchill had the key and I was sent with him to find some alcohol. After searching around for a time, we finally came across a square five-gallon can with a label "Pharmaceutical Ethyl Alcohol" on the outside. I remember the label but it meant nothing to me. I recall Mr. Churchill saying "I don't know if this is the right stuff, but alcohol is alcohol." We did not see any other kind, so he told me to take it.

When I got back to the ship with the five-gallon can, one of the men said, "My God, you can drink that stuff." As soon as the crew was informed that there were five gallons of ethyl alcohol in the paint locker aft, they got a small jug and went aft, when the officers were absent, and tapped out some for personal use. They charged the coffee in the morning and afternoon with a small shot, making a drink they called "coffee royal".

The mate could not understand why the gang no longer went to the Rendezvous for afternoon coffee/beer break. Neither the squareheads, the bo'sun, nor anyone else ever abused the ethyl alcohol. They restricted it to a small shot in their coffee. I never saw them drink it other than that.

As time went by, however, the newer crew members tapped the alcohol until it reached the point when the last gallon and a half ended up being stored in a locker in the crew's head. The mess boy and I mixed the alcohol in a bottle of Bacardi white rum—about half and half. We gave it to one of the afterguard who might be described as a "professional drinker", saying it was too strong for us. He thanked us for it. He did not surface for about three days, his eyes blurry and red, and badly in need of a shave.

About five months after the ethyl alcohol came aboard (we were in Cuba at this time) Chief Mate Karlson decided to shellac the alleyway (passages) below. I was in the paint locker passing up the shellac, when he asked me for the alcohol. I knew full well that it was in the locker in the crew's head and not in the paint locker. I told him I could not find any. He asked me, "Vat the hell did you do vit it, drink it?" That question made me laugh.

I felt compelled to tell the mate where the can of alcohol was. He retrieved the almost empty can and reported the matter to the captain, who, by this time, was Gilbert Oakley, a strict disciplinarian; Oakley was appalled with the idea that the crew had been drinking the shellac alcohol. I believe he thought it was methanol or wood alcohol. We were called aft, including the mess boys and me, who never touched a drop of the stuff. We were all given a very stern lecture by the captain. He told us of all the dire effects that methanol could cause, including blindness and even death. He could not understand why they would drink such stuff with all the cheap rum then available in Cuba.

The mess boys and I, when talking it over later, decided the captain would probably hang us on the spot if he ever knew of the half rum and alcohol (it was nearer one-third rum and two-thirds alcohol) that we gave to the "professional drinker" who was berthed well "abaft the mast".

Felix—His Rations and Adventures

Shortly after we arrived back in Woods Hole from one of the short cruises that autumn, AB Willie G. became concerned about the ship cat Felix's diet. The cook and Willie did not agree on what the cook gave Felix to eat. "You tink Felix likes to eat the yunk you feed us? Ve vant him to have his own rations." The cook made some remark about the "goddamn cat" to which Willie paid little attention. "Ve take care of dis ourselves, ve know vat cats like, dey like milk and fish." Then he said that I should go ashore with him.

Atlantis was laying at the main dock of the Oceanographic, so it was just a short walk out the guard gate and across Water Street to the small A & P store where WHOI had an account. The clerk in the store was Henry Parker, who greeted us with a smile. Willie put in his order: "Ve vant two cases of canned milk and two cases of the best damn tuna fish you got, for Felix." Henry rounded up the two cases each of milk and tuna fish, and, while I was surveying them and considering the weight involved, Henry got out the invoice and presented it to Willie for his signature.

Willie, taking the pencil in hand, asked Henry, "How do ve spell the skipper's name?" "K-N-I-G-H-T", Henry said slowly, as Willie signed the invoice "Captain Knight". "Dot iss the vey ve cuts red tape", he said, as we hauled the cases of milk and tuna fish out of the store while Henry held the door open for us.

We got Felix's rations on board and stored them in the forepeak. After sampling this diet of milk and tuna, Felix's palate became very sophisticated, and very, very fussy.

We never heard anything about Willie signing the captain's name to the

Atlantis on port tack in heavy weather. Photo courtesy WHOI Archives © Woods Hole Oceanographic Institution.

Land birds commonly alight on ships far at sea. Pictured here, probably in January or February, are Common Redpolls, a northern species that is sporadically found off New England in winter. Photo courtesy WHOI Archives © Woods Hole Oceanographic Institution.

invoice. It would not have mattered to me anyway. I was only ordinary seaman, no responsibility, no authority and no cares.

Atlantis spent the fall and early winter in ten day to two week trips off the Continental Shelf, which can be a very rough place at that time of the year. In November of 1945 the weather had been chilly and windy, especially offshore. We had been working near the 100 fathom curve, on sound wave transmission, through warm water to cold. We were usually out ten days and in for three or so. That year we suffered through many intense gales and storms, especially from the NW. These gales would sometimes last two or three days. During one particularly fierce NW storm, even the big liner *Queen Mary* was held up on her approach to New York, for over a day. That made us feel a little better.

We spent a lot of time hove-to, mostly to lower a hydrophone over the side. We were working with the U.S. Navy's Research vessel *Mentor*. She was diesel-powered with a Navy crew. She had a difficult time with the inclement weather, especially on the back side of Nantucket. *Mentor* was the vessel sending out the underwater sound signals while steaming on various courses. *Atlantis* carried the hydrophone, attempting to pick up those signals.

Because of the gale force winds, *Mentor* could not maintain her courses, and, as it was difficult for her to heave-to offshore, she ran in for shelter when given the chance. *Atlantis* could not make the speed that *Mentor* could, and as a result we would heave-to near the Continental Shelf and ride it out.

During our trips offshore that fall, we had on board a radio officer whose name I can't recall. His job was to operate the wireless and keep in contact with *Mentor* wherever she was or whatever she was doing. I can't tell now exactly what it was that we were doing, except we lowered the hydrophone a great deal.

During the many gales from the NW that we experienced, *Atlantis* would be the resting place for many birds blown offshore. The radio man and Chief Backus were both interested and concerned for these birds, giving them fresh water and food. Felix, being a normal cat, was also interested in the birds, probably the first he had ever seen. The birds could stay high enough up on the top of the deck lab and engine room fiddley, well out of Felix's normal reach. Although he did study the birds curiously whenever he was on deck, we never saw any evidence Felix ever caught a bird. The radio man, however, did not like Felix's presence on deck if any bird was aboard.

Mumbling to himself one day, he said in a voice loud enough for Willie Gustavesen to hear, "If that damn cat harms one of those birds, I'll be tempted to throw him over the side." Willie walked up directly to him and said, "I hope you can swim, Sonny Yim (Willie said this as an insult), because if you touch dot cat, overboard you'll go." From the look in Willie's eyes, the radio man saw that he meant it. Never again did he ever mention Felix and the birds. Willie Gustavesen was one tough hombre.

Felix Goes Missing

In the windy, squally weather, we were continuously working with the sails, setting them whenever underway or taking them in to heave-to, as necessary. If we were working forward and it was not too wet, Felix would sometimes come and play with us, as young cats will. Many times he would climb the jib as it lay on deck prior to being furled, or dart in and out of the folds of heavy canvas just after we had hove-to.

He was doing this one evening while we were trying to furl the jib. This was a heavy job for two of us, and we did not have any time to play around with him. After we had the gaskets around the jib, pounding it down with our fists to get as tight a furl as possible, we hoisted the clew high enough to clear the jib from the deck. When the job was finished, we got a chance to look around and saw no sign of Felix. We guessed he was disgusted because we did not want to play, and must have gone aft or below.

That evening we did not see Felix anywhere, but did not worry because we did not always know where he might be sleeping. As we were going on watch the following morning, Willie had Felix's breakfast ready and asked if we had seen him. Felix usually bugged Willie as he came off the 4-8 watch, wanting breakfast, but, "Oh well, he is probably asleep somewhere aft." Noontime came and still no sign of Felix. Willie began to be concerned and the watch below in the fo'c'sle began to comb the ship. There was no sign of Felix. It had been quite rough during the night hours, and we began to believe he might have been washed over the side, somehow.

Toward evening, when he did not appear for his food, we accepted the awful truth that we had lost him. The squareheads particularly, at this time, were very quiet. By morning of the next day, with no sign of Felix, we now knew the worst must have happened. Felix was lost at sea. We often wondered why he hadn't fallen overboard before this. After 8 bells that morning, the captain ordered us to set the jib. We lowered the jib on to the deck, to get at the gaskets, feeling sad, as it was here that we last saw Felix.

We untied the gaskets and, with one man on the halyard winch below, the sail began to rise slowly. As the head went up the stay, a heavy part of the sail unfolded, and lo and behold, back from the dead, tumbled out Felix! He had been furled up in the sail for a day and a half! I picked him up, carried him over to the fo'c'sle companionway and hollered below, "Willie, here is Felix returned from the dead, and hungry as hell."

Later, in November of 1945, we lost three squarehead seamen from the fo'c'sle. Willie and Ernest Gustavesen and Norwegian Nels decided winter in the North Atlantic, off the East Coast, in a small sailing vessel, was not for them. They had seen too much of this kind of life in the past. The old sailors used to say "You have never been to sea, until you go to sea in the wintertime."

Before he left *Atlantis,* the tough old squarehead seaman, Willie Gustavesen, gave Felix a farewell hug. The kitten had held Willie's affection for the past three months. Years later, I realized that Felix was probably the only creature Willie had given affection to for a long time in his life. With Willie gone, Felix soon found a new source of protection. That was the Second Mate Arvid Karlson. Felix was now berthing with the second mate during the night. He still took his meals in the crew's mess. He would visit the fo'c'sle during the day, if it was not too rough. ABs Willie and Ernest left *Atlantis* to sail on larger ships, to warmer climes, shipping in late 1945 still being plentiful. This left the bo'sun, Ernest Siversen, the only squarehead in the fo'c'sle. He was getting old and having trouble with his previously injured back. Back trouble slowed him down enough to make my life easier.

For the remainder of the year, we had an unbelievable turnover in crew, which included many different types of ex-service men and Merchant Marine sailors. So many, in fact, I cannot remember them all, let alone, their names. Some of these people, whose names I can remember, included: Bob Baker, later a well-known wooden boat builder from whom the Woods Hole Historical Museum obtained the *Spy,* one of the last of the "Woods Hole Spritsail boats". Also, a fellow with a chief mate's license who served as ordinary seaman, Bob Harris, many years later a yacht designer living in Vancouver. Besides many ex-merchant seamen, ex-Navy armed guard men, an ex-Army Air Force man who had been a POW in Romania, we had other strange characters, some said by the men in the fo'c'sle to be Section 8 discharges [discharged as mentally unfit]. Most only stayed for the short trip, be it a week or ten days. Conditions were so rough, miserable and hard, that new crew would leave as soon as *Atlantis* returned to port.

Atlantis was, in rough water, a real lively vessel, which kept her dry in breaking seas. This liveliness gave her a quick motion, especially when pitching into a head sea. As anyone who has been to sea knows, pitching will bring on seasickness very quickly, more so than rolling. I remember we had one ex-Merchant Marine sailor come aboard who was pretty sure of himself. When we told him that it was possible he would get seasick in the fo'c'sle, since he had never slept so far forward before, he replied, "I've sailed all over the world on Liberty Ships, I don't think this piss pot will bother me." He was out, groaning and sick in his berth in the fo'c'sle, before we even cleared Gay Head, and had to be forced out, when his time came to go on watch.

Life aboard *Atlantis,* when she was hove-to, could be very pleasant as she was a good sea boat and the decks remained dry most of the time. I must admit, the sight of the large waves with combers breaking, coming at the vessel from weather side at night, put the fear of God in one, if he happened to be on deck at the right moment. When the sea would almost be upon us and we were looking up at the breaking crest and expecting it to crash down on you, the "old girl" would gently roll down to leeward and raise her weather side up. The sea, with hardly a sound, would past harmlessly underneath the hull.

The weather was cold, but for the most part when we were hove-to, it was dry on deck. At this time of the year we wore our oilskins most of the time at sea, to keep dry and break the cold penetrating wind.

A number of times, when we were ready to sail from Woods Hole, we were short a seaman. To make up for this, the Marine Superintendent and number two man at the Oceanographic, John Churchill, would ship out as ordinary seaman, but he did not act as ordinary seaman nor did he stand watch. Instead he took charge of the 8-12 watch (the bo'sun's watch) where he could stay dry and warm in the wheel watch. He also slept aft and ate in the saloon mess with the officers and the few scientists we were carrying, mostly electronics men. The bo'sun acted as seaman whenever John Churchill was aboard. Captain Knight called him "Ordinary Seaman Churchill".

Lightships

Sometimes when I stood a wheel watch or standby watch in the wheelhouse, I would hear Captain Knight and John Churchill talking. One of the things I heard John Churchill say, some 65 years ago, was that in a few years all the lightships would be gone, replaced by automatic light buoys. That did not sound good to my romantic soul. Thinking of all the big liners going into New York Harbor at the time, I asked Mr. Churchill if even *Ambrose* Lightship would be replaced. "Yes," he replied, "Ambrose Lightship and eventually *Nantucket* Lightship. Just when, I don't know, but you can count on it." How true that prophecy turned out to be; in 30 or 40 years after that time, there were no lightships left afloat, only automatic lighted buoys.

Quick's Hole Buoy

In the evening watch, 8 PM, returning to Woods Hole, my wheel watch began just about the time we had the Vineyard Sound lightship in view. It was a relaxed time, near the end of the trip, with Thanksgiving a day away. At the time, *Atlantis* was under sail and power, carrying jibs and mizzen. After we fetched the lightship, we made the turn to run up the Sound. The mizzen was slacked well off, with the wind astern. Compared with the stormy conditions we had endured during the past week or so, the weather was very mild, with a light breeze astern. Ernest, the bo'sun, was on lookout forward. John Churchill was in the wheelhouse gazing out the open wheelhouse door at the passing shore. I was at the wheel, steering the course that would take us to the next mark, the Quick's Hole lighted buoy.

Through the open pilot house door, I could hear the water swirling by the hull. I could also see the flashing light of the Quick's Hole buoy ahead, but that was not my concern. My job at the moment was to steer the compass course given me. After a while, I thought that the light seemed to be getting brighter on the bow. All of a sudden I got a glimpse of the bo'sun coming aft from the bow saying something in an excited voice to John Churchill. Mr. Churchill was not used to translating Ernest's dialect, especially when he was excited, so it took a moment for him to understand what he was saying. When he did, he rushed aft from the break of the poop deck

Landing at the main dock, Atlantis' deck crew in oilskins snubs the bow hawser. Photo courtesy WHOI Archives © Woods Hole Oceanographic Institution.

and hollered in through the pilot house door to me: "Hard starboard, full right rudder!"

I had been taught to obey all orders instantly, so I immediately began to turn the wheel, 3 1/2 turns to starboard. Running at that speed, about 7 knots, there was a great deal of pressure on the rudder, so it took all the strength I could muster to turn it to hard right rudder. I no sooner had accomplished this task, then, before I had a chance to look up the order came: "Full left rudder!"

Now I had to turn the rudder from full starboard to full port, almost 7 turns. The first three turns from starboard to mid-ship were easier, but from mid-ship to full port was the same difficult operation. As I finished the turns, I had a chance to gaze out the pilot house door and saw the Quick's Hole buoy pass close to our port side, just clearing the mizzen boom, the mizzen sheet, foot ropes on the boom, and the boom tackle. How the buoy cleared the latter, I don't know. As the boom cleared, the white light flashed as if saying "Good-bye."

The captain had been down in his cabin when he heard the orders to the helmsman. To satisfy his curiosity, he arrived in the wheelhouse just after the Quick's Hole buoy had passed astern. "Well, Lambert," said Mr. Churchill to the captain, "we almost ran down the Quick's Hole buoy!" Then, laughing, "I would loved to have seen the look on the chief's face if we had hit the buoy and it had bounced along the side of the ship." The chief was the chief engineer, Harold Backus. "That would be almost worth bouncing off the buoy."

Change of Command

While lying in Woods Hole, one evening early in December 1945, one of the men in the fo'c'sle came down from being on deck and said, "I just saw Captain Knight throw his hat overboard from the bow." We did not understand what that was all about. The next day, we were informed that Lambert Knight was replaced as master by Gilbert Oakley, ex-commander, US Coast Guard. Lambert Knight would now sail as chief mate. It was said that the Oceanographic was the Harvard Yacht Club. Captain Oakley was a Harvard man, where Lambert Knight had attended Princeton.

That evening, Captain Oakley paid a visit to the fo'c'sle and introduced himself, and, in a short speech, said that the pay rate would be standardized at $150.00 per month for ordinary and $175.00 for AB. He told me that I

Captain Gilbert Oakley (left), seen here with Paul M. Fye (who later became the 5th WHOI Director), came from Coast Guard experience in Arctic waters. Photo courtesy WHOI Archives © Woods Hole Oceanographic Institution.

Above: *The ship's cats independently discovered the best heavy weather berth for cats, under the gimbaled table in the scientists' main saloon. Seen here is a Woods Hole six-toed cat, a successor of Felix. Photo by Jan Hahn © Woods Hole Oceanographic Institution.*

Below: *Icing up:* Atlantis under sail in the *wintertime. Photo by Harold Backus © Woods Hole Oceanographic Institution.*

Above: *Scientist Alfred Woodcock braves the icy fore-deck to capture a wind speed measurement. Photo courtesy WHOI Archives © Woods Hole Oceanographic Institution.*

would receive a $50.00 a month raise immediately. I liked this man, and by his demeanor, we knew there was no doubt he was the master. My pay was now $150.00 per month, pretty good when you consider I also got room and board. Technicians ashore at WHOI received $100.00 to $120.00 per month without room and board. In 1945, seamen were well paid.

We received the first LORAN set (Navy surplus) on board *Atlantis* in early December, 1945. The 110-volt DC power the ship's service supplied was wrong for the LORAN. An inverter was installed aft in the chartroom to supply the AC current the LORAN needed. The early LORAN sets were difficult to operate with the system of lining up the slave station with master station and the necessity of reading off the measurements from the scope itself. At first, Captain Oakley was the only one who could operate it. The LORAN, however, was a tremendous aid in coastal navigation.

Felix's Heavy Weather Berth

The fo'c'sle in *Atlantis* was a bad place to be in rough weather, particularly if we were driving and plunging in to the sea. In rough weather, Felix never slept in the fo'c'sle. He had many other places he could sleep farther aft where the motion was not half so bad. In December 1945 the new master, Captain Oakley, drove *Atlantis* relentlessly in the miserable weather. He had been master of a converted trawler in the Coast Guard, and had two years experience on the Greenland Patrol, and the weather we were experiencing did not faze him in the least. He ordered everything well secured and battened down forward, full speed ahead, and "bring the lookouts aft." This latter order made Captain Oakley the hero of the men before the mast. Coming aft away from the wind, spray and crashing seas made our life on lookout in the bitter cold a lot more pleasant. When salt water freezes to your oilskins, you know that it is cold.

All in all it was a very rough period. It was at this time that I first saw Felix in his rough weather berth. The dining table in the main saloon in *Atlantis* was "gimbaled" or a swinging table. The table had a bracket which formed the legs at each end, to which the table itself was attached with a pin. This arrangement allowed the top of the table to tip from side to side, so that in the case of the ship's heeling over on one side, the top of the table would remain level. In order for all this to work, there was a steel channel iron 6 inches to 7 inches wide. This channel piece was in turn filled with lead which gave the top of the channel a flat, smooth surface. Now, to make the action of the table steady and to prevent anyone from upsetting it easily, the lead counter-weight was very heavy. With the ship driving ahead in rough weather, there was a great deal of movement, even if heeled down, carrying sail. This movement made it look as if the table itself were swinging and gyrating about something awful, when in reality the table was very steady and it was the ship that was doing all the moving around the table.

When I was relieved from wheel-watch at 8 AM one morning during a particularly rough period, I proceeded to go forward below in the ship which would take me through the main saloon at breakfast time. We had permission, in rough weather, when relieved from watch, to pass forward below in the ship, through the scientists' area, officers' quarters and main saloon with strict orders, however, to remove our hats before entering the main saloon.

I entered the saloon at a time when the ship was heeling well to starboard, but also moving about a great deal from the send of the sea. As the lead weight in the bottom of the gimbaled table swung well out, I caught sight of Felix also seeming to fly through the air. He was fast asleep on the top of the lead counter weight, which, in reality, was almost stationary, while *Atlantis* was violently gyrating around him. Here he was in his "rough weather berth". When I told the men forward where Felix was sacked out, they all laughed, including old Ernest. Ernest then said, "Dot cat might yust as well be sleeping under an apple tree, as far as he is concerned." According to the bo'sun, "The best cure for seasickness is fifteen minutes under an apple tree."

Back Before Christmas

Captain Oakley was driving the "old girl" pretty hard in some real rough weather. It was nearing Christmas and Captain Oakley wanted to finish our work and be in Woods Hole in plenty of time for the Christmas holidays. To the great surprise and joy to us all, we finished our work and arrived in Woods Hole a few days before Christmas. We in the crew were all given leave for the holiday.

Laying in Cuba

13

Atlantis sailed to Guantanamo Bay, Cuba, in February 1946, Captain Oakley in command. We were to work out of the naval base there, a continuation of the anti-submarine warfare project we had been engaged with in the Tongue of the Ocean. Working out of Guantanamo Bay, we'd heave-to at an ocean station and flying boats would come over and drop depth charges. Destroyers would go by and they dropped more depth charges. I don't know why—the war was over. But every night we would go back in and we'd lay in what they called the Ordinance Dock. To get into the Ordinance Dock we would turn hard—the *Atlantis* would spin very easily if you stopped the engine and turned the rudder hard left and then give her half ahead. She would go right around—but we would usually hit the dock. Oakley was the roughest captain of all; he put more dents in the ship than anybody. We'd spin around and tie her up and we'd be ready to go out to sea again at 5 AM in the morning.

The Ship's Wheel

One day toward the end of March 1946, Chief Mate Arvid Karlson called me and another man aft, saying he had a "good yob for you two." The mate took us into the wheelhouse and pointed at the ship's wheel: "Ve iss going to take all the warnish off the veel so it can all be warnished again."

He then proceeded to tell us about the time he spent on big steam yachts and how they stripped to bare wood many parts of the deckhouses, rails, and brightwork every year. "Ve used paint remover, vire brushes and burlap. Dot vos all. I vant you to use vire brush and burlap on dis veel and noting else. I picked you two guys because I vant a good yob, you under-

Above: *By age 19, Bill had been promoted to able body seaman. He is pictured here at St. George, Bermuda, in about 1945. Photo from Cooper family collection.*

    Above right: *Bill Little was one of the crew before the mast who participated in a cruise to Cuba. Photo from Cooper family collection.*

    Right: *Refinishing Atlantis' wheel was a "good yob" that got Bill into trouble. Photo from Cooper family collection.*

stand?" "Yes, Sir" we replied. "Good, then cover the deck vid tarpaulin and anyting else dot needs to be covered to protect them from any remover that gets splashed around. Now, remember, I vant a good yob."

"Yes, Sir, Mr. Karlson, we understand. Only remover, wire brush and burlap to take the old varnish off the wheel."

The mate left us in the wheelhouse and we sized up the job. The other sailor was a Boston Irishman named Joe, about 25 or 26 years old. He had been on yachts before the war and was a Navy veteran who had served mostly as a gunner's mate in the armed guard on merchant ships. As I remember, he was a real nice fellow, easy-going and had a good sense of humor. Joe and I procured the necessary pieces of canvas to cover the deck, compass binnacle, and what not, to protect them from the paint remover that we were to liberally put on the ship's wheel.

Atlantis' wheel, as I remember, was about five feet or so in diameter outside the spokes. The wheel spokes themselves were made of ash turned in the classical shape as columns and balusters, and set into a brass hub. The outer pieces near the rim were beautiful dark mahogany with filler pieces between the spokes and cheek pieces on either side to make the assembled wheel or rim. These mahogany pieces also had the various mouldings, all in the classical sense. It was because of these details of mouldings and carvings in the wood that the chief mate wanted us to be extra careful in the removal of the old varnish. He reasoned, from experience, that, with the paint remover and only a wire brush and burlap to remove the old varnish, we could not do much harm to that beautiful piece of equipment.

For Joe and me, this was really a plush job. The mate was busy on deck and he never bothered us at all. We would slap on remover, and then sit back on the settee in the wheelhouse and give it time to work. Joe told me about visits to Pacific Islands during the war. Talking it over, we could not understand why we were stripping off the varnish in the first place. The wheel had looked perfectly fine to us and we reasoned another couple of coats of varnish was all that it needed. But ours was "not to reason why, ours was to do and die"— obey!

We continued to apply the remover and, after a while, wipe it off with the burlap cloths. Before noon, we gave the wheel another liberal coat of remover. Then Mr. Karlson arrived and knocked us off for lunch. We were close approaching the point where the "vire brush" would be needed. The mate looked at our work and seemed satisfied.

We tackled the job again after lunch. It was very warm in Cuba at this time of year, and we did not wear any shirts. When we tackled the wheel spokes with the wire brush, we were showered on our bare chests with drops of paint remover which burned like hell. Neither Joe nor I liked the idea of using just burlap and a wire brush, especially on the spokes. The old varnish was in the grain of the wood and hard to get out, and, after feeling the stinging pain of the remover, we paused to sit awhile on the settee and think about it.

Twenty years and a few months later, I would be working in the mold loft at Minnefords, in City Island, New York, where the America Cup Defender *Intrepid* was under construction. The head loftsman was a 75 year old Norwegian named Nels Halvorsen. He had been a boat builder and loftsman for over 50 years. He had been in charge of the mold loft at Henry Nevin's yard all through the 1920s, 30s and 40s. He laid down the Cup defenders *Columbia, Constellation,* and *Intrepid*; in short, he had a great deal of experience.

We were getting out templates for the main keel section. Nels had us make a template for the top of the 6-inch thick keel and a template for the bottom also. After we completed the templates and delivered them over to the shop, I asked Nels why there was a need for a top keel template and a bottom one also. After all, I reasoned, they were boat builders in the shop and would know how to get the keel out from the top template with sections laid out on it. His answer to my question was "Ve don't let dem tink, because ven dey tink iss ven dey gets in trouble."

True to form, when Joe and I, sitting alongside in Guantanamo, Cuba, paused to think, we got into trouble. Sitting on the settee, I told Joe the story an old seaman had told me when I was in a schooner yacht, about scraping and varnishing spars on a ship waiting a cargo in Shanghai, China, in 1886. He said they used their sheath knives to scrape varnish off the spars and "that no goddamn Yankee skipper would ever supply sandpaper". They then varnished the spars, dipping their hand in the varnish and rubbing it on by hand.

Joe got up and went over to the wheel and started to scrape one of the spokes with his sheath knife; it seemed to work. So I joined him with my knife. After a while, we thought a scraper might work a little better on the flat areas. *Atlantis* only carried ship scrapers used to scrape paint and rust off steel. Joe and I got a couple of these and sharpened them as best we could on the hand grinding wheel located in the sail loft.

With our new tools, sheath knives, and scrapers, we attacked the wheel with a vengeance. We worked steady and each became lost in his own world, scraping and scratching away. With this diligent activity, we managed to get most of the old varnish off. Stepping back to view our work, Joe and I did notice a few digs and scratches here and there. Just then the chief mate stepped into the wheelhouse. When Joe saw him, he said in his cheerful Irish manner: "There, Mr. Karlson, we got the wheel all stripped. How does it look?"

The chief mate's face seemed to have frozen with his eyes ready to pop out. "How does it look?" he answered, "It looks like a f—g rabbit has been schewing on it, dot's how it looks!"

The next day and for a few days after, Mr. Karlson had us working with Garnet sandpaper on the ship's wheel to remove "the marks of that f—g rabbit's teeth". After awhile, the skin on our fingers began to wear thin and we wondered when we would ever get the job done to the mate's satisfaction, and, above all, what the next "good yob for you two" would be.

Above left: *Bill Cooper and Jim Bailey in a playful moment atop the main boom. The two became lifelong friends. Photo from Cooper family collection.*

Above right: *George Swanson and Jim Bailey were shipmates aboard* Atlantis. *Photo from Cooper family collection.*

Above: *Don Fay was one of the ship's crew who was fond of the cats. Photo by Scott Bray © Woods Hole Oceanographic Institution.*

Right: *While working out of Guantanamo Bay, Cuba, the Atlantis crew found time to sail the Number 2 whaleboat. Photo from Cooper family collection.*

What Happened to Felix

Felix never had shore leave every night before Guantanamo. He got so he was running and coming into his manhood. Now it didn't occur to us that this would ever happen, we thought he was always going to be the kitten. He would be right on the chock as we came in—the chock was a hole on the bow on the bulwarks—he would lean out of that chock until the bow hit the dock and then he would jump off and he'd walk up the dock, and everybody would say, "You going ashore to have a good time tonight, Felix?" He'd look back and go, "Meow-meow", and would disappear for the evening.

In the mornings we left about six in the morning, but the cook got up at five and Felix seemed to know that he had to be back at six, because he always came down the dock about quarter-to-six. When he'd come in sight of the *Atlantis*, he would start yowling, this screeching yowl, and the cook would run up on deck and say, "It's ready Felix, it's ready!" He wanted his breakfast ready when he stepped on board. After they fed him he'd go back and sleep in the captain's berth.

By the time we were ready to head back to Woods Hole, Felix got to like Cuba pretty well. The last day there, the crew was headed up to a Cuban bar room to have some Cuban beer, and they put Felix in the chief mate's cabin so he couldn't go ashore that night, because it was coming on 5 PM and Felix went ashore every night at 5 PM, without fail. One of the mess boys wanted to get something in the chief mate's cabin and he opened the door accidentally while everyone was ashore. The kid told me later Felix went out the gangway and up the dock. That evening the mess boy never told anybody that Felix wasn't there. So hands came back about a half an hour or so later, and we cast off the lines and we left him at Guantanamo Bay. When we got near the Windward Passage, which is at Cape Maisi, the eastern point of Cuba, they discovered that Felix wasn't on the ship, so Oakley sent a wireless back to a Navy tug (that laid on the opposite side of the dock from us) and said, "We've lost our cat, keep your eyes open for him." The next day, we got a wireless back from the tug saying that Felix had come back at five in the morning and we weren't there, but he didn't care what ship he was on, so he just went aboard the tug. So that was that. They gained a cat. We were too far out to go back and get him. Today they'd probably fly him home to Woods Hole.

Months later I saw the tug in Bermuda, and one of the engineers was still on board. So I asked him, "Well, what happened to Felix?" "Oh," he said, "Felix started coming back less and less. He would spend two days away—typical tom cat. Then rest up for two days, then spend three days away and he must have really got taken with those Cuban Senoritas, because we never saw him again. He stayed in Cuba."

So that's what happened to Felix.

Back to Guantanamo Bay

In September 1946, *Atlantis* headed south out of Woods Hole to the same waters, Captain Adrian Lane now in command on his first *Atlantis* cruise. The objective was to find the depth of the natural sound SOFAR channel in the water between Bermuda and Puerto Rico. We spent over two months making a number of runs between these points. There were four of us in the crew who had been on the earlier SOFAR Cruise: Don Fay, Chief Engineer Backus, Assistant Engineer Hans Cook, and myself, now an AB. We made many hydrographic stations, sending Nansen bottles to various depths, and taking BT readings every half hour or so. All this was for a rocket range survey. Before the mast, we had no idea what the whole cruise was for. We certainly knew nothing about a rocket range. I only found out about this when I read it in Susan Schlee's book, *On Almost Any Wind*, forty years later.

On the trip south, we were sailing along with sheets well out on starboard tack, before the wind. The boom tackles were rigged on both main boom and mizzen boom (to hold the booms in position), and the engine was not running. Suddenly a rain squall hit, and immediately after that, the wind changed and blew hard from the opposite direction. I was an AB, nineteen years old and with the wheel watch at the time. I knew instinctively that, as the wind went around with the sun, we should change course steering to starboard, keeping the wind aft until the squall cleared and the wind settled in the proper quarter.

Captain Lane rejected my suggestion and made me hold course. I had to keep the helm hard aport, trying to head into the squall. As the wind hauled around toward the east and southeast, we were suddenly caught aback. With the booms held out by the boom tackles, all sails including the

Captain Lane, known for his commanding pose on the wheelhouse top, brings the ship alongside the WHOI dock at the end of a cruise. Photo by Jan Hahn © Woods Hole Oceanographic Institution.

jib were caught aback—that is, the wind came around to the leeward side of the ship.

Atlantis came to a stop, and the pressure of the wind on the sails caused her to lay over with the starboard side deep in the water. The mate's staterooms were on the starboard side, and I believe Chief Mate Karlson, who had turned in about an hour before, had his port light open. When we were caught aback, the ship heeled hard to starboard and that side was submerged. Water poured in the mate's cabin right on top of Mr. Karlson and woke him up with a start.

Atlantis lay down real hard with the rail level with the water and slowly began to go astern. With the wheel (rudder) hard to port, the stern went to port and the bow began to fall off. All the time this was going on, in the dark night with the wind screeching, I had no idea where the captain and the bo'-sun were, and I could not change course unless ordered to do so.

About this time, Chief Mate Karlson arrived in the wheelhouse, mad as a wet hen. He immediately slacked away on the mizzen boom tackle, taking the pressure off the mizzen. As the vessel's head fell off, he ordered me to come to full right rudder. This action finally brought the ship round to the wind on the starboard quarter, but going in the opposite direction. The bo'-sun and the two ordinary seamen of the watch got the gear straightened out, with the mate's help, and *Atlantis* resumed her course, but now close hauled on the port tack. When the rain squall cleared, the men forward sighted a ship dead ahead. She signaled to us and identified herself as a Coast Guard cutter. She had seen us on radar in the squall and wondered what we were doing.

When all was in order again, the chief mate came to the wheelhouse, and, in the presence of the captain, gave me a real bawling out for the stupid action of being caught aback in the squall. "Didn't you know that in a squall you have to keep the wind aft and turn with it? Yesus that is one of the first tings a man learns at sea. Ships are lost by that kind of stupidity."

I knew Mr. Karlson was really not speaking to me but to Captain Lane, for what the chief mate considered an incompetent action on the part of the captain. I took it all in and only said, "Yes, Sir, Mr. Karlson." Later, on thinking over the incident, I wondered if that was the cause of the loss of the *Kobenhaven,* a five-masted bark lost off Cape Horn with all hands. One thing I noticed, however, was that the sails did not "blow out of the bolt ropes" when the power of the squall hit and knocked the ship down on her starboard side, as Mr. Nordquist hinted they would.

Time Off in Woods Hole—
Einar Edwards

I STAYED home from a cruise of the *Atlantis* in the winter of 1946-47 and rented a room from Einar and Mrs. Edwards in December of 1946. I wanted a place to study and draw for a correspondence design course I was taking from the Westlawn School of Yacht Design [now the Westlawn Institute of Marine Technology, located in Eastport, Maine]. In the evenings, when I was tired of drawing, I would go to the kitchen and visit with Einar and Mrs. Edwards. They had a combination kerosene and electric stove in the kitchen, so, during winter nights, it was always warm and cozy there.

Einar Edwards was born into a family of fishermen in Norway and immigrated to the U.S. in the mid-1920s. With his brother, he settled in the Sheepshead Bay area, in Brooklyn, New York, which at the time had a larger Norwegian population than Oslo. He went fishing out of Sheepshead Bay. The boats they used were very similar to the New Jersey Sea Skiff model power boat, the same model that Einar used afterward for the boats that he built.

In the 1930s, he went to work in the winter on the large skyscrapers that were being built in New York City. I remember him telling me that he worked on the Empire State Building and the Radio City Music Hall.

Einar came to Cape Cod in 1940 to work in the construction of Camp Edwards, and lived on Millfield Street in Woods Hole in Susie Swain's boarding house. Later on, he said that when he first came to Woods Hole, he thought that the people here were half asleep—compared to the New Yorkers.

Einar and Susie Swain (who was divorced from Albert Swain of Quissett) married after the war. Einar started lobstering out of Woods Hole

In December 1946, Bill Cooper rented a room in Susie Swain's rooming house on Millfield Street, where Einar Edwards also lived. Later, Susie and Einar, shown here, were married. Photo courtesy of Charles Swain.

with an open lapstrake boat about 26 feet long. He always used open lobster boats even though he fished his lobster pots mainly off Noman's Land and Cox's Ledge at the entrance to Buzzards Bay.

The open boat, without a pilot house or windshield, enabled Einar to enter and leave Eel Pond anytime without the need for the bridge to open. Susie Edwards' yard, which borders on the Eel Pond, had a small marine railway. Whether Einar installed the railway or it was there before, I do not know. With this railway, he could haul his boats at anytime.

While knitting heads for his lobster pots, Einar would tell me stories about his early life fishing in Norway, working on the skyscrapers, his early days in Brooklyn, when he neither spoke nor understood English, and fishing and lobstering out of Sheepshead Bay. One night he told me about coming home from Cox's Ledge with a load of lobsters and running before a southwest sea. His boat was pooped by a big wave and almost completely flooded. The engine stalled and the boat came to a stop.

In the process of bailing the water out of the boat, he decided it was too short in length. After he had unloaded his lobsters at Sam Cahoon's, he took the boat into Eel Pond and hauled her out on his railway. Before he could consider the consequences, he took a hand saw and cut the boat in half, forward of the engine, amidships, while she was in the cradle. He then pulled the bow section forward and the stern aft so the boat was four or five feet longer. After that he started to fill in the area between the two halves with a new keel section, planking, frames, clamp and deck.

Einar was a hard worker and in a few days the boat was almost whole again. When doing this kind of job, his step-son, Pete Swain, would always give him a hand (Pete Swain lived most of his life in Quissett and died in 2004 at age 94). "I thought my pots would be alright for a week or so", he said, and the boat was rebuilt and back fishing before the week was out.

In December 1946, Einar was planning to build a new 30-foot lobster boat and at that time was getting the materials together. He bought the white cedar planking and oak for frames and keel from a sawmill in Rochester, Massachusetts, and loaded the lumber on top of his pre-war Studebaker, without any roof racks, with the load well lashed down. There was a small opening in the pile of wood over the driver's windshield. I never could understand how he could see well enough to drive. He said it was like driving the car looking through a periscope. The car, as I remember, when I saw it in Woods Hole, looked like a lumber pile with four wheels.

Einar, while in Woods Hole, built all his boats with only hand tools,

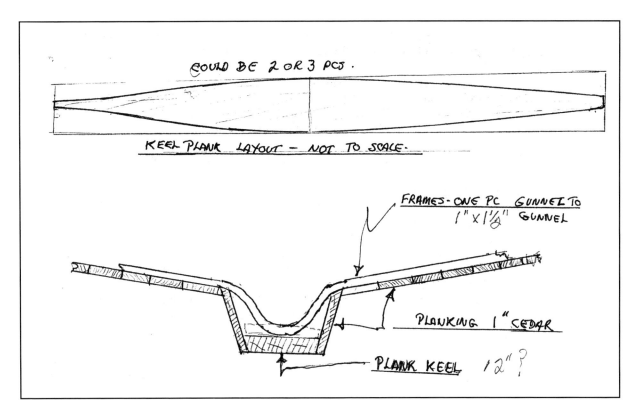

COULD BE 2 OR 3 PCS.

KEEL PLANK LAYOUT — NOT TO SCALE.

FRAMES - ONE PC GUNNEL TO
1" X 1½" GUNNEL

PLANKING 1" CEDAR

PLANK KEEL 12"?

although he might have had an electric drill. The lobster boat he started to build in January 1947 was smooth planked, whereas all the previous boats he had built were lapstrake, as were the small fishing boats of Norway and the Jersey Sea Skiffs. The Jersey Sea Skiff model had what is called a hollow box keel. As I recall, the natives of Woods Hole and Quissett had never seen this type of keel or construction before and as a result, they did not have much use for it. The bottom of the box keel was oak, about 12-inches wide and 2-inches or so thick and 24-feet long.

Although we did not see many circular saws in those days, there were band saws in the boat yards. To use a band saw the oak plank would need to be taken to a boat yard—Hilton's in Woods Hole or MacDougall's in Falmouth.

I don't know exactly how many boats Einar built in Woods Hole, but know of at least four. They were all the Jersey Sea Skiff model and all built on the same molds, with different spacing, 24 to 40-feet and all round bottom and the same keel construction.

Einar and Mrs. Edwards bought Henry Davis' boat yard in October 1950 and moved from Woods Hole to Waquoit at that time. Sixty years later I have many fond memories of the times I spent with Einar and Susie and those days in Woods Hole.

The Jersey Sea Skiff was a workboat designed to be launched from an unsheltered beach, through the New Jersey surf. The box keel served to keep the boat upright in the sand before launching and after retrieval. The spritsail rigs of the 1880s providing sail power were later replaced by engines. Drawings by William B. Cooper.

Judith Eldred Cooper

Soon after seventeen-year-old Bill Cooper first arrived in Quissett Harbor on the schooner *Segochet*, and became aware of the boatyard there, he was told that the yard owner's oldest daughter was named Judith. At that moment, having never seen her, Bill had a premonition that she would one day be his wife. As part of Bill's welcoming into the small community they soon met.

Three years later Bill returned to New York to ask his estranged father for permission to marry. After that, he would never need to see his father again. On September 6, 1947 Bill Cooper and Judy Eldred were married. Their backgrounds couldn't have been more different, but the marriage endured for over five decades.

Judy was born in 1928, into the sixth generation of Eldreds in Falmouth. The large Eldred land holdings bordered on Quissett Harbor and extended northward to include an area now called Racing Beach developed for house lots. Judy's forebears had farmed this land for over a century before concentrating their efforts on the boatyard. The early Eldred homestead, a stately house that still stands facing the harbor, was likely built by Lemuel Eldred in about 1790 and was later the home of Judy's father and grandparents. Her grandmother had been a teacher at the nearby Quissett School, now long since gone.

Judy grew up in a house built for her parents directly opposite the homestead, uphill from the boatyard her father ran. The boatyard and house are still there. As a child she wandered the wooded paths and boulder-studded shorelines that had belonged to her family. In summer she sailed and swam in the harbor and bay and watched sunsets from the hilltops; in winter she skated on woodland ponds, and sledded down the snow-covered hills— always with her sister and cousins. As teenagers they would walk to Woods Hole for frappes and to listen to the juke box, returning in the dark along the Woods Hole Road.

Bill Cooper and Judith Eldred were married on September 6, 1947. Judy is seen here in November 1944 outside her childhood home at Quissett Harbor. Photo from Cooper family collection.

Judy's father, Charlie Eldred, allowed the young men, some employed in his boatyard and some serving in the military in Woods Hole, to visit and play ping pong in the basement with the local girls. Bill Cooper was one of those young men. After their marriage, Bill made only one more cruise on *Atlantis* before "swallowing the anchor" and moving ahead with his boat-building profession.

Douglas Cooper

Source:
Smith, M.L. [Ed.], 1986. *Book of Falmouth, A Tricentennial Celebration: 1686-1986.* Falmouth Historical Commission, Falmouth, Mass. 582 pp.

Captain Adrian Lane in a moment of relaxation works on a ship model in his cabin.
Photo by Don Fay © Woods Hole Oceanographic Institution.

The Med Cruise

In March of 1948, *Atlantis* was lying in the port of Piraeus, Greece. We had been out working in the Aegean Sea for the past 21 days in the terrible weather that winter can bring to that part of the world. We, those of us who served on deck, wore our oilskins most everyday, watch in and watch out. The oilskins, being coated with linseed oil, began to wear out towards the end of the period at sea. We usually tried to recoat them with linseed oil (boiled linseed oil if available, otherwise we added Japanese dryer to the oil), particularly our sou'westers (hats) at the first chance we got. That way, our foul weather gear and the linseed oil could get a chance to dry before we went to sea again.

After a tranquil Atlantic passage, the Mediterranean Sea brought storms and rough seas. Photo by Jan Hahn © Woods Hole Oceanographic Institution.

The Med Cruise

The Med Cruise was the longest *Atlantis* cruise to date, December 1947 to June 1948, and it made several interesting and exciting port calls. Bill was by that time a newly married man and this was to be Bill's last cruise aboard *Atlantis*. Curiously, Bill recorded very few memories of this cruise.

Sponsored by the Naval Hydrographic Office, the central mission in the Mediterranean Sea was to survey the bathymetry of the Aegean Sea, leading to the Dardanelles and the Black Sea, where a growing Soviet naval force was based. These were the years when the Cold War was ramping up and the U.S. Navy wanted information about the Aegean for patrol and submarine operations to bottle up the Soviet Navy. The captain was Adrian Lane with Chief Mate Arvid Karlson. Don Fay had by this time worked his way up to second mate. Gus Lindqvist replaced the retiring Ernest Siversen as bo'sum. Backus and Cook were joined by a third engineer to ease the watch schedule in the engine room.

What began as a leisurely transit in fair weather in the Atlantic changed with the often-violent winter weather of the Mediterranean. In one gale of 60 knots Schlee relates, "Billy Cooper, a seaman, and one of the messmen, Albert Leonard, preferred to ride out the storm above decks, and they sat on the galley trunk hanging onto the half-open hatch. The ship, hove-to

At this time, we had arrived in port and were kept busy doing various jobs on deck in the morning when it began to rain. The bo'sun, Gus Lindstrom, a Dane, had been directing the work on deck. When the rain started, as senior AB, I told the bo'sun we wanted to "knock off" so that we could re-oil our foul weather gear. The bo'sun went below to ask Chief Mate Arvid Karlson, a squarehead, if this was agreeable with him. Karlson, being of the old school, said, "No, let them mix up a bucket of soojee and vash the bulvarks." "But, it is raining", said the bo'sun. "Zo," replied the chief mate, "dey can vear their seaboots and oilskins." The bo'sun came on deck and gave us the chief mate's reply.

As the senior AB the bo'sun directed his conversation mainly to me.

again, was lying nearly broadside to the wind, and from where they sat, each glittering, foaming wave that came roaring toward the vessel as she rolled down to windward seemed about to crash its tons of green water straight down upon the decks. But at the last moment the ketch gave a lurch to lee-ward and, with her masts describing frantic arcs across the low sky, lay over on her other side and heaved herself sideways over the oncoming wave. A fifteen-foot wave picked her up in this manner and rolled her down fifty degrees, putting her lee rail out of sight underwater. The roll sent Cooper and Leonard flying off the galley trunk. As Cooper was catapulted into the main rigging Leonard made a grab for the hatch, which shut on his hand, breaking one of his fingers and bruising the others. The two men scrambled below then, Leonard to get his hand bandaged and Cooper to join the crew at dinner."

To the never-ending severe weather problems and associated seasick-ness was added the antics of an exhausted and often mischievous ship's complement when in port.

Arthur Gaines

Source:
Schlee, S., 1978. *On Almost Any Wind.* Cornell University Press, Ithaca and London. 301 pp.

When he repeated to me what the chief mate had said, I told him we did not want to do that and for him to tell the chief mate.

Val Worthington, a scientist, happened to be in the main saloon at the time and it was he who told me this part of the story later on. Val only heard the conversation between the chief mate and the bo'sun, not knowing what we on deck had said. When the bo'sun went below again, he informed the chief mate that we "refused to soojee the bulwarks in the rain." Chief Mate Karlson's reply, between sips of his coffee was, "Vat the hell do you tink ve brought dese kids along on dis ship for, a f—g yoy ride? Soojee the goddamn bulwarks!" The poor bo'sun, who sympathized with us, came back on deck and gave us the chief mate's reply.

Atlantis and her crew spent long days buffeted by sometimes rapidly-appearing storm winds. Photo courtesy WHOI Archives © Woods Hole Oceanographic Institution.

Atlantis was lying stern to the wharf, in a Mediterranean moor, with a bow anchor out in the stream. On our port side lay a World War II corvette that belonged to the Greeks, and on our starboard side, looming high above us, was the Italian liner *Surtainia*, sailing the next day for New York, a ten day voyage for her. Looking at *Surtainia*, I told the bo'sun I would probably be aboard her tomorrow morning, bound home, if I refused to soojee the bulwarks. "No," said the bo'sun, "you would have to be fired before you can be sent home, and they will not fire you, but only dock your pay (two days for one)." "Yes, Gus," I replied, "but tonight when all you people go ashore, and I take the fire axe (in a rack on the aft side of the wheelhouse) and chop down the mizzen mast, you can bet I would be on *Surtainia* tomorrow morning."

The bo'sun did not answer, but instead disappeared quickly below. When he again arrived in the main saloon, he told Chief Mate Karlson in an excited voice, "They refuse to soojee and Cooper says he can chop down the mizzen mast in the night."

Val said this caught old Karlson aback, who then smiled and gave the bo'sun his reply. The bo'sun came back on deck with the verdict, "Mr. Karlson says you can knock off." In all fairness to the chief mate and the bo'sun, they did not know for sure whether or not I would cut down the mast. The trip so far had been terrible and the chief mate had been pushing us hard. I never heard the mention of "soojeeing" in the rain for the rest of the voyage. The chief mate, being a squarehead officer, was always fair and never vengeful.

Captain Adrian Lane

Adrian Lane was born in 1919 and grew up on Skipper Street in West Mystic, Connecticut. The street was so named in the 19th century because of the large number of vessel captains who lived along it. Adrian was fond of saying he was "the last leaf of the tree", as he was the last captain from there.

His sea-going career started on the Mystic River in a 10 foot sailing skiff named the *Downit* when he was 11. *Log of the Downit*, made up of the cryptic log Adrian kept, briefly chronicles 221 voyages he and his mate (his cousin Jack Wilbur) made over four years up and down the river on the *Downit*. The editor of the published replica describes the log as "local history at its best" as the voyages detail local vessels' and people's comings and goings on the river and along the shore; "all that goes on in a little village that opens on a sound leading to the sea".

In 1946, just discharged from the Coast Guard at Woods Hole, after service during World War II and his first command (the Corvette *Pert*), he walked down the street to the Oceanographic and applied for a job. After a short stint as Port Captain, Adrian took command of the *Atlantis*. He was

Adrian Lane by the wheel-house of Atlantis *alongside the WHOI dock. In the back-ground is the 85-foot, yawl-rigged yacht,* Saluda, *in Navy service during the wartime years.* Saluda *was driven across Great Harbor attached to Atlantis' bow in the hurricane of 1944.*

229

27 years old. "A Brief Biographical Sketch of Adrian Kingsbury Lane" by editor Richard M. Morris in *Log of the Downit* states: "this began 16 years in sail. His license read, 'Master of Sailing Vessels of any tonnage on any ocean and 3d Mate of Steam Vessels on any ocean.'"

In addition to his time on *Atlantis* he served as: third officer on the three-masted R/V *Vema* once operated by Columbia University, in which he sailed to the Beagle Channel; Captain of WHOI's ketch R/V *Caryn*; 3d Officer on the 3-masted schooner *Atlantic* on her record-breaking passage in the 1949 Bermuda Race; three cruises as a deck officer on the USCG bark *Eagle*; and Captain of Mystic Seaport's Olin Stephens-designed sail training schooner *Brilliant*, from 1953 until the mid-1960's.

He then returned to powered research vessels, first at Groton, Connecticut, as Captain of Electric Boat's R/V *Sea Surveyor*—which sank in the Gulf Stream in the winter of 1969. A plate had failed and the vessel sank very quickly. Adrian said he knew things were going badly when, as he headed to his cabin to get some papers, he ran into the engine room gang "coming up from below". All on the crew made it into a life raft and were rescued 26 hours later by a Norwegian freighter, which took them to Norway. His last berth was as Captain of the University of Rhode Island, Graduate School of Oceanography's R/V *Endeavor*.

I first met Adrian in the mid 1950's when he was Captain of the *Brilliant*, and had the pleasure of sailing with him aboard the topsail schooner *Shenandoah*, on which I was the first mate from 1966 to 1970. One time as we entered the narrow channel leading into Nantucket Harbor under full sail and travelling at about 10 knots, Adrian turned to me at the helm and said, "I guess you have to say we're committed." In 1964 when *Shenandoah* was being built Adrian had given her owner and Captain, Bob Douglas, a plaque which Bob installed above the top step of the forecastle companionway ladder, which reads; "Growl You May, But Go You Must". It's still there today.

Adrian was adroit at turning a phrase, and the crew and other passengers were captivated with tales of his sea-going experiences, which were always understated as there was no need for additional drama. He described an incident aboard one of the newer research vessels on which he sailed when "the Loran got into an argument with the Sat Nav, so I settled it with my sextant."

Adrian's last sailing days were out of Noank on the Mystic River; back where he started. This time he was in the 21- foot catboat, *Dolphin*, built in 1917 by Wilton Crosby of Osterville, Massachusetts, which he co-owned with his friend Ned Watson. *Dolphin* had a 40 horsepower Lathrop engine which power Adrian accounted for by saying "well boys, if you're going to put power in a boat you might as well put enough." That may be true of the engine but I know I could never get enough of Adrian's stories or the twinkle in his eyes when he told them. His family later donated *Dolphin* to Mystic Seaport where she remains a part of the small craft collection of the museum.

He was indeed "the last leaf of the tree".

Matthew Stackpole

Sources

Lane, A.K., 1993. *Log of the* Downit. R.K. Morris [Ed.], Noank Historical Society, Inc., Groton, Conn. 53 pp.

Schlee, S., 1978. *On Almost Any Wind*. Cornell University Press, Ithaca and London. 301 pp.

First Mate Arvid Karlson, an old-school seaman, repairs a sail. Photo by Jan Hahn © Woods Hole Oceanographic Institution.

Famagusta, Cyprus 1948

We spent three months in the stormy and gloomy Aegean Sea. We lay in the lee of Chios, which provided shelter from NE gales. We had a hard time getting out. The waves in Aegean Sea were short and high, and *Atlantis* took seas over the bow, which had never happened in the Atlantic.

In April, 1948, at 6 AM off the Island of Rhodes in the Mediterranean, Chief Mate Karlson and I alone set all sail including the mainsail. In all the time I served on *Atlantis*, this was the only time that all sail was set by only two men. We left the Aegean Sea, off the Island of Rhodes on April 1st. The weather changed completely and suddenly it was spring in the Mediterranean. We made surveys in the eastern Mediterranean, and had on

board a Hydro Oceanographer of the Royal Navy. He told us stories about his service in the British Army in World War I— how each regiment had a different language for drill. If you did not use the right words, the troops would not move.

We arrived off Famagusta, Cyprus, before dawn. We could smell the sweet aroma of the land in the morning watch at 4:00 AM. None of us had ever heard of Famagusta before. We received a quick lecture of the place from one of the scientists, Frank Mather, while we were waiting for the pilot to come out. The harbor was walled in, as well as the city itself, by the Venetians in the 15th century, a fortified port of Venice in the Eastern Med. The Lion of Venice was over the main gate to the city. There were high walls with a road way on top and also a moat. We rode bicycles on the road on top of the wall.

A bathythermograph is deployed to obtain temperature data. Photo courtesy WHOI Archives © Woods Hole Oceanographic Institution.

Bill Cooper (right) with other crew row one of the whale-boats out to Atlantis, *seen anchored offshore. Bill's left hand ring-finger sports a gold band, one reason this was to be his last cruise. Photo courtesy WHOI Archives © Woods Hole Oceanographic Institution.*

Cyprus was the location of the Jewish internment camps, holding those Jews who illegally attempted to enter Palestine the previous year. From what the British soldiers told us, they were mostly European Jews. We could see the outline of the camp from the dock, a wire fence circling a tent city.

There were British troops guarding the dock area where we tied up. The soldiers had a patch on their left shoulder—"24th South Wales Borderers". The badge on their green berets was a pyramid and the word "Egypt". I think it was the 2nd Battalion, a very famous regiment from the past, but we did not know that at the time. The troops, on the whole, were young conscripts, National Service men they said, rather shy, but friendly. In those days, we were proud to have our large (in port) flag— the Stars and Stripes— flying from the stern staff, proud to be Americans.

We were not unusual to the people of Famagusta, as there were a large

number of American Jewish aid workers there who stood out from the local Turks, Greeks, and Jewish locals. There were lots of big fancy station wagons. The dock, which was about 1000 feet long, was guarded 24 hours a day. Rifles were loaded with only five rounds. The troops told us if they fired a round at any time, they had to bring back the empty cartridge to prove that they had not sold it to a "Yip" (or Jew) or a "Sip" (Cyprian Greek or Turk). The rifles were Enfield model IV, 1917, marked "property of the U.S. Government". The soldiers showed us the stamp. The rifles were equipped with a short spiked bayonet which none of us had ever seen before, as none of the crew had served in the European Theatre in World War II. At night the troops on guard duty wore a sleeveless leather jerkin over their uniforms to ward off the evening chill. The Aegean Sea had been so much colder, so that the cool weather did not bother the *Atlantis* crew.

While in Piraeus, Captain Lane (right) purchased a Greek dinghy, carried home as deck cargo on Atlantis. *Bill Cooper is at the stern (far left) attaching a stern line. Photo by Jan Hahn © Woods Hole Oceanographic Institution.*

Most of the British soldiers were about my age, and mostly shy and bashful. However some of the older men who had served around "Yanks" were much bolder. All were very friendly. The first evening I had the deck watch. About 11 PM, two soldiers came walking by and one said to me "Would you like a cup of tea mate?" The other one replied right away: "This is a Yank ship, they have coffee." I told them they could have tea or coffee, and the cook had just baked some nice fresh bread— would they like a piece of that with butter and jam? It is strange to see how much people enjoy a food we all take for granted. The two "Tommys" ate the bread, butter and jam with sheer delight. We became very friendly with the troops and we fed them quite often on the night watches—sometimes made fried egg sandwiches for them. They told us although the battalion was a Welsh regiment, there were not many Welshmen serving in it. They said Queen Victoria had given the battalion a silver wreath that they carried on the regiment colors and they did not want to become a royal regiment as they would have to break the wreath.

They rotated their guard duty from the dock to the perimeter fence of the internment camp. They hated that duty as, after dark, the Jews would throw rocks at them. Many soldiers were severely injured. They had unloaded rifles on fence guard, with only their bayonets. They also felt very sorry for the Jews interned on Cyprus.

The Jews who had been in German concentration camps gave no trouble. It was the Polish and Russian and other eastern European Jews that were the trouble makers—also the English and American. The Commandant of the camp told the internees to pick their representative and the Commandant would negotiate all problems with the person they chose. If the Jews did not like the terms the representative agreed to, they would commence to beat him. The British troops with fixed bayonets would have to enter the camp and try to rescue him. At this point, the Jewish women would rush toward the troops with "fixed bayonets" and push their babies and children to the front. "They knew we would not hurt those children", one British soldier told me.

By the time they got the camp representative out he would be half dead, if alive at all. They also told us that on warm days, the young Jewish girls would strip down naked and taunt the guards along the fence. If any soldier was foolish enough to move near the fence to get a better look, the girls in

Above: *A last Mediterranean port stop of this cruise was at Malta, where Atlantis moored stern-to in the Grand Harbor, Valletta. Photo by David Owen © Woods Hole Oceanographic Institution.*

    Left: *While at Malta Captain Lane (left) and Bill Cooper (right) launched the Greek dinghy, a traditional lateen-rigged felucca, and took her for a sail. Photo by Jan Hahn © Woods Hole Oceanographic Institution.*

237

certain areas would move aside quickly and the rocks would come out in a barrage.

One time the Jewish internees decided to burn their tents. After the fire was extinguished, the internees had to live in the open until the new tents arrived. The American Jews outside the internment camp complained bitterly to the International Red Cross. When the new tents were sent in a few days later, they were also burned. The poor people in the camp had to live in the open a long time after that as the new tents had to be made. A great deal of suffering was caused because of the actions of a few.

At times a ship would come in with people captured trying to enter Palestine and would unload them into trucks to take them to the camp. Later on, some of the trucks came back from the camp with people that were on the list to enter Palestine. Some of the people riding on the trucks would pass the British soldiers lined along the road, and wave and cheer them, others, the younger ones, would give the World War II "f—k you" salute. We would watch all this from the decks, fascinated—history in the making.

View of Atlantis' *after deck from the mainmast. The smoke from the starboard side is from the engine's cooling water discharge. Photo by Alfred Woodcock © Woods Hole Oceanographic Institution.*

Broader Issues

In reflecting on the Med Cruise, the Chief Scientist, Martin Pollak, later wrote, "The experience of the past six months indicates that *Atlantis* is too small to carry out a complete oceanographic program with modern instrumentation." Perhaps more to the point, she was not up to winter conditions at sea. Having worked with large naval vessels during the war years, and ever more aware of the limitations of sailing vessels, even Columbus Iselin began to hint that *Atlantis* was becoming inadequate. She lived up to the prevailing conditions surrounding operations of a summer program at an academic oceanographic laboratory. With large-scale govern-ment-funded ocean programs and growing competition the rules had changed.

Arthur Gaines

Bill Cooper (center) sits aboard Atlantis *in Woods Hole with his shipmates John White (left) and Frederick Thurber (right). Photo from the Cooper family collection.*

Quiet Times and Sailors' Tales

D URING my years aboard *Atlantis* at "cocktail time" in the fo'c'sle, I could ask the ABs and the bo'sun questions, as the mood was relaxed. The questions went like this: "Ernest (the bo'sun), when you first went to sea (about 1894), did they carry fresh water in barrels?" "No, ve carried fresh vater in tanks. Who the hell do you tink I sailed vid, Columbus?"

Willie G. told us that before the war, he sailed in the school ship *Nantucket.* "Were you a cadet, Willie?" I asked him, knowing full well he wasn't. Looking at me with a scowl, he replied "Hell no, I vas the bo'sun!"

"Ernest, did you ever work ashore?" "Yes, I cut vood for my mudder."

"Ernest, how did you keep warm beating round the Horn in the square-riggers?" "Vel, sometimes ve vould be up to our 'schests' in vater hauling on the lee braces. To keep varm ven vet, ve alvays vore long voolen undervear."

"That's all that kept you warm when wet, even in wintertime, a suit of long woolen underwear?"

"Oh, no, in the vintertime, ve vore two suits of voolen undervear."

One of the stories that Willie and Ernest Gustavesen told us was about a fall from aloft on a square-rigged ship. I never knew if this really happened, but it does reveal the deep-water sailor's sense of humor. It went like this: an AB working aloft got careless and fell from the upper part of the main topmast. On his way down, he hit one of the yards which knocked him out, and then he was caught on the hook of a block which caused a tear in his stomach. When he landed, his small intestine spilled out on the deck. First aid in sailing ships was administered by the chief mate and/or the captain. On this particular vessel, both considered themself proficient to do the job. After it was ascertained that the man was still alive, he lay on the deck while the chief mate and the captain argued about the proper way to coil the intestine back in his stomach. They could not agree if it should be done "right-handed" with the sun or "left-handed" against the sun. Finally they reached a compromise; they coiled half the intestine "with the sun" and the other half "against the sun". With that accomplished, they let the sailmaker sew up the wound. I never knew if the unfortunate sailor survived this experience.

A Piece of *Titanic*

The older ABs, Karl Johnson and the French Canadian called "Frenchie", played cribbage every evening before turning in. The cribbage board they used in the game belonged to Frenchie. It was larger than the ordinary boards that I had seen and was a beautiful piece of dark polished mahogany. One evening, before the game, I had a chance to pick up and examine the cribbage board carefully. On the bottom was carved the date, "1912". Frenchie noticed my interest in the board, and told me it was a piece of furniture from the *Titanic*.

Titanic!

Good God, I had grown up hearing stories about the *Titanic*. When a small boy and living in New York City, I could remember clearly when my father took me to see and go aboard RMS *Olympic*. I also remember him telling me "This is what the *Titanic* looked like", for *Olympic* was her sister ship. I could not imagine that a ship that size could sink! I always had a feeling of romance for the big transatlantic liners I used to see so often.

A few years before, I had been chums with a boy whose mother kept a scrapbook of all the newspaper clippings of the *Titanic* disaster, a book his mother let us look at many times. Here now, 33 years after her sinking, in the fo'c'sle of the *Atlantis*, I was holding a piece of *Titanic* in my hands! What a strange feeling!

When I asked Frenchie how he came by this piece of wood, he told me this story: he said he was serving in a Canadian cable ship (years later I learned she was the *MacKay-Bennett*) in 1912 when the *Titanic* foundered. His ship was sent out into the area of the wreck to recover the many bodies still floating around in lifejackets. When they arrived near the scene of the sinking, the sea was covered with floating wreckage, as well as bodies. The ship launched two boats to pick up the dead and Frenchie was sent in one of the boats.

While in an area of wreckage to pick up a body, Frenchie saw a nice piece of mahogany floating right next to the boat. He fished it out of the water and placed it in the bottom of the boat. He told me they picked up bodies and looked for identification. Those with identification were placed in the hold of the cable ship. The ones without identification were sewed in a hammock shroud, weighted and buried at sea. All this was very disagreeable work and the men did not like it. They found if they came across a corpse with no identification they could take off the life jacket and the body would sink into the sea. They did this in the boat he was in. When I asked him how many bodies they had recovered, he said "hundreds". Time for the cribbage game arrived, so the story ended.

Whom of us, in the fo'c'sle of *Atlantis* in that early spring evening of March 1945, could have even imagined what would happen forty years into the future? That in 1985 a research ship from the Woods Hole Oceanographic would locate and photograph the wreck of *Titanic* in the ocean depths. Even more fantastic would be that the same small institution that very few even knew about in 1945, would send a deep diving submarine down the following year and land on *Titanic*'s forward deck! The artifacts since recovered from the *Titanic* wreck make Frenchie's cribbage board seem very insignificant now, but to me, in March 1945, it was a magical piece of wood.

Channel Fever

I had heard the expression "channel fever" used a few times by the crew, but had only a vague idea what it meant. One afternoon during "cocktail time", when the bo'sun appeared to be a little more relaxed than usual, I asked him about it. After thinking about it a minute he replied: "Veil, 'channel fever' iss ven you have been 180 or 190 days out on the voyage and now, at last, have a good slant up the channel (the English Channel)."

The captain, who never spoke a word to the AB at the wheel before, offered his version of channel fever: "What is your heading, Jack (he is asking what course Jack is steering)? Jack does not look at the compass at all, but answers 'twelve pounds, thirteen shillings, truppence, ha'penny, and a farthing, Sir.' That is the exact amount of wages he has coming. That is 'channel fever'."

Yarns About Heavy Weather

In the evening, while on wheel watch, I can remember Captain Knight sitting on the settee in the aft end of the wheelhouse, with cigar in hand, talking in his quiet way, telling Chief Backus a yarn about rough weather. I always enjoyed listening to seamen tell yarns about their experiences, especially to one another, without any BS involved. I believe this is the best way I could have learned the profession of a seaman. I cannot, after all these years, remember exactly what Captain Knight said, word for word, or even all his colorful expressions, but his story went something like this:

In April 1932, Knight was an AB in the 328-foot bark *Parma* with Allan Villiers. Captain Knight had also been an AB on *Atlantis* in 1931. The skipper was a man of lots of experience, named Captain du Cloux. They were running their "easting down" nearing the Horn and making good time. In the late afternoon the wind from the west was blowing about 60 knots. By sundown it began to increase. He said he would always remember that the glass fell to about 28.1 inches (in comparison, during Hurricane Bob in 1991, the barometer fell to 28.78 inches). In my time with him, Captain Knight was a constant observer of the barometer.

This was a bad sign. The squalls of snow and sleet came on with greater fury of almost hurricane force, as night came on. Under a brand new foresail, lower topsails and main upper topsail, she was making about 13 knots. At that speed and wind, everything on a square-rigger begins to vibrate and shake. They knew they were pushing her to the limit.

The seas were getting higher and higher, with the tops beginning to break off. The watch on deck was hiding under the fo'c'sle head, near the bow, trying to keep out of the snow and sleet, waiting for the order to take in the foresail or any other sail. A large sea lifted the stern high in the air and the ship seemed to be driven ahead at a great speed, almost like going down hill. Then she drove her bow under the sea ahead. At this moment, she took a mountain of water over the fo'c'sle head. This sea passed right over the watch on deck and gave them the feeling of being under a waterfall.

Parma started to broach (lay down) to starboard, when a giant sea broke high over the poop, driving tons of water the whole length of the ship. In other words, *Parma* was pooped and broached, down to starboard (broadside to the sea), and laying there as if she were never going to come up. At this time, the brand new foresail blew out of the bolt ropes and when the crew attempted to get in the other sails, they blew out also. The wind shrieked through the rigging with the fury of hell. The captain could see plainly now that it was too dangerous to keep running, so he ordered *Parma* hove-to. This was the first time that Captain du Cloux, in his thirty years or so, of rounding the Horn, had ever been broached so badly that he had to heave-to. The seas crashing aboard caused a great deal of damage on deck and below.

It was a hard night for the *Parma* and Captain Knight said he did not expect to live until morning. They thought for sure, laying there in the pitch black darkness, that the seas crashing aboard would rip the tarpaulins off the hatch covers. If this had happened, and water got into the hold, *Parma* would have foundered. *Parma* was carrying a cargo of Australian grain.

At the end of his yarn, Captain Knight said, "As you can see, chief, anything can happen. I was on a well-found ship, with a very experienced skipper, and yet I can never forget that incident, as I most certainly did not expect to live." I repeated this story later to the men in the fo'c'sle. The older seamen and the bo'sun seemed rather blasé about what I regarded as a very exciting tale!

What had always impressed me through the years was the fact that, to even a skipper of great experience, nothing like that had happened before in 30 years of rounding Cape Horn. However, the bo'sun did tell me later that "most captains carry on with too much sail, too long before a gale." He also said that there is always a "Cape Horn greybeard" that will catch and poop you. Many ships have been lost that way, such as the *Kobenhaven*, a five-masted bark lost with all hands. "One can go to sea for 40 years and get pooped or knocked down, but the first time this happens can be the last. I tink dose guys in *Parma* were lucky."

"Between the Catheads, Sir"

In 1945, *Atlantis* had two magnetic compasses, the standard compass and, inside the wheelhouse, the steering compass. For younger readers, I would like to explain that in the days before GPS (global positioning system), LORAN C, the gyro compass and Radar, complete reliance had to be placed upon the magnetic compass. This was usually the "standard compass". All navigation was done with this compass. In a steel ship, many factors could cause a magnetic effect upon the compass including, believe it or not, the north, south, east or west direction the vessel faced while under construction. It was, therefore, considered best to place a magnetic compass as far as possible from the magnetic effects of the steel hull. Also it had to be placed in a position to take the sun's azimuth, or pelorus, bearings for coastal navigation.

In most ships the best location for the standard compass was as high as possible on top of the wheelhouse or bridge. In *Atlantis*, the standard compass was placed just forward of the wheelhouse on top of the trunk cabin, below which were the captain's quarters and the chartroom. This location worked out well for taking the sun's azimuth (bearing) with the azimuth's prisms on top of the compass. The standard compass was mounted in a binnacle, or stand, that supported and protected the compass. *Atlantis'* binnacle was of traditional design, made with teak and brass for the trim and cover, and a compensating ball on each side. It looked the way one would expect a seagoing binnacle to look.

Because the standard compass was the primary compass of the vessel, all courses and bearings were taken from it. Corrections and adjustments were made to the compass quite often. This was accomplished by taking azimuth bearings of the sun, which were given in the Nautical Almanac for the date and latitude and with various corrections for the time of day. On the SOFAR Cruise, Captain Knight took the sun's azimuth bearings with the standard compass during the 8 to 12 forenoon watch. In *Atlantis* in 1945, the steering orders were given in points, such as: East by North, a 1/2 North. However, the sun's azimuth was given in degrees in the Nautical Almanac, so corrections of the standard compass were done by degrees. If the course given were East by North, a 1/2 North, the captain (or officer in charge) would order the change of course to the nearest degree, while the sun's azimuth was being taken.

There was always a difference in readings between the standard compass and the steering compass. Since it was daily recorded, there was no problem to convert the standard compass reading to the steering compass or vice versa. While a comparison of the readings of the two compasses was being made, the most aggravating question to the man at the wheel was "What's your heading?" (meaning what compass heading is the vessel on).

Sometimes, especially in a seaway, the vessel would roll quite badly and the compass would go from one full point to port and one full point to starboard off the course. If one tried too hard to keep on the exact course

(*Atlantis* steered very easily, half a spoke of the wheel, one way or the other), the tendency would be to oversteer, and naturally *Atlantis* would deviate from the proper course more often. The captain, when comparing compasses or taking the sun's azimuth, wanted to know that the vessel was on her proper course. He would call constantly to the helmsman thru the open skylight on the top of the wheelhouse asking "What is your heading?" The helmsman, struggling to keep the vessel on course, would be slow to answer or only answer when the lubber line of the compass passed slowly thru the correct point.

When I was an ordinary seaman and at the wheel, I once experienced a real difficult time trying to hold the exact course. I only tried to answer when the vessel rolled, and the lubber line passed thru the correct course. Captain Knight became annoyed and asked again "What's your heading, goddammit?!" Again I tried to give the course he wanted when the lubber line passed thru the correct reading. It was really a wearing wheel watch for me.

Later that day in the fo'c'sle, I was explaining the problem I had to my watch mate, Don Fay. Norwegian Nels was playing cribbage and heard my story. He laughed and said the next time you are asked "What's your heading?" for me to answer, "between the catheads, Sir." It was a joke, but in all seriousness, the answer was correct. My heading was straight down the centerline of the vessel and would pass through the bow forward between the "catheads", that is, if *Atlantis* had catheads, which she did not.

All seamen and certainly Captain Knight knew what catheads were: timbers canted out either side forward to secure the anchors. The captain really wanted the ship's heading and not "your" heading. The squarehead ABs considered me to be "sassy" at times, and I believe now they hoped I would give that answer. I must admit, though tempted, I never dared answer the question "What's your heading?" with "between the catheads, Sir".

Schooner *Thomas W. Lawson*

During one of Chief Mate Nordquist's evening visits to the fo'c'sle, the conversation got around to the old schooners, the four- and the five- and six-masters, and to the giant of them all, the *Thomas W. Lawson*, which carried seven masts. Chief Mate Nordquist was sitting on the settee-locker near the bo'sun's berth, smoking his cigar, with glass of rum in hand, and carried on his conversation, in spite of the cribbage players' seeming obliviousness, and the bo'sun's only partial attention while reading his paper.

The chief mate, as I remember him, was a cheerful, outgoing sort of man compared to the other squareheads. I, for one, found his stories fascinating. In regard to the *Thomas W. Lawson,* he said she was really too big and clumsy, just "too big" as far as he was concerned [475-feet]. He went on to tell us that he was outward bound from England on a ship in late 1907 and saw the *Thomas W. Lawson* bottom up off the Isles of Scilly, a few days after she was wrecked. "Ve did not know almost all the crew had been lost."

One of the able seamen, Karl Johnson, who was the same age as the chief mate and the bo'sun, told me later he had never sailed in the *Lawson* but he had served in five-and six-masted schooners. On these schooners, they called the masts and sails by numbers, starting with the foremast.

The Bo'sun Tells his Tale

Ernest Siversen, a squarehead, was the bo'sun of *Atlantis* at this period in 1945. He was a real old shellback in every sense of the word. When I served under him, he was about 65 years old and had been 50 years or more at sea. All the old sailors and officers had a great deal of respect for him. I don't believe there was anything about the ship he did not know.

I served as ordinary seaman under him for a total of two years. At times he would be very hard on me, correcting my every action, but constantly taught me the seaman-like way things should be done, whether it be making fast to a cleat, the proper lead of mooring lines, the proper way to make fast the main halyard, a sailor's clothesline, rope yarn grommets, or how to sew canvas. When I first came aboard *Atlantis* in early August 1944, Chief Engineer Backus gave me this advice: "Mind you now, listen to Ernest for he is a real deep-water man from out of the past and he can teach you a great deal."

Ernest was born in Sweden about 1880. He never said anything at all about his family or his home life. Once he went to sea, he never went home again. This was common of many of the older squarehead seamen. He shipped out as a boy of 14 on a German four-masted bark. Life was very hard for boys on German ships in those days. He told me that they were told only twice the names and locations of the many halyards, braces, lifts, buntlines, and other rigging, and after that, the officers kicked and beat you if you did not know. This action encouraged one to learn quickly.

On his first voyage, the bark rounded the Horn, from east to west during the dead of winter. According to Ernest, old-time seamen only considered an east to west rounding of the Horn a Cape Horn passage. For him at that young age it was a living hell. All this time, as a boy, he was constantly being harassed by the officers and senior crew members. One thing that stood out in his memory was that he had to polish the second mate's sea boots. When one realizes that the leather sea boots of that period (late 19th century) were generally coated with mutton tallow to keep them waterproof, polishing would seem almost impossible. Evidently this duty really bothered Ernest, as he told this story to me a number of times. It was the only yarn he had ever repeated.

He had just finished telling me a yarn about a ship he served in, when innocently I said to him, "It must have been exciting sailing on those big square-rigged ships, around the Horn, when you were young." This statement brought him up all standing: "Exciting!" he said, looking at me with fire in his eyes, "You tink it vas exciting? I tell you now, if I had a son I vould rather kill him myself then see him suffer the vey I did on dose goddamn ships!" That, for me, ended the romance.

The bo'sun had many interesting things he could talk about, but he was usually very brief, and one had to ask questions all the time to get the details. Some of what he told me about the various ships is as follows: "Limejuicers were usually good ships, and the 'Limey' was a good seaman'. Limey officers 'knew their yob, and generally were fair and polite, yust like Chief Backus." The British had a law about the number of crew required, and the ships did not sail short-handed, but the food was terrible and ships were hungry. That is why serving in them was called "starvation and ease".

American ships often had "bucko mates" who carried a belaying pin "in each sea boot". On the Limejuicers the officers rarely struck a man, but on American ships, this was common. They would sail short-handed and the mates would try to beat the men who were not seamen into being seamen. The food was far better than on a Limejuicer, but "you vorked for it and you earned your vages."

On German ships the food was also better than the English ships, about the same as the American ships. "At first I thought the German officers vere hard on me because I vas a Svede, but dey vas yust as hard on the German boys."

The best yachts he ever sailed on were the big American yachts around 1900. The sailors were well fed, beyond what he had ever dreamed it could be. The clothes and oilskins they were issued were the very best. The crew also received bonus money from $5 to $25 if the yacht won or did well in a race. This would be equivalent to up to $500 in 1996 dollars. But you had to be a first-class seaman or they wouldn't keep you. You also had to shave every day with a tea cup of hot water.

Heaving-To

During the evening watch, while hove-to, we were only required to have one man on watch at a time. One evening, during my time on deck with the bo'sun, the tropical weather being beautiful, and the bo'sun very relaxed, he began to explain the principles of heaving-to. The bo'sun, Ernest Siversen, would not normally give me a long discourse or explanation. I usually had to ask questions continuously to keep the conversation going.

However, this evening, he began to explain in simple terms how a ketch such as *Atlantis* was hove-to and how it was different from a schooner, and that in heavy weather, a square-rigged ship could be hove-to with a "goose winged" fore or main topsail, and sometimes with a tarpaulin lashed in the weather mizzen rigging. He certainly told me more than I could digest at the time. When I asked him a question about schooners, he said he had experience in small schooners, as he served in the Boston Pilot schooner *Columbia* when he was young. He first came to the U.S. in early spring 1898, when he was 18 years old. While in New York City, he and a friend deserted the German bark they had been serving in. They had intended to get a job on one of the big American yachts.

They boarded a train in New York and went to Boston, to a sailor's boarding house. Jobs for seamen on yachts and other vessels were posted at the boarding house. Together Ernest and his chum signed on the Boston pilot schooner *Columbia*, which looked very small to Ernest after the big German, four-masted bark from which he had deserted. *Columbia* was one of a few vessels Ernest served in that he ever mentioned by name to me (the other two were the schooner *Wildfire* and the bark *Intrepid*). He said he liked

Columbia very much, the food was good, and he began to learn English. As a pilot schooner out of Boston, she was hove-to a great deal of the time, and as a schooner, she could be hove-to in many different ways. On board her, Ernest learned the principles and tricks involved.

When I asked him why he left her, he said he did not like the idea of "vinter" in a small vessel in the North Atlantic. Therefore, about the middle of November, 1898, he left *Columbia* and shipped out on an American square-rigged ship, bound for Shanghai, China, loaded with case oil (kerosene in five gallon cans). His friend stayed in *Columbia,* and Ernest never saw him again. In the American square-rigger he had his first experiences with "American bucko mates" with a "belaying pin in each sea boot", as he expressed it.

Many years later, while reading about the great "Portland Gale" of late November, 1898, I discovered that among the many vessels lost was the Boston pilot schooner *Columbia*. She was lost off Scituate with all hands. I have often wondered since if Ernest ever knew that she had been lost shortly after he left her. . . most likely not.

The bo'sun told us, "On American ships, especially the Down East schooners, you had to watch out you don't get paid off with the main boom." Supposedly, when sailing into the harbor at the end of the voyage, the schooner captain would call all hands aft to be paid off. With the sailors lined up on the quarter deck, the captain, at the proper moment, would jibe ship all standing, knocking the crew over the side. Any time you were cheated out of your pay, it was called "being paid off with the main boom". In 1946, when we were in Cuba, I used to help Ernest Siversen with canvas work. He was sailmaker his last few months on the *Atlantis*.

A New Era

Atlantis had, in my time aboard, three masters, five chief mates, three second mates and two bo'suns. We also used up a number of cooks. Only one stands out in my mind, "Stew-pot Charlie", so called because he came aboard with what appeared to be a 10-gallon aluminum kettle and everything he cooked, everything, was cooked in that kettle. Anything he served us was served in a soup bowl. The bo'sun said Stew-pot Charlie could probably use his pot for a life raft.

We had one poor soul for a cook, who had only worked in restaurants on shore. He took the job on *Atlantis*, and I am sure no one ever told him how rough the winter sea could get, or the fact that he might get seasick. We went out in December for a ten-day trip and this poor fellow, with two first-voyage mess boys—so full of bravado while we were still at the wharf—all became seasick. One evening everything was so bad, the galley crew just left all the dirty dishes and pots and pans on the leeward side of the galley. We had been on the port tack since about noon the previous day, and at about 10 PM that night, we tacked over to starboard. The crash of the pots and pans and dishes resounded all the way aft to the wheelhouse.

I was at the wheel at the time and Captain Oakley was in the wheelhouse also. "My God, what the hell was that?" he asked. "It sounds like all the dishes, pots and pans in the galley slid down to leeward, Sir." The captain went forward and roused out the poor seasick cook and ordered him to clean up the mess in the galley. I think all the cook did was stack everything on the now leeward side and get back to his berth as quickly as possible. About midnight, just before the change of the watch, we again tacked ship. All the dishes and pots again went crashing over to starboard with the same loud noise heard throughout the ship. Again the captain went forward to rouse out the cook. The cook, terribly seasick, almost as limp as a rag, replied, "everything on the now leeward side." As we were coming off watch, the bo'sun said in his cheery voice, "Oh why, oh why did I ever sell the farm and go to sea?" After we were below in the crew's mess, he looked into the galley and said, "We will probably need a bulldozer and a fire hose to clean up this mess."

By 1946 only Don Fay and I remained of the men before the mast, and before long he would become an officer. The old-timers, mainly the square-head seamen who had been trained on the hard road to Cape Horn and the North Atlantic in winter, who sailed in the big schooners, the large racing yachts of the past, including the magnificent J-boats of the 1930s, were gone. This type of seaman would never again occupy the fo'c'sle. In their place would be a much younger and far less professional type. Looking back over 50 years, I realize a new era had begun for *Atlantis*.

Bill Cooper at the Acropolis at Athens, Greece, May 1948.
Photo from the Cooper family collection.

Moving On

On one of the *Atlantis'* last port stops, at Piraeus, during the Med Cruise, Bill and others made their way to Athens, where they were drawn to the Acropolis. This would be Bill's last cruise, and I think of this visit to the temple of Pallas Athena, Goddess of Knowledge, as Bill's commencement exercise. His cap-and-gown was the dress of the tenured Able Bodied Seaman. He had studied for four years with the masters—the squarehead seamen—in the classrooms of the wheelhouse, the fo'c'sle, and the sea-washed deck. Perhaps one of the most important lessons he learned was not a nautical one—that your most important obstacles in life are often those you hold in your mind. Beyond that many things are possible.

Bill was ready to move on. He began his new journey by going home.

Arthur Gaines

Right: Random *was designed by 22-year-old Bill Cooper and constructed at the Eldred Boatyard by Bill, Sam Weeks, Charlie Eldred and others. In October 1950* Random *was christened at launching in Quissett Harbor by Florence Eldred, Bill's mother-in-law. Photo from the Cooper family collection.*

   Lower right: *Bill and Harold Morris at work on the new Cooper house in 1951. The house is still owned by the Cooper family. Photo from the Cooper family collection.*

Epilogue

Bill Cooper
Boatbuilder, Raconteur, Teacher
by Douglas Cooper

Cooper-Eldred Boatshop

AFTER leaving *Atlantis* in 1948 Bill made his home in Falmouth, Massachusetts, building his own house near Buzzards Bay and raising five children. Most of his life was devoted to boatbuilding and design, crafts at which his mastery was widely acknowledged. When he first came ashore, having a young wife and child, he worked for his father-in-law, Charlie Eldred, at the Eldred Boatyard at Quissett Harbor.

In 1949 Charlie decided that he needed to build a new work boat for himself. Though only 22 years old, Bill convinced Charlie that he could do the design. Bill had been reading voraciously on the subject and had taken the reputable Westlawn correspondence design course. The boat was built at Quissett in the winter of 1949-1950 and the result was *Random*, a 30-foot lobster-style powerboat.

Using the drawings he made for that boat as proof of his abilities, Bill applied for a job at and was hired by the famous Luders shipyard in Stamford, Connecticut. Luders had been awarded a contract to build seven, 180-foot wooden minesweepers for the Navy, a dream come true for anyone interested in wooden shipbuilding. Bill lived in Stamford, staying with a former shipmate, occasionally returning home to spend time with his family. Quickly excelling at the job, he worked his way out of the drafting room and into the shop itself. Bill thrived at Luders, earning the respect of the Navy inspectors and "old man Luders" himself. Next to his service on *Atlantis* this was the determining experience of his life.

Luders Shipyard, Stamford, Connecticut, when Bill worked there in 1951. Photo from the Cooper family collection.

Tired of living apart from his wife and feeling that he had learned what he needed to, Bill left Luders in early 1954 and returned to Falmouth. There, with more children to support, he worked where the best opportunities were, mostly in the marine trade, but also house-building and general carpentry. He was always ready to help out Charlie Eldred at the boatyard when necessary.

By 1958 the strain of maintaining the large number of wooden boats of Quissett and Woods Hole, year after year, overcame Charlie. In debt and emotionally spent, he sold the yard. This decision was a huge disappointment to Bill and he bitterly opposed it. He loved the Herreshoff 12 1/2 and S-boat fleets that the yard maintained and he loved Quissett and its surroundings. It was the first place, since his early childhood, where Bill had felt welcome and at home.

Not to be deterred by this setback, Bill soon found a boatbuilder in Mattapoisett, Alan Vaitses, whom he liked and who needed help. There he once again excelled. But by the mid-1960s Bill longed to be his own boss and build boats in his own shop. He built a small barn at his home in Sippewissett, with no exact idea of what he would do in it. Through his connections with Vaitses he quickly got a job building a small powerboat for a local man. Soon after, he designed and built a very small (11-foot) ocean-going ketch for a man intent on setting a record for a transatlantic crossing. The client, William Willis, set out to cross the Atlantic twice, but was towed

Above: *A wooden mine-sweeper (Luders hull Number 973) under construction at Luders in 1951. Photo from the Cooper family collection.*
Left: *The completed minesweeper, USS Aggressive (MSO 422) seen here underway, was commissioned in 1953. U.S. Navy photograph.*

back in both times. Following his third attempt, the boat was found floating in the ocean with no one aboard.

Keen to expand his experience, in 1967 Bill was hired to help loft (draw out full size) the America's Cup defender *Intrepid*. She was a wooden 12-meter class sloop designed by Olin Stephens and built at Minneford's yard in City Island, New York. Bill worked on the loft floor alongside the famous loftsman Nels Halvorson, a Norwegian with a heavy accent who reminded Bill of his days on *Atlantis*. As at Luders, Bill didn't restrict himself to lofting but also took to the shop floor, where he interacted with the boat-builders, the designer, and the owner's representative. *Intrepid* was a ground-breaking boat that defended the Cup twice and influenced yacht design for years to come.

Soon after coming home from working at City Island, Bill took up naval architecture on a large scale. Ever since going to sea and seeing big ships first-hand, coupled with his boyhood infatuation with the ocean liners of the '30s, he had been interested in their design. The idea had been percolating in his mind about solving the inherent problems of structural weakness of cargo ships as they became larger and longer. In 1968 he came up with the idea of "the Multi-Section Ship", or more descriptively, a flexible, segmented ship made up of adjoining "sections". Encouraged by a friend, who oversaw the construction of tankers for ESSO, Bill threw himself at this idea and worked to develop the details, undeterred by the immensity of the task.

He formed a corporation and, through the force of his personality, got some financial backing. He built a large working model, almost 60 feet long, complete with connecting hydraulics, that he named *Audacity*. Experts in ship design came to view the craft as it plied the waters of Buzzards Bay to demonstrate the feasibility of the concept. Bill even traveled to Washington and presented his case to U.S. Naval officials, who liked the idea of interchangeable weapon systems. Buoyed by the positive reception and afraid a large company would steal it from him, Bill hired an attorney to pursue a patent. Unfortunately the attorney, who perceived Bill as naive and overly trusting, exploited the situation and accomplishing next to nothing. Delayed by the patent process, underfunded, and burdened by the need to support his large family, the corporation folded.

Bill returned to the more modest profession of boatbuilding on a small scale. *Audacity* was partly left to rot and partly recycled as a float for mooring work. When it was all over, his long-suffering wife, Judy, was philosophical yet somewhat unforgiving, dubbing the abandoned test model in her backyard, "Cooper's folly".

Bill produced many boats over the 1970s and 1980s, some built to his own designs and some by other designers, such as L. Francis Herreshoff, Ray Hunt, Dick Newick, and George Crouch. Included among these boat designs were: a shallow-draft cruising ketch, an offshore sports fisherman, an ocean-crossing trimaran, and a replica racing powerboat from the roaring twenties.

Though his shop was small and to the casual observer "under-capitalized", Bill was always ready to take on any challenge, sometimes to his detriment. Size and complexity rarely discouraged him and, though he loved to talk about economics and business theory, it was the technical challenge, not the monetary success, that motivated him. All of this was done with

Opposite: *Judy and Bill's children in 1959: (l to r) Amy, Katherine, William, Matthew, and Douglas. Photo from the Cooper family collection.*

Lower left: *Bill inspects one of his students' work at a Saturday morning boatbuilding class in February 2010 at the Woods Hole Historical Museum. The young women, Abby Heithoff (left) and Elise Olson (right), were also Ph.D. candidates at the MIT-WHOI joint program. Photo courtesy of Susan Fletcher Witzell.*

Lower right: *In his shop in 2014, Douglas Cooper examines Atlantis' cedar whaleboat bucket Bill saved from the trash heap in 1944. Photo by Emily Ferguson.*

great confidence, capability and humor. The men who worked for him were always captivated by his charm and his love of storytelling.

To help him when he had a big project he hired "old-timers"—carpenters and boatbuilders—who had learned their trade in the '20s and '30s. One of these, Al Windle, was a boatbuilder who had started out at the Bristol, Rhode Island, Herreshoff yard in 1925 and who taught Bill much about how the Herreshoffs did things. Later on, in the late 1970s, it was the younger generation he hired, mostly college-educated men who had dropped out of the career track to return to simpler times. Bill became a surrogate father to them, mixing strict standards with his personal allure.

Sometimes it was difficult for his workers to get things done when he told a story or lectured on an unrelated subject. In the words of one employee, "when Bill talks to you he demands eye contact." Bill always made time for those who dropped by the shop on a daily basis to listen and tell their own stories.

Lamenting how his beloved Falmouth had changed since the 1940s, Bill did his civic duty and was elected Town Meeting Member eight times, from 1981 to 2002. He was known for challenging the status quo on numerous occasions. In 1986 he came to believe that the Town Harbormaster's system for issuing mooring permits was unfair and illegal, a blatant example of small town cronyism. Representing himself he sued the Town officials in Federal Court claiming the Town Selectman had no authority on Federal waters. The court ruled against him so, on his own and through his own preparations, he filed an appeal to the U.S. Supreme Court. The Court declined to hear his case.

Like his own mentors, the squarehead seamen of *Atlantis*, Bill was committed to passing along his skills and knowledge, the boat shop serving as his classroom. In addition to the people who worked for him, over the years his students and acolytes (many with Ph.D.s) attended his evening hands-on classes to learn boatbuilding and marlinspike seamanship, and bask in the atmosphere of a working boat shop. In 2000 he helped organize the Woods Hole Historical Museum's "Small Boat Restoration Program" that operates year round each Saturday morning, the neighborhood resounding with the sounds of woodworking tools and collegial banter.

In 2009, at the age of 82, Bill saw his boatbuilding career come full circle when a replica of *Random*, his first design more than a half century earlier, was launched. He helped his son build the 30-foot wooden power boat for his longtime friend Carol Reinisch Suitor. She christened the new boat *Marjorie* in honor of her mother. A year and half later in early January 2011, after struggling for five years with congestive heart failure, Bill passed away. His ashes were scattered off the stern of *Marjorie* by his family, at the first government buoy in Quissett Harbor, not far from where he had first entered the harbor 66 years earlier.

Atlantis Sails On

by Arthur Gaines

After Bill Cooper departed *Atlantis* in 1948 the ship carried out 148 more cruises, many of them chronicled in books by Susan Schlee (1978) and by Dana Densmore (1995). During the 1940s, as Bill relates, the Institution had begun to work with power vessels, and by the late 1950s the Institution leadership had arranged for operation of the ex-Navy salvage tug *Chain*, a 213-foot steel motor vessel capable of operating in the North Atlantic in winter. R/V *Chain* arrived on scene in 1958.

The same year, the new Institution Director, Paul M. Fye (who had been Chief Scientist on the 1945 Tongue of the Ocean Cruise) decided an aging sailing vessel in need of maintenance was no longer appropriate for the kinds of research called for in the ever-accelerating, advanced and competitive field of oceanography. Mirroring the earlier view of Columbus Iselin, he set a goal early in his administration of obtaining a new power vessel specifically designed for ocean research. The R/V *Atlantis II*, which entered service at WHOI in September 1963, was 210-feet in length, 44 feet in beam and drew 17 feet. She was powered by two Skinner Uniflow steam engines, rated at 700 horsepower each, had a cruising speed of 12 knots and carried a complement of 33 crew and 25 scientists.

It was not until 1966, however, that the original *Atlantis* departed WHOI. She was conveyed to CONICET, the National Research Council of Argentina, to be operated by the Argentinian Navy. After a sentimental last visit to Woods Hole in November 1966, the ship sailed to Buenos Aires

On November 8, 1966 Atlantis was transferred to the Argentinian Navy at a ceremony at the WHOI dock in Woods Hole. Photo courtesy WHOI Archives © Woods Hole Oceanographic Institution.

under her new name, *El Austral*, to be welcomed by the President of CON-ICET, Dr. Bernardo Houssay.

Beginning in 1970 *El Austral* made 40 research cruises in Argentinian waters basically under her original configuration. But by 1978 the ship had deteriorated to the point she could not go to sea and was abandoned by the Navy. She was stripped of her equipment, masts and rigging and by 1980 her fate hung in the balance: two of the options considered were a return to WHOI, or deep-sea disposal.

Instead, as a third option, *El Austral* was towed to Puerto Madryn, Argentina, for rerigging and modest renovations, and by 1982 she was back at sea as a research vessel, this time operated by a Merchant Marine crew. Continued hard economic times put an end to this phase of operations and, still under custody of the Navy, she had lost her Certificate of Seaworthi-ness. *El Austral* lay abandoned in Puerto Belgrano, Argentina.

Amazingly, in 1996 the Argentinian Prefectura (Coast Guard) took charge of the ship in collaboration with the Navy and CONICET, under yet

Above left: *An Argentinian Navy crew raises the Argentinean ensign on the stern flagstaff. The ship was renamed El Austral. Photo courtesy WHOI Archives © Woods Hole Oceanographic Institution.*

Above: *Under the command of her new master, Ricardo Rennella, El Austral set sail the next day for Buenos Aires. Photo courtesy WHOI Archives © Woods Hole Oceanographic Institution.*

Above: *After many years of service in Argentina, El Austral was surveyed in 2006 at the Tanador Shipyard, and found to be beyond repair. Photo courtesy of Marcelo Recio.*

Above right: *A new ship, named R/V Bernardo Houssay, was built based on the lines of Atlantis. Launched in 2011, she has new shipboard laboratories and will continue conducting oceanographic research and training of young ocean scientists. Photo by the Prefecture Naval, Argentina.*

Bernardo Houssay *has an ice-strengthened hull, improved bridge facilities, and expanded space, allowing her operation in the southern ocean among floating ice. Photo courtesy of the Prefectura Naval, Argentina.*

another new name, R/V *Dr. Bernardo Houssay* (after the Argentinian 1947 Nobel Laureate in Medicine, and former President of CONICET). Manned by a Coast Guard crew, she was brought to the Tanador Shipyard in Buenos Aires, the preeminent shipyard in Argentina.

The ship was thoroughly surveyed, a process that entailed cutting her in half, which survey is documented in sometimes startling photographic detail. The hull and superstructure were found to suffer from 70 years of massive corrosion and ad hoc repairs. In the face of changes in ship materials and fabrication technology since 1930, the decision was made to build a new ship rather than to attempt to incorporate some marginally salvageable parts of the old vessel. Nevertheless the new design was based on that of *Atlantis*, an acknowledgement of the value to Argentina of the ship's historical acclaim and prestige. Reference was made to distinguished scientists who had sailed aboard *Atlantis*, such as August Krogh, and Selman Waksman who, like Bernardo Houssay, had received the Noble Prize in Medicine. Where possible, token parts of the old *Atlantis* were incorporated into the new ship, including certain deck fittings and teak companionways.

The final design of the ship, however, incorporated some important changes: the draft was reduced by 4 feet; the stern section was redesigned

Bernardo Houssay *has a modernized sailing rig, improved engine room machinery and new shipboard laboratories. Photo courtesy of the Prefectura Naval, Argentina.*

to accommodate a new 5-blade propeller and a new engine; the teak wheel-house, originally located in the stern, was replaced by a larger steel structure amidships, elevated nearly 9 feet over the deck to improve visibility; the bow was ice-strengthened to allow operations in floating ice; and a bowsprit was added. Overall, the ship was enlarged to accommodate a complement of 53 crew and staff. One estimate puts the cost of the new ship at $10 million USD.

El Renacimiento (the Renaissance)

This skillful and extensive effort and substantial cost was not expended solely to rebuild a ship. Instead, the endeavor was seen to signal a rebirth: renewed national pride in shipyard capabilities; renewed awareness of Argentina's sovereign seas, their stewardship and promise; and renewed commitment to ocean research and education.

The fate of a ship after long and distinguished service is usually not a happy one: the breaker's yard, the sea bottom, entombment in a remote mudflat. But not for *Atlantis*, now enshrined in the *Bernardo Houssay*. The gala launching ceremony of the new *Bernardo Houssay*, in September 2011, was presided over by the Minister of Justice, Security and Human Rights; the Head of Cabinet of the Ministry of Defense; officials from the Tanador yard; and the Commandant of the Argentina Coast Guard (the agency designated to operate the ship). Speeches proclaimed: This 'state of the art' refurbished scientific vessel with new labs and equipment, which carries the legacy of three Nobel Laureates and global ocean discovery, will continue in research and teaching to prepare new generations of Argentina to make the best of the Argentine Sea. The graceful lines of *Atlantis* are reborn in *Bernardo Houssay* and she sails again today.

Perhaps, beyond her lofty goals, the ship will once again inspire young people in the course of their lives and self-confidence, as *Atlantis* did so long ago for a 17-year-old boy from Brooklyn.

Appendix
Atlantis Sailing Orders

April 23, 1945.

Captain Lambert Knight
Research Vessel "Atlantis"
Woods Hole, Massachusetts

Dear Captain Knight:

The scientific party on Cruise #129 will consist of the following, some of whom will not join the vessel until you reach Florida:

Paul M. Fye (scientist in charge)   Charles Slichter
Robert H. Cole   Ralph Spitzer
Wm. G. Schneider   Charles Wheeler
John Decius   Robert Price
John Eldridge   Paul Smith (Lt. (jg) USNR)

You will leave Woods Hole on Monday, April 23rd and proceed to Port Everglades, Florida, following the inshore route designated to you by the Navy, in so far as it is practical to do so. When conditions are such that it is advisable to use both sail and power in getting to windward it will, of course, be necessary to tack. In daylight it is believed to be perfectly proper to take fairly long tacks, but at night until you are past Cape Hatteras it would seem best not to get more than three or four miles off the designated course.

At night you will use, whenever the visibility is not good (less than 1 mile) lights, unless instructed otherwise by a responsible representative of the Navy. The route assigned to you is considered to be safe, and except for keeping a sharp lookout for other vessels there is nothing to worry about.

After securing fuel and provisions at Port Everglades you will proceed via the Northwest Providence Channel to the vicinity of Nassau and the Tongue of the Ocean where the work will be carried out at anchor, once suitable conditions have been located. The Navy has agreed to provide an escort until you return again to Florida, but it is not considered that this is essential. Under present conditions I have no objection to the "Atlantis" proceeding on her own in the Florida Straits or in Bahaman waters.

The question of whether or not you should clear for Nassau can best be decided when you have reached Florida in consultation with Dr. Fye. It seems likely that you will want to put in to Nassau for rest and supplies, and if clearance is required, it will obviously facilitate your entry to have your crew list and the other necessary papers in order. On the other hand, if you are to be escorted by a

Captain Lambert Knight   - 2 -   April 23, 1945.

Navy vessel these formalities may well be unnecessary.

It is believed that you will find the conditions suitable for anchoring near the eastern side of the Tongue of the Ocean about 15 miles south of the western end of New Providence Island. If the tidal current at the surface is strong and of the reversing type, it is suggested that you try the conditions further south near the head of the Tongue of the Ocean. As you know, the requirements are smooth water and lack of a deep current. Once successfully anchored, it may turn out that there will be no reason for interrupting the scientific work. If the Navy can furnish the necessary supplies and water, the crew and scientific party can perhaps take turns in going ashore via one of the Navy boats. Again such questions can best be decided in consultation with Dr. Fye after it has become clearer just what facilities will be provided by the Navy.

The scientific program is very full and much of it is of considerable urgency. Thus there is an advantage in aiming to keep it going without interruption. If you can avoid the loss of time involved in taking the vessel in and out of Nassau, so much the better, but obviously all hands will need periodic rest and recreation.

The objectives of the cruise have been outlined to you and in order to avoid classifying this letter they will not be repeated. Something like two months' work is now planned but it is most difficult to estimate now the total amount of time involved. It may even be necessary to break off the program now planned, either because of instrumental difficulties or because of the lack of availability of special Navy equipment. In this event some or all of the scientific party may return to Woods Hole to rejoin you later and I may issue supplementary orders for a completely different scientific program to fill in the time until the Project 7 work can be resumed.

It is considered safe for you to remain in Bahaman waters at least until July 15th. If it seems necessary for you to reamin longer, arrangements will be made for you to received hurricane warnings and supplementary orders will be issued.

Presumably the war in the Atlantic will be over before the time comes to head north again, in which case we will probably arrange for some hydrographic work that will take you offshore on your way back to Woods Hole. This would also involve a change in the scientific party, the new men presumably joining you in Florida. While it is expected that you will be back in Woods Hole by July 1st, it is possible that you may be as much as a month later than this, depending on the success of the work directed by Dr. Fye and the cooperating facilities which the Navy can provide.

You will be in touch with Woods Hole by mail and you will keep Mr. Churchill informed as to your needs for supplies, money and crew. He will stand ready to make such arrangements at this

CAPTAIN LAMBERT KNIGHT   - 3 -   APRIL 23, 1945

end as may facilitate the work and improve the comfort or safety of those on board. You will also submit to him periodic statements concerning the ships accounts and requests for such additional funds as may be needed. You are hereby authorized to advance such money to the scientific part as may be required for equipment, travel, and pocket money.

Finally, you are cautioned to maintain strict measures to protect the gasoline and explosives against fire.

With best wishes for a successful and pleasant voyage.

Sincerely yours,

WOODS HOLE OCEANOGRAPHIC INSTITUTION
Woods Hole, Massachusetts

August 14, 1945

Captain Lambert Knight
Research Vessel "Atlantis"
Woods Hole, Massachusetts

Dear Captain Knight:

The scientific party on Cruise #131 will consist
of the following:

Worzel (In charge of acoustical program)
Klebba
Riley (BT work)
Woodcock (Convection)
Fuglister

You will leave Woods Hole on Tuesday August 14
so as to arrive at New London, if possible, on Wednesday
morning about 8 o'clock. It is expected that you will be
able to berth at the U.S. Navy Underwater Sound Laboratory.
At New London certain sonic recording equipment will be
installed and the "Atlantis" radio will be tuned up. Two
Navy radio operators will join the ship at New London and
also most of the scientific party.

While it is not contemplated that there will be
any necessity of stopping in at Bermuda, if you feel that
it is desirable to have clearance for Bermuda this can be
arranged at New London. However such clearance should
not delay your departure.

You will leave New London, weather permitting,
on Thursday evening, August 16, and proceed towards
Lat. 29°N, Long. 55°W so as to arrive there, if possible,
by daylight on August 23. In any case, at that time you
will begin anchoring, either at the assigned position or
as near to it as you have been able to get.

You will use the same anchor as on Cruise #129,
but it will be rigged somewhat differently. Your heaviest
chain will be made fast to the anchor, followed by the
weight and then a second length of chain leading to the
end of the cable. When the end of the cable has been
lowered to within 4000 ft of the bottom a special

hydrophone will be attached to the cable at deck level.
As you continue lowering, the hydrophone cable will be
made fast to the anchor cable at intervals of about 500 ft.
Assuming zero wire angle, when the hydrophone is at 4000
ft, your anchor and all of the chain will be on bottom.
The only further scope that you will use will be whatever
is required to maintain the hydrophone at a depth of about
4000 ft.

It is more important for the purposes of the
experiment that the hydrophone remain near the assigned
depth than that you do not drag the anchor. You will
determine the initial anchoring position as accurately as
possible and likewise you will secure frequent sights as
long as you are anchored to determine any changes in your
position. The acoustical work is the primary objective
of the cruise.

If present plans can be carried through, you
will remain at anchor, weather permitting, for about 11
days, that is until September 2. You will then return
directly to Woods Hole, unless it becomes necessary to
stop at Bermuda. Provided no emergency arises, all of
the scientific party will remain on board until you are
back at Woods Hole.

Throughout the voyage you will be informed by
radio from New London if it should become advisable to
deviate from the schedule outlined above because of a
hurricane. In other words, we will monitor the weather
situation from New London and instruct you by radio if
it becomes necessary to avoid a hurricane.

Two secondary observational programs will be
undertaken as time permits. On both the outward and the
return voyages bathythermograph sections will be secured.
Tests will be made of a bathythermograph designed to work
down to a depth of 1000 fathoms. While you are at anchor
the bathythermograph will also be used frequently, provided
the anchor cable does not lead aft. If any dispute arises
as to whether or not the BT program is interfering with
the acoustical work, the final authority is Mr. Worzel.
In addition to the bathythermograph observations, Mr.
Woodcock will undertake a study of convection, both in
the air and in the water. For this purpose while in
passage it may become advisable for short periods to
deviate from the shortest course.

Captain Lambert Knight   - 3 -   August 14, 1945

     During the period when you are at anchor it will be necessary from time to time under Mr. Woodcock's direction to secure observations from the whale boat or skiff. These should be made well to windward of the "Atlantis" and it is your responsibility to determine whether or not it is safe to launch the boats. Since it is desirable to obtain some observations in winds of at least force 4, you will first watch the handling of the boats closely in more moderate weather and convince yourself that the seamanship is up to a sufficient standard to make it advisable to work at stronger wind velocities. Your advise and cooperation in this phase of the scientific program will be particularly appreciated.

                         Sincerely yours,

                         C. O'D. Iselin

CC-
   Comdr. Knight
   BuShips (Code 940D)
   Lt. Newhouse
   Mr. Worzel
   Dr. Ewing
   Dr. Riley
   Mr. Woodcock

WOODS HOLE OCEANOGRAPHIC INSTITUTION

WOODS HOLE, MASSACHUSETTS

Cruise #140

February 6, 1946

Captain Gilbert Oakley, Jr.
Research Vessel ATLANTIS
Woods Hole, Massachusetts

Dear Captain Oakley:

The fundamental purpose of this cruise is to make studies of the following problems for Project #7 in the clear water south of Cuba:

    A. Underwater photography
    B. Cylinder damage studies
    C. Bubble pulse and period studies
    D. Underwater travel of bombs

You will leave Woods Hole, weather permitting, at 4:30 p.m., February 6, 1946 and proceed to the Naval Operating Base, Guantanamo Bay, Cuba, which you will make your base. Arrangements for basing at Guantanamo have been made by Lt. T. Cotter, who will be Liaison Officer between the Project and the Navy.

On the trip to Cuba, the scientists representing Project #7 will be:

    Mr. Shultz
    Lt. Cotter
    Mr. White
    Mr. Hull
    Mr. Woodward

Mr. Shultz will be in charge of this group and responsible to you. This group will be joined later by:

    Dr. Swift
    Mr. Gever
    Mr. Brown
    Mr. Price
    Mr. Sullivan

and still later by:

    Mr. Decius
    Mr. Wheeler

Dr. Swift will be Chief Scientist for Project #7, or in his absence, Mr. Decius.

-2-

On the trip to Cuba, Mr. McCurdy representing Project #17 and his assistant, Mr. Quinlan, will accompany you for the purpose of making Intensity Measurements on Deep Bombs. You will facilitate his making an average of two stations per day. However, conditions may occur which, in his opinion, will warrant making the stations oftener, and in this case you will assist him in so doing, but in no case shall he make more than a total of 24 stations. Mr. McCurdy and Mr. Quinlan will leave the vessel at Guantanamo.

You will also make BT observations and Hydrographic Stations, and this work will be your charge. Mr. Spalding and at least two other persons, who will be designated by Mr. Shultz, should be assigned to making the necessary observations.

On the run from Woods Hole to Guantanamo, starting at Gay Head, observations are to be made every half hour using the 900 foot instrument whenever possible. Whenever the observation is delayed appreciably, it should be omitted. Special care should be taken so that no observations are missed while crossing the Gulf Stream and on approaching the Bahamas and Cuba. On the BT Log sheets, the following information must be entered for each slide: Slide No., BT No., Day, Local standard time, log miles, Lat. and Long. in degrees and minutes, wind direction and force, a surface temperature taken from a dip bucket, and the soundings. Every two hours a sample of the surface water should be taken and the bottle number entered in the log. Also, every two hours the weather, sea, clouds and wet and dry bulb temperatures shall be noted.

This program is to be repeated on the return trip from Guantanamo to Woods Hole. While on station in the Caribbean a thorough study of diurnal warming should be made using a shallow BT. At least two deep lowerings day and night should also be made. An exact plot of the position of the observations should accompany the log sheets.

The first Hydrographic Station will be No. 4388. One station is to be made each day on the run from Woods Hole to Guantanamo, simultaneously with one of the Intensity Measurement Stations. Temperature observation and salinity samples to be taken at even 100 meter depths, the surface temperature and salinity sample can be taken from a dip bucket.

You will return to Woods Hole in time to dock not later than midnight, April 15, 1946.

I trust you will have a very pleasant and successful trip.

Sincerely yours,

John Churchill
Administrator

cc: Mr. Iselin
    Dr. Fye
    Dr. Swift
    Mr. Allen
    Mr. Fuglister
    Mr. McCurdy
    Mr. Shultz

Cruise #143

September 5, 1946

Captain Adrian K. Lane
R/V ATLANTIS
Woods Hole, Massachusetts

Dear Captain Lane:

You will leave Woods Hole before dark on the fifth of September, weather permitting, on Cruise #143 and proceed to Bermuda conforming as nearly as possible to the course laid out on the master chart which is in your possession, except that on reaching Cape Hatteras area, Mr. Fuglister will request that certain changes from the course laid out be made in order to get a full section across the Gulf Stream. Cruise #143 is in four sections as indicated on the master chart - Section #1 starting from Woods Hole and Sections 2, 3 and 4 from Bermuda. These are all parts of Cruise #143.

The purpose of this and the three cruises departing from Bermuda is to conduct a Hydrographic and BT survey of the areas indicated. There will also be bottom reflection work to be done in conjunction with the Hydrographic work. Also, continuous recordings of soundings will be made whenever the tape will record. When in water beyond the depth of the tape, soundings will be taken every fifteen minutes. The sounding work will be done by the BT observers.

Under normal weather conditions you will make three Hydrographic stations per day. This may be varied if you are held up by bad weather or by taking an unusually long time to make any one Hydrographic station. In other words, you should try to have the Hydrographic stations reasonably evenly spaced, the normal spacing being based on a speed of seven knots and at a rate of three stations per day. Your crew will assist the scientific party when taking Hydrographic stations and the watch officers should become proficient in the handling of the Nansen bottles and the crew in the handling of the winch and gear. If soundings indicate any pinnacles or sea mounts, you are authorized to conduct a box survey in order to determine the extent of such sea mount, and you will make every effort to locate it accurately. The scientist in charge should be consulted in this matter.

The scientific party will consist of Mr. Fuglister, who will be in charge until the vessel first reaches Bermuda, then Mr. Worthington will

-2-

assume charge of the party which will consist of the following members:

Arnold Clarke	Lewis Post
David Owen	Stanley Bergstrom

It is realized that it may not at all times be possible to conform to the tracks laid down on the master chart. It is, however, very desirable that every effort be made to conform as closely as conditions will permit. You should make every effort to maintain a speed of seven knots when weather permits. Power should be used only when speed under sail drops below seven knots.

It is also desired that you tie in the southern legs of the trips out of Bermuda to an actual landfall making a detour if necessary to do this. Particular attention throughout these cruises should be made to accurate celestial and Loran fixes as the actual position of the ship is of greatest importance. To this end it is suggested that you train as many of your officers, including the radioman, in the use of Loran so that frequent fixes can be obtained with this instrument.

If any difficulty develops with the new main engine, you will make every effort to continue the cruise which you are then on under sail and to effect necessary repairs to the engine. However, if upon completion of a cruise the engine is not in satisfactory operating condition, you will report same to us and we will give you instructions. In case of any emergency you are authorized to proceed to the nearest port.

During one of your stays in Bermuda, you may be requested by Dr. Seiwell to do some work off Bermuda during your in-port period. You are authorized to assist him, and you should make an effort to contact him each time you are in Bermuda. He can be reached through the Bermuda Biological Station. You should also check with the Bermuda Biological Station for any messages that we may have for you.

There is a possibility that it may be necessary to have your vessel return to Woods Hole prior to the completion of the three trips out of Bermuda. However, it is hoped that this will not be necessary and that you will return to Woods Hole sometime between the tenth and twentieth of November. Notify us of your arrivals and departures from Bermuda. Also notify us by radio your ETA on the first run to Bermuda two or three days in advance so that we may secure reservations for scientists who are leaving the ship after your first cruise. Also advise us of your ETA Woods Hole in advance when you return so that we may make arrangements with Customs Officials for your entry. Except when in port, you will make every effort to send us a message notifying us of your approximate position by indicating the station number most recently completed. These messages should be sent on Mondays and Thursdays.

Upon arrival in Bermuda you should contact the Commanding Officer of the Army Air Force Air Field at Bermuda. He will have a dispatch authorizing him to provide you with commissary stores. You can at that time make

-3-

arrangements for the regular supplying of the Atlantis by the Air Field.
The Bermuda Biological Station may be able to assist in transportation
problems that you have ashore in Bermuda. You should also notify the
Customs Officials at Bermuda when you enter that you are carrying explosives. They will instruct you as to a docking at anchorage berth.

You should take all reasonable precautions to avoid hurricanes determined to be crossing your track, and you are authorized to deviate
from your course when such deviation seems advantageous. Your first
Hydrographic station will be No.4410. Wishing you a pleasant and successful voyage.

Sincerely yours,

Gilbert Oakley, Jr.

cc: Mr. Iselin
      Mr. Allen
      Dr. Redfield
      Dr. Ewing
      Mr. Fuglister
      Dr. Woollard
      Mr. Worthington
      Mr. Mather
      Dr. Hersey
      File

go...va

6 December 1947

Captain Adrian K. Lane
R/V ATLANTIS
Woods Hole, Massachusetts

Dear Captain Lane:

You will depart on Cruise # 151 at 0800 Sunday, 7
December 1947, weather permitting and the ship being ready for sea.

The scientific party will consist of the following:

M. J. Pollak - Scientist in Charge
D. F. Bumpus - Senior Scientist
R. D. Campbell
L. V. Worthington
E. K. Krance
N. Corwin
D. M. Owen
R. D. Abel
F. J. Mather, III

Krance and Corwin will not join the vessel until
she reaches Bermuda and the following men will accompany the vessel
only as far as Bermuda, to do biological work en route.

Dr. Ketchum
Dr. Ford
Dr. Riley

The trip to Bermuda should be of about 6 days dura-
tion and Dr. Ketchum will be in charge of this phase of the work.

After leaving Bermuda, you will proceed to Gibraltar
and thence to Malta. You should make every effort to fully fuel and
provision at these ports as provisioning may be difficult beyond Malta.
The Piraeus should, except in emergency, be your only port of call in
the Aegean Area. The American Consul should be contacted by you in each
port prior to any other personnel going ashore. The American Consul
will also serve as your mail address in these ports. Particular attention must be paid to seeing that all attached personnel observe local
regulations as instructed by the consul.

The work to be done is contained in a memorandum
which Mr. Pollak will have. You will cooperate with him in an effort
to complete the work outlined in that memorandum. Persons aboard should
be cautioned not to discuss their work freely ashore.

Captain Adrian K. Lane   (2)   Cruise # 151

Communication with us should be via usual commercial
channels and we would like to receive one report from you each week, in
addition to arrival and departure reports from each port.

It is not possible to write detailed orders, as the
situation may change as time goes on. We do, however, have every confidence that you and Mr. Pollak will bring the voyage and the work to be
done to a successful conclusion. Your first Hydrographic Station will
be # 4619.

Wishing you a pleasant and interesting trip, I am

Sincerely yours,

G. Oakley, Jr.

CC: Mr. Iselin
    Dr. Redfield
    Mr. Pollak
    Dr. Ketchum
    Dr. Ewing
    Mr. Fuglister
    Mr. Allen
    File

Stan Bergstrom and J. Wenzel launch a depth charge as Atlantis powers ahead. Photo by Jan Hahn (C) Woods Hole Oceanographic Institution.

Acknowledgments

THIS BOOK stems directly from the efforts of Judy Cooper who produced and collated typed copy from Bill's musings, recollections and hand notes. Based on that start, we are pleased to have played a role in bringing the book to completion.

We are grateful to several retired WHOI employees with first-hand experience on *Atlantis* for their discussions of parts of this book and suggestions for improvements: Mike Palmieri, John Leiby, Tom Stetson, and Dick Dimmock. Their contributions to this book could not be obtained in any other way and none as enjoyable.

Scott Peterson brought to our attention a manuscript that formed the Prologue chapter for this book, and clarified several points regarding his father, Capt. John Peterson. Dr. Renée "Bunny" O'Sullivan provided the letter in Bill's handwriting that appears on the half title page.

Most of the photos in the book are from the extensive Archives of the Woods Hole Oceanographic Institution and we owe thanks to Dave Sherman, Institution Archivist, and Ann Devenish, Publication Services, for easing access and for their help and patience along the way.

We are indebted to staff and Steering Committee of the Woods Hole Historical Museum, publisher of this volume, for providing previously published materials of Bill Cooper's writings, a transcript of his 1997 oral history presentation, and photographs of wartime Woods Hole used in this book. Susan Witzell, Archivist, and Jennifer Gaines, Executive Director, reviewed drafts of the book as it came together, adding significantly to the quality of the final product.

The several sidebars added to Bill's account were written by: Douglas Cooper, Cooper-Eldred Boatshop; Matthew Stackpole, Mystic Seaport; Phillip Richardson, Woods Hole Oceanographic Institution; and Arthur Gaines, Woods Hole Oceanographic Institution.

Finally, thanks to the late Paul Ferris Smith who embraced and invigorated the idea of this book, as he and his late wife Mary Lou have so many other publications and projects of the Woods Hole Historical Museum since its beginnings.

May 17, 2014

References and Further Reading

WE frequently consulted Susan Schlee's book, *On Almost Any Wind—The Saga of the Oceanographic Research Vessel* Atlantis (Cornell University Press, Ithaca and London. 1978. 301 pp.) a thorough and skillful account of many *Atlantis* cruises, from her maiden voyage through her conveyance to the Argentinian Navy in 1966. Schlee's book was written at a time when many of the cast of characters she wrote about were still available as primary information sources.

In his book, *A-boat: Six oceanographic cruises in the world's biggest ketch.* (Village Printer, Falmouth, Massachusetts, 1995. 195 pp.) oceanographic technician C. Dana Densmore gives an inside account of shipboard activities on *Atlantis* over, perhaps, the ship's most productive period, the late 1950s and early 1960s. Densmore participated in the last *Atlantis* cruise in 1966.

Vicky Cullen's 2005 book *Down to the Sea for Science.* (Woods Hole Oceanographic Institution, Woods Hole, Mass. C&C Offset Printing Co., China. 174 pp.) produced in celebration of the Institution's 75th year of operation gives a concise, illustrated history of WHOI.

For those interested in an international perspective on the history of oceanography a starting point is *Oceanography—The Past* (Edited by M. Sears and D. Merriman, Springer-Verlag, New York, Heidelberg and Berlin. 1980. 812 pp.) the proceedings of the Third International Congress (1980) on the History of Oceanography, convened in Woods Hole in celebration of the Institution's 50th anniversary. Susan Schlee served on the planning committee and contributed a chapter on *Atlantis*.

On a local basis, two books deal with the history of Falmouth and of Woods Hole. *Woods Hole Reflections* (Mary Lou Smith, editor, Woods Hole Historical Collection, Woods Hole, Massachusetts. William S. Stillwold Publishing Inc., Taunton, Massachusetts. 1983. 301 pp.) contains over 60 chapters and photo essays by local authors addressing the history of organizations, activities, and other interest points in Woods Hole. Historical top-ics addressed in this book are enlarged upon and added to with the biannu-al periodical journal *Spritsail,* also published by the Woods Hole Historical Museum.

The Book of Falmouth—A Tricentennial Celebration: 1686-1986 (Fal-mouth Historical Commission, Falmouth, Massachusetts. 1986. 582 pp.) also edited by Mary Lou Smith, addresses the villages and communities of the Town of Falmouth, including Woods Hole, in their many dimensions. A chapter by Judy Cooper records memories of her childhood growing up at Quissett Harbor.

Photo courtesy WHOI Archives © Woods Hole Oceanographic Institution.

Donors

Patrons:

In memory of John F. Austin Jr.
Douglas E. and Katherine H. Cooper
Judith Eldred Cooper
The Friendship Fund
Jalien G. Hollister
In memory of George Frederick Jewett, Jr.
Robert B. Ryder
Paul Ferris Smith
Lori Austin Spilhaus
Dr. Carol Reinisch Suitor

Sponsors:

Margaret T. Stone
Susan Wigley and Jay Burnett

Contributors:

Family of Elliot and Priscilla Billings
George and Yara Cadwalader
Pete and Vicky Lowell
John and Frederica Valois
Mary and Redwood Wright

Supporters:

Dorothy and Duncan Aspinwall
Donald Aukamp
David and Nancy Babin
Annette and Jerry Baesel
Molly Bang
Craig and Amy Cooper Barry
Julie and Frank Child
Judy and Steve Clark
Dr. Joseph and Elizabeth Cook

Willie Cooper
Bruce and Carol Lynn Courcier
Joseph P. Day
Frank R. Lillie Egloff
Ruth Alice and Konrad Fitz
Richard Foster
Barbara P. Gaffron
Jennifer Stone Gaines
Joyce and Bill Gindra
David H. Graham
David and Caroline Green
Cynthia E. Haigh
James J. Heriot and family
Whitney and Fred Keen
Jim and Alice Liljestrand
Arlene and Mark Lowenstein
San Lyman
Joseph and Constance Martyna
Samuel McMurtrie, Jr.
William D. and Charlotte Emans Moore
Captain Christopher Olmsted
Elise Olson
Elmer A. Richards
Alison and Dana Rodin
Cecily Cannan Selby
Chip Shultz
Dorman and Joan Swartz
Dr. T. Sean Tavares
Bob and Marilyn Werner
Joan R. Wickersham
Roland and Nancy Wigley
Isabelle P. and Albert J. Williams 3rd
Helen and Al Wilson